FINANCIAL INDEPENDENCE

FINANCIAL INDEPENDENCE

Through Buying and Investing in Single Family Homes

DAVID J. GRZESIEK

PELICAN PUBLISHING COMPANY
GRETNA 1985

*To the greatest investor I have ever had the pleasure of knowing,
my father, Joseph E. Grzesiek.*

Library of Congress Cataloging in Publication Data

Grzesiek, David J.
   Financial independence through buying and investing in single family homes.

   Includes index.
   1. Real estate investment. 2. Real estate management.
3. House buying. 4. Housing, Single family. I. Title.
HD1382.5.G79   1984   332.63′243   84-1135
ISBN 0-88289-440-4

Manufactured in the United States of America
Published by Pelican Publishing Company, Inc.
1101 Monroe Street, Gretna, Louisiana 70053

Contents

ACKNOWLEDGMENTS

Without the help and encouragement from my loving wife Christine, I never would have started this book, or finished it. The time she put into helping me with the manuscript was only outdone by the time she put into helping me achieve my goals as an investor. For all of this I thank her from the bottom of my heart.

I also would like to thank the people who gave a hand to seeing this book in print. Because they are all important, I will list them alphabetically: Ilona Brustad, Cliff Carey, Mike Ready, Susan Trickett, Victor Weipert, and Robert Wohlgamuth, CPA.

Last, but not least, I want to thank all the people who have helped me throughout my life to grow, not only as an investor but also as a person.

FINANCIAL INDEPENDENCE

PREFACE

This book will show you how you can become financially independent by owning as few as four single family homes. You will learn how easy it is to find and finance these and other properties in any market, even if you don't have any money, assets, or visible means of support. You will also learn how to do this in your spare time, no matter where you happen to live. Best of all, you will learn how to create real wealth in any economy and how to cut your income taxes legally all the way down to zero.

Unlike most books that deal with real estate, this one is easy to read and easy to understand. It is even enjoyable. Unlike most books, it covers the whole process of investing and managing property from beginning to end, without skipping any important steps. You will learn about the four returns you should get from any real estate investment, and you will learn how to figure out what those returns will be before you invest your first dollar. You will learn how to spot bargain properties, and you will learn why most buyers pass them up. You will learn how to find the hidden problems that catch most buyers and how to turn those problems into profits. You will learn how to spot motivated sellers and how to make them ridiculous offers they will want to accept. You will learn how to negotiate the lowest price you would think possible, and you will learn three techniques you can use to lower the price even more. You will learn what improvements make you money and which ones do not. You will learn how to get more money out of your property by refinancing it than you could by selling it. You will learn how to find and keep good tenants, how and when to raise rents, and how to get your tenants to ask you to raise their rents. You will even learn of an eviction technique that saves you time, money, and possible damage to your property.

It doesn't matter if you are looking for financial independence, help in managing your properties, help in getting started in real estate, or help in setting up a retirement program that is sure to be there when you need it. It doesn't matter if you are looking for a way to buy your first home or a way to acquire your first fortune. It doesn't matter who you are or what your present situation is—as long as you are serious and definitely want to better yourself and your circumstances, this book will go a long way toward helping you attain your goals. In short, this book will help you achieve the kind of life you have always dreamed of, by showing you how to invest in real estate—especially single family homes.

CHAPTER ONE
PLAYING THE GAME

Winning isn't everything; it's the only thing.

VINCE LOMBARDI

I never wanted to become a landlord. By the time I woke up to realize that I was one, I was living too good a life ever to give the role up. From time to time I have ventured into various businesses and other investments, but I have found that nothing offered the lasting freedom and almost effortless income that being a landlord could provide.

Being a landlord wasn't always as easy and rewarding as it is for me now. When I started out, I made all kinds of mistakes and I had all kinds of problems. Back then I figured that my problems were just something that came with the territory, and therefore an indication that I must have been doing something right. It wasn't hard for me to come to this ridiculous conclusion, because everybody I talked to either had, or knew someone who had, similar or even greater problems. As it turned out, my biggest problem was the fact that I was talking to the wrong people and getting the wrong information.

The answers to all the problems I encountered along the way appeared to be some very well kept secrets. Knowledgeable people, worthwhile books, and even adequate formal schooling were hard, if not impossible, to find. Feeling that my only practical option at the time was to continue my education in the "school of hard knocks," I paid my dues and learned my lessons. Although this proved to be a slow and expensive education, it was quite thorough and effective. Because of the beatings I had to take to get where I am, I can tell you what to look out for. Because of the success I have had, I can tell you what to look for. I can now give you the answers I wished someone could have given me so many years ago.

What you are about to learn can help you to become a successful landlord, investor, and wealth-builder. If you are presently any of these things, it can help you to become even more successful. Before we start, I want to state again that I never had as my goal becoming a landlord. In fact, I never had as my goal becoming a real estate investor. My goal was financial independence. Investing in single family homes was the safest and surest means I could find of attaining that goal. Becoming a landlord was merely the by-product, and, as it turned out, not a bad one at that.

SUCCESS

We human beings are an odd lot. We are brought up with the idea that we are all individuals, all unique. Yet don't we all really share the same desires and the same fears and inhibitions? Sometimes it is hard to comprehend that our own personal feelings are felt and shared by others. We may act and react in different ways, but that doesn't mean we want different results. For example, we all like success and the feeling that comes from being successful. None of us likes to fail or to be looked upon as a failure.

There are all kinds of success. Success even means different things to different people. To some it may mean learning the Bible. To some it may mean graduating from high school or college with honors. To some it may mean raising a good family and being a loving spouse. To others it may mean owning a business, being one's own boss, or doing one's own thing.

The definition of success varies from individual to individual; it also changes as each individual changes or redefines what is and is not important. Success can also be measured in different ways. It can be measured in terms of one's personal, or psychological, satisfaction, or it can be measured in terms of one's accumulated wealth.

I find it amazing that many of the people who measure success in terms of dollars never attain any degree of financial independence; presently, only about five percent of the people in this country ever do so. Some of these people actually end up doing very well—someone once illustrated just how well by using a set of children's wooden toy blocks. After assigning a value of $1,000 to each block, he said some of the highest incomes would be represented by a stack of blocks higher than the Eiffel Tower. He went on to say that the incomes of ninety-five percent of the people would be represented by a stack of blocks less than three feet high. It seems a shame that in a world where most people can jump higher than that, financially they never get over three feet off the ground.

What is even more disheartening is the fate that awaits the ninety-five percent that don't make it. At age sixty-five, over half will be dependent upon friends, family, charity, or the government for their very existence. Over a third of them will be somewhat luckier; they will be dead and will have left their problems or their meager estates to someone else. The remaining members of this unfortunate group will still be working, out of either habit or necessity.

If all this doesn't seem like much to show for a lifetime of work, you are right; it isn't. These unfortunate people don't end up where they are because they want to be there, but because they have been given the wrong directions or because they have failed to learn the rules and then apply them until they succeed.

LEARNING THE RULES

Life often seems unfair. It seems to reward those who don't deserve it and passes over those who do. Examples abound in all our lives. Have you ever had a boss who had less brain and ability in his entire body than you have in your little toe? Have you ever lost a job or promotion to someone with less experience and fewer qualifications? Have you ever busted your backside and received little or no recognition for it? Have you ever stood by in total amazement and disbelief as someone who doesn't have as much on the ball as you goes out and becomes a great big success?

Have you ever heard the expression "life is a game"? Actually, life is a whole series of new and different games occurring on ever-changing fields. Although there are some basic rules that apply to all games, each game has its own set of rules that must be adhered to. Most people fail to realize this fact; consequently, they go through life never quite understanding why the rules that once worked so well don't work anymore. Bewildered and frustrated, they either continue to play a losing game or join the crowd of spectators on the sidelines and watch life and all its rewards pass them by.

On the other hand, there are the successful people of this world.

They are the ones who eventually come to realize that life is not always the same old game that can be played by the same old rules. As a matter of record, most people do not achieve their greatest success until after age forty. The main reason appears to be that it takes most people that long to unlearn old rules and habits and to discard all the false and inaccurate information they have been given up to that point. Regardless of how long or how short a time this takes, all successful people know that knowing the rules and then applying them is often the only thing that separates the winners from the losers. All successful people also know that luck has nothing to do with their success; they make their own luck.

I was never a particularly lucky individual. In fact, I was never a particularly intelligent individual either. Until my graduation from high school, I was never better than a mediocre student at best; I even spent some time in summer school making up some of the subjects I had failed. As much as being a failure bothered me, it didn't bother me half as much as knowing that I had tried my best and still couldn't make it.

Everyone knows that it takes much more ability to make it in college than it does to make it in high school. When I went away to college (yes, I found one that would accept me), I didn't think I would last over a semester or two at the most. Knowing that I couldn't work any harder than I had in the past, I decided to spare myself the agony of trying and failing. Since I figured it was downright crazy to work for an "F," I decided to enjoy my stay in college and treat myself to a long-overdue vacation.

As a token gesture, I decided the only thing I would do was to show up for all my classes. Since that was my only concession, I didn't even take any fancy notes as I had done in high school; all I did was sit there and observe. I was amazed to find that many of the so-called good students really didn't have any more natural ability than I had. I discovered that what made them successful was their knowledge of the rules by which the game of education was played.

What amazed me most about all this was that the rules were not that difficult to discover or to put into use. I was even more amazed when they worked for me as well as they did for the other successful students. For the first time in my life I became a good student, and I remained a good student (if good students are judged by the grades they get). I found that success comes from working more intelligently and not necessarily from working harder.

GETTING INTO A NEW GAME

After graduating from college, I went out and got a job. Like most people I found myself working for a living, and like most people I found I had a problem, a problem not so different from the one I had had as a student. My problem was that I was working so hard just to earn a living that I didn't have time to make any money. I found that I was playing a losing game, a game where someone else made up the rules, a game where someone else benefited from my efforts more than I did.

It wasn't until I was twenty-seven years old that I really noticed that, financially, I wasn't getting anywhere. I knew that I didn't want to live the rest of my life worrying where the next dollar was coming from. I wanted more than that. I knew I only had one shot at life and that if there was anything I wanted, I had to get it this time through.

I started reading everything I could find on success. I questioned all the successful people I knew. I watched people who were doing things, and I analyzed their results in order to find the basic rules they used to bring about their success. My efforts paid off. I discovered that all successful people set a goal for themselves and then set out to realize it.

Since I wanted to be financially successful, I set a goal for myself: to be worth $50,000 in five years. (It may not sound like much to you, but at the time it was an awful lot of money to a guy who didn't have anything.) Now I had a goal, but I still had a problem. My problem was I didn't know how I was going to reach my goal. Nothing I had learned up to this point seemed to help. I needed someone or something to put me on the right road, the road to success.

It was then that I remembered the time, a few years back, when my father took the whole family into the basement and proceeded to prove on the blackboard that a person could buy a house, arrange a ten-year payoff, and have the tenant's rent cover all the expenses. He also worked out a table that showed how, once that person bought the first house, it would help buy the second. The first and second would help buy the third, those houses would help buy the fourth, and so on.

He even went into detail on how inflation, which was very low in the 1960s, was a bonus that would automatically raise rents and provide extra cash. I think he was trying to prove all this more to himself than to us, because it all seemed unbelievably simple and absolutely possible.

I remember all this so vividly because all the while my father was talking, my mother was in tears. She was sure that my father had lost his mind and that the mortgage he wanted to put on her house (in reality, their house) would leave her without a home to live in. I don't know how he ever talked her into it, but he did. I'm glad he did because otherwise I may never have had the chance to do what I did and share this information with you.

THE FIRST MOVE

There I was, twenty-seven years old, living in a mobile home, married to a good wife who shared my goal, and looking for a place to invest the few thousand dollars we had managed to save. Every night I scanned the want ads in our local newspaper for a house that I could buy and thus start on my way to the good life. It wasn't long before my prayers were answered by an ad that offered a house for sale for $2,500. That's right—two thousand five hundred dollars! That was not the down payment; that was the full cash price. Even back in 1970 that was an awfully low price for a lot, and this one had a house on it! I didn't waste any time getting over to see the house and meet the owner.

Although I would have been embarrassed if anyone ever found out I owned that junker, I bought it since the eighty dollars a month it brought in was better than the seventy-five dollars a year I received in interest by leaving our money in the bank. It didn't take many brains to figure out that eighty dollars a month adds up to almost one thousand dollars a year, a very good return on a twenty-five hundred dollar investment. What I didn't figure on was that the city building department would come along and condemn my beautiful money-maker. To add insult to injury, I had to pay a private contractor to tear it down and haul it away.

At this point, I could have taken a solemn oath never again to invest another dollar in the dastardly game of real estate. I could have started looking for something else that I didn't know anything about and try again. Many people do this, and finally quit after too many defeats.

(This is probably what led Benjamin Franklin to observe, "Many young men die at age twenty-five but are not buried until they are seventy-five.") Rather than give up, though, I recalled from my earlier reading and research that every failure held within it the seed of an equivalent or greater success. If this was truly the case, I was determined to squeeze every ounce of success out of this failure. Since I had paid my dues, I figured that I had a right to receive the benefits.

What did I get for my money? I got an education that was far more valuable than my college education, at a cost that was considerably less. I learned that I should check a house out from the roof right on down to the ground it sits on. I learned there were things like building codes and landlord-tenant laws. I learned that there were more ways to find, finance, and fix up a house than I ever thought possible. I even learned how to use some of those unusual and puzzling tools found on the shelves in many hardware stores.

My greatest discovery, though, was learning how to become financially independent by investing in single family homes. Talk about squeezing lemonade out of a lemon! I found that if one home could generate $1,000, six homes could and should generate $6,000. Since my salary as a teacher at that time was less than $6,000 a year, I concluded that six properties could provide me enough income to quit my job.

The realization that owning six homes could free me from the bonds of a lifetime of work (whose only rewards were a very modest existence and an even less desirable standard of living upon retirement) set my mind racing. I quickly figured that if I were to buy two houses a year for the next three years, I would be able to retire by age thirty.

The thought of early retirement opened up all kinds of possibilities. There was the possibility of having more time to spend with my family and my friends. There was the possibility of going into various businesses and naming my own hours. There was a whole world of possibilities out there, and I would have the time and the money to take advantage of them. I could, in effect, have the kind of life I had always wanted.

Now you are probably thinking, "How can anyone in his right mind call $6,000 a year financial independence? That's poverty!" Financial independence is different for everybody; some people need more money, and some people need less. Back in 1968, when I graduated from college, many people, including myself, started out earning less than $6,000 a year. And I'm talking about gross income. (Gross income is what you tell your friends you make; net income is what you actually bring home.)

Thanks to inflation, the value of my property and my rental income both increased. Since neither my debts nor my payments on them increased, my net income automatically increased. The end result of all this is that the same properties that made me financially independent allowed me not only to remain independent, but to do so with a much higher income than I had at first. I should add that I was not satisfied with just this continuing automatic increase in my income. I continued to buy property after I became financially independent in order to increase my income and my standard of living even more.

As it turned out, my first failure was the best thing that ever happened to me. It taught me a lot of the basic rules I would need to know in this new game I had chosen to play, and it reconfirmed my commitment to make it, even though I had struck out my first time at bat. My first failure also taught me a great moral lesson. It taught me never to buy a home to rent out to others if I wouldn't live in it myself.

When I started out, I set out to be the world's greatest slumlord. I did so out of pure and simple greed. I thought that I could get a much greater cash flow (money that goes into my pocket) by owning and renting out junkers than I could from owning and renting out decent homes. My first failure scared me enough to make me start living and investing according to my own conscience. Once I started doing that, a funny thing happened. I started feeling good about my properties and myself. And you know what else happened? I started making more money and I started creating more wealth than I had ever thought possible.

GETTING A GOAL

In addition to everything else my first failure did, it also caused me to change my original goal. I didn't want $50,000 anymore; I wanted financial independence. What made this such an appealing goal was that I knew how I could attain it. Like the successful people I had studied, I now had a goal and I knew the steps it would take to attain it. All I needed were six homes that produced $1,000 a year and three years in which to get them.

A funny thing about goals is that once you can define them and determine how they can be met, they almost seem to take care of themselves. It doesn't take all the time and effort that you may think to realize them. And once your goals are all set, you begin to notice opportunities that you never noticed before, even though they may have been there all along. It's like when you buy a new car. You know how you select the color, the interior, and all the other options? When you order that car, you probably think it's going to be a one of a kind, a personal statement about you and your good taste. You have probably never seen another car like it on the road. But the day you pick it up and drive it home, you see not just one car like yours on the road, but a whole bunch of them. They've been there all the time; you just weren't looking for them before.

Opportunities are like cars; they pass all of us by each day of our lives. It's only when we have a goal that we recognize them or even notice them at all.

Don't worry if people say you are crazy. Except for my wife, no one gave me any moral support when I first set my goal. In fact, everybody I knew told me I would never find what I was looking for. My friends, my relatives, and the people I worked with all told me I was crazy. They all told me that making money just wasn't that easy. Even the realtors who sold me most of the properties that eventually brought about the realization of my goal told me I would never find what I was looking for.

But the properties I needed did exist, and I was able to buy them. In fact, I was able to reach my goal eight months ahead of schedule. Some people may attribute my good fortune to luck, but I don't. I attribute it to having a goal. If luck played any part at all in all of this, it was the part it played in my electing to set a goal.

Do you want to be worth a certain amount of money? Do you want legally to lower or eliminate your taxes? Do you want to be financially independent? If so, you have to set a goal. Below is a fancy version of a simple but effective goal card. If you don't want to use anything this fancy, use a three-by-five file card like I did. If you don't like to write things down, that's okay. Your goal (what you want), the steps (number of houses you will need), and the timetable (number of years you want to reach your goal in) can easily be kept in your head.

I encourage you to take the time now at least to determine what your goal will be and how soon you would like to reach it. As for the

This is my own personal one-way ticket to

FINANCIAL INDEPENDENCE

DESTINATION ☐ An Annual Income of $_____, within _____ years

☐ A Net Worth of $_____, within _____ years

☐ A Reduction of my Income Taxes to $_____ within _____ years

DEPARTURE: _____ ARRIVAL: _____

BY WAY OF: Acquiring _____homes per year for the next _____years

Compliments of   I'll be there in _____years or less
David J. Grzesiek Seminars
Helping to arrange successful
trips into your future   _____

number of houses you will need to reach your goal, you'll be able to figure that out yourself by the time you are finished with this book. You will also know how you are going to find them, finance them, and fix them up.

Don't feel that the goal (financial independence, zero taxes, or a certain net worth) you set for yourself at this time has to be set in stone and can never be changed. As time, conditions, and your own desires change, you should feel free to change or modify your goal. As I said earlier, when I started out, my first goal was to be worth $50,000, but I soon changed my goal to financial independence. After I reached that goal, I set another: to reduce my income taxes legally to zero. After I reached that goal I set yet another: to be worth half a million dollars and, later, a million dollars. You should feel free to be this flexible, too.

IT'S UP TO YOU

This fascinating and exciting game of buying and investing in single family homes is open to everyone. One of the nicest things about this game is that everyone can be a winner. It's one of those games in which the more players there are, the more winners there are. Winning is even easy; you don't have to be super-smart, you don't have to cheat, you don't have to take advantage of anyone, and you don't have to do anything illegal. On the other hand, losing in this game is darn near impossible; you have to try to lose money, and even then it can be hard to do. If this is the kind of game that appeals to you, you have come to the right place. Your goal card is your ticket, and this book is your set of rules. I'm ready if you are, so let's get going!

CHAPTER TWO
FINANCIAL FREEDOM

It's not the sweat on your brow,
but the size of the crop that matters.

HENRY FORD

Your success and this whole book are based on the concept that it is possible to create or otherwise acquire enough wealth to become financially independent. Most people would find it very difficult, or even impossible, to save enough money to become financially independent. Our present tax system serves only to make this approach to financial independence even more difficult. The more you make, the more the I.R.S. seems to take, and this point should be kept in mind by anyone who thinks he can become financially independent or even wealthy through earned income alone.

Besides believing in the fallacy that earned income can make you wealthy, many people have a lot of other misconceptions about what it takes to become financially independent. If you were to ask a hundred different people what it takes, you could get at least a hundred different lists of items or qualities. If you were to combine those lists and then arrange everything into categories, you would probably end up with everything falling under four main headings. These headings would be brains, hard work, money, and luck (and not necessarily in that order).

Although I believe that it certainly wouldn't hurt to have any or all of these things, I don't see that they are all that important. I became financially independent without much help in any of these areas, and if I did it, anybody can do it. After you have examined these four "unnecessary necessities," I'm sure you will agree also.

"UNNECESSARY NECESSITIES"

Brains. If you have been able to read this far, and you are able to do basic arithmetic, you already have the intelligence necessary to succeed—you don't have to have a Ph.D., be a college graduate, or even have a high school diploma. Too much formal schooling may even hinder you by giving you too many reasons why something won't work and not enough reason why it will. All you have to have is enough sense to recognize the road to wealth when you see it, and to take it.

Hard work. If hard work were all it took to become rich, a lot of people would be wealthy today. For those of you who can't or don't want to work any harder, there is a solution. Work smarter.

Working smarter doesn't depend on how well you use your back, but on how well you use your spare time. Nobody, no matter who, is busy twenty-four hours a day, seven days a week, fifty-two weeks a year. Everybody has some spare time.

The people who do television surveys have found that most people have a lot of spare time and spend a good deal of it turning on their television sets and not themselves. The average adult watches about three hours of television every day. That's about twenty-one hours a week, or over one half a normal, forty-hour work week. Add to that figure all the time spent on video games, video recorders, and disc players, and you begin to see why some people never get anywhere.

If you are already watching less than twenty-one hours of television a week, congratulations, you may already be spending some of your spare time wisely. But any time you spend watching television you can put to better use starting your investment program by working smarter instead of harder for your money.

Money. It's been said so many times that it takes money to make money that many people believe it. Furthermore, they believe that since they don't have any money, the prospect of their becoming rich is out of the question.

Many people who fail to accomplish all they could in life fail because they look at life backwards and let lack of money stop their progress. They put the cart (money) before the horse (a deal that can make them rich). They don't realize that the first step is to find the right deal (in this case, property). Once they have done that, finding or attracting the money (necessary financing) usually isn't a problem at all.

It's a well-known fact that many fortunes were started with a few hundred or a few thousand dollars the wealth-builder was able to save. It's also a well-known fact that the more money one has, the more opportunities will be available. All this is a good argument for starting or increasing a savings program, but it still doesn't provide the key to how most fortunes are built.

Many people are unaware, or simply fail to remember, that most fortunes were started with and built on something called OPM (Other People's Money), not the founder's own money. The world is full of individuals and institutions that have money to lend. They are always looking for people and places that can make their money grow. Once you learn how to find and use these sources, you will realize that you don't need any money of your own to get started or to keep growing. You will also realize that you will run out of places to buy before you ever run out of places to get the money you need.

Luck. If it weren't for bad luck I probably wouldn't have had any luck at all. Every property I ever bought brought with it some degree of misfortune. Usually my bad luck took the form of an expensive oversight or an unexpected problem. Although at first these obstacles appeared to be misfortunes, many proved to be blessings in disguise. My first investment (the condemned house mentioned in chapter one) is an excellent example. I had to take a good hard look, but I found in that first failure a way to invest successfully in real estate and become financially independent.

Even with all my bad luck and all my blunders, I was still able to reach my goal. I even reached it eight months ahead of schedule. Many people look at me today and try to tell me that I was just lucky. They try to tell me that I was lucky to be in the right place at the right time, lucky to have gotten the buys that I got, and lucky to start when I did. They even try to tell me that the time for making it big in real estate is gone. Rather than get upset, I listen and I understand. I understand because I used to look at other people and other times and feel the same way. I know now that the people who appear lucky are the people who have a goal and are working towards it. I also know that now is the best time to start to do anything, especially when "anything" is how you are going to spend the rest of your life.

Most people spend more time planning their vacation than they do planning the rest of their lives. Yet they look at people who do plan their lives and then work their plan, and call them lucky. If you want to appear lucky and receive all the benefits that seem to come from luck, you have to set a goal and then work to attain it. After you realize your goal and people start coming up to you and saying, "You sure were lucky," you can tell them what I tell them. Tell them that if they set a goal and then work toward it, it won't be very long before people come up to them too and say, "You sure were lucky."

THE BEST TIME TO INVEST

I believe the best time to invest is *now*. If you sit around waiting for the right time, you could end up spending your whole life in a very unprofitable position. Doing the right thing at the right time is the most important part of being successful. Knowing that different times call for different responses is the key. When times are good and everybody is out looking for investments, you may have to search high and low to find a really good deal. Then you have to be a smart shopper and a shrewd negotiator. When times are bad and bargains abound, you literally have the pick of the crop. Then you have to be a good judge of quality and you have to be aware of the number of new deals you can handle effectively.

As you can see, changing markets should change the way you invest, but they should never stop you from investing. This book can help you invest successfully, but first you have to decide that *now* is the best time, and the right time, for you to begin. Don't be like a young man I once met. His excuse for not investing was that current market conditions weren't right and that it could take him five years to get where he wanted. He thought five years was too long. He thought he would be too old to enjoy his success. He thought he would wait until the market improved. I asked him how old he would be in five years, and he said, "Thirty-one." I then asked him how old he would be in five years if he didn't do anything, and he said, "Thirty-one." I think he got the point.

The point I am trying to get across here is, don't procrastinate. Too many people look back on their lives and all the opportunities they have missed and say, "I wish I had . . ." Even if you are one of these people, it's not too late. You can change your life for the better. You can start having the kind of life you have always wanted. You can get out and stay out of the "could have, would have, and should have" club, but you have to act now. And now is the best time to start investing.

AN UNDERSTANDING OF MONEY

Many people who just get by in life have a hard time understanding, acquiring, and controlling money. Wealthy people, on the other hand, don't seem to have these problems. They seem to attract money like a magnet. Why? Because they understand money for what it really is.

Money is anything people accept as a medium of exchange. Unlike money from the past (gold, silver, or other valuable commodities), our present-day money has no real value. It is nothing more than paper with a little bit of ink on it, and, as such, it should not be confused with what it really takes to make one wealthy. Aside from serving as a medium of exchange, money is also an excellent device for keeping score. It allows you—and other people—to have an up-to-the-minute report on how well you are doing.

The outcome of most people's income is usually zero. The main reason is that these people don't control their money; it controls them. Every paycheck goes to pay the butcher, the baker, and the candlestick-maker. If there is anything left over, and usually there isn't, it goes into savings. This kind of behavior won't make a person wealthy, and it won't keep a person wealthy either.

One of the best things you can do for yourself is to learn to control your money, and the best way to do that is to learn to pay yourself first. You do this by taking five or ten percent of each paycheck and putting it into the bank. Then take what is left and divide it among the butcher, the baker, and the candle-stick maker. If there isn't enough money to go around, cut their services, but don't cut your share.

If I were to ask you who made more money, a man who earned $10,000 a year or a man who earned $50,000 a year, what would you say? Before you answer, let me tell you that the $10,000 man managed to save $10 a week during the course of a year, and the $50,000 man saved nothing. Except for this one small difference, both men spent all their income. Although the $50,000 man may have been able to enjoy a better life-style than the $10,000 man, he actually ended the year no richer than when he began. But the $10,000 man was ultimately worth $520 more than at the beginning of the year.

The example above may sound a little unrealistic, but estate planners have found that it's not far removed from real life. They have found that most individuals with high incomes end up spending all or most of their income, while those with lower incomes tend to be the savers. If all this proves anything at all, it proves anyone can pay himself first. No one has to be a slave.

Saving a part of each paycheck depends more on the amount of your determination than it does on the amount of your paycheck. As long as there is someone around who gets by on less than you do, there is always the possibility that you can get by on less. When that possibility exists, you have the opportunity and the obligation to pay yourself first. Don't blow it!

The habit of paying yourself first will be of great benefit to you as an investor. Developing and continuing this habit will mean that you will have the funds to take advantage of even more of the opportunities that come your way.

AN UNDERSTANDING OF WEALTH

Many people fail to get all the money they desire because they work for money rather than work to acquire wealth. To become rich or financially independent, you must acquire or create wealth. Earning a lot of money is the result, not the cause, of your becoming wealthy.

For our purposes, you will create wealth by buying homes below value or fixing up homes to create more value. Earning an equal amount of money by any other means usually creates only one thing— taxes. Paying taxes won't make you rich.

There are two basic forms of wealth, and you want both. One is tangible wealth and consists of things (houses, tools, furniture, equipment). The other is intangible wealth and consists of what you know and what you can do (the ability to put deals together or acquire and manage property). Once you have a sufficient amount of tangible and intangible wealth, you will be able to convert, exchange, or use it to generate all the money you desire. In short, you will be wealthy.

THREE MAIN SOURCES OF MONEY—
WEALTH, CAPITAL GAINS, EARNED INCOME

Wealth. Of all the ways of getting rich, creating wealth is the easiest and the most desirable method. The main reason for this is that it is the only way to amass a fortune without ever having the monstrous income tax system take its bite.

If you were to buy a house and then see it double or triple in value, all that appreciation (wealth creation) would be yours tax free. This wealth could be converted into money (via mortgage or loan) and used for any purpose you desire, even creating more wealth and getting more tax-free money. If there is any secret to how fortunes are made, the creation of wealth is it. If there is any secret to how fortunes can be left to grow without danger to principal or profits, this is also it.

Capital gains. Next to financing tax-free money out of your wealth, the best method involves selling it to get the money you want. Any time you sell an investment that you have held for at least one year and you realize a gain by doing so, that gain is called a long term capital gain.

As of this writing, sixty percent of that gain is tax free and the other forty percent is taxed at whatever your tax rate happens to be. Although this may not appear to be as desirable a way of getting your money out as the method described above, it still affords you a pretty good tax break. Add to that the possibility that the tax that is due can be postponed, paid in installments, or even eliminated, and you have a source of money nearly as good as financing your money out of your wealth.

Earned income. As a method of obtaining money, working for it is at the bottom of the list. Don't get me wrong; I have nothing but admiration and respect for those people who earn their own way. The problem seems to be with the I.R.S. The tax laws are written in such a way that the average person is penalized for working for a living. This penalty even follows the average wage earner into retirement, where certain amounts of earned income (but not investment income) can reduce their social security benefits.

TAXES

As we have just seen, the source of a person's money can make a considerable difference to the amount of income tax he pays. When I was growing up, I didn't know any of this. The information wasn't taught in any of the schools I attended, and I doubt if it is taught in any schools today.

My upbringing led me to believe that income taxes were an inescapable fact of life. I even foolishly believed that all people paid income taxes according to the amount of their gross income. It wasn't until I started reading the newspapers that I found out that a lot of people with incomes many times higher than mine were paying less income tax than I had to pay. Some of them even paid no income tax at all: Needless to say, this made me very angry and very frustrated. I didn't like paying all the tax I was forced to pay, yet I didn't understand how someone operating under the same system as I could legally pay little or no income tax.

I suffered with this problem for years. I came to expect an acute attack every year around tax time, but what I didn't expect was the eventual realization that I was my biggest problem and my own worst enemy. I found that Uncle Sam wasn't forcing me to play a losing game. He left that up to me. I found that it was entirely up to me how I got my income. Since I had found out that people pay less tax on capital gains than they do on earned income, and that they pay no tax at all on appreciation of their assets, I decided to switch rather than fight. Once I did that, I came to love the system I used to hate.

Let's look at three different people who received an extra $10,000 and see how the system treated them. The first person financed the money out of an investment, the second person sold an investment that he had held for at least one year, and the third person worked at a part-time job. Assuming that all three people were in the thirty percent tax bracket before their good fortune, here are the results. The first person would owe absolutely no tax whatsoever on the $10,000. The second person would owe around $1,200 in tax ($4,000 × 30% = $1,200. The first 60% or $6,000 of his capital gain is tax free; only the remaining 40% or $4000 is taxable). The third person would owe at least $3,000 in tax ($10,000 × 30% = $3,000). Can you now begin to see why I came to love the tax system after I changed the source of my income?

If this illustration isn't enough to make you want to change, consider the following. If these three people had all been retired and drawing social security benefits, the system would still penalize the person who gets all or most of his income through earned income. Had that $10,000 been their only income apart from social security payments, the first and second people would both be able to draw full social security benefits, while the third person would find his social security benefits cut. All this may not seem fair, but these are the economic facts of life under our present tax system.

The noted humorist Art Buchwald once wrote, "Tax loopholes are available to the rich as well as the poor; it's just the poor choose not to take advantage of them." Although his intent was humor, his message rings of truth loud and clear. You do have a choice. How you exercise it is entirely up to you. If you don't like your present situation or the tax consequences the future holds, you can change things. You can start to take advantage of the so-called loopholes yourself.

Choosing to avoid paying income taxes legally is quite different from choosing to evade paying taxes. The biggest difference is about fifteen years if you get caught and a life of constantly looking over your shoulder if you don't. People who legally avoid paying income taxes are not freeloaders. They can also contribute to the system, society, and the country, just like the people who do pay income taxes. By using the incentives built into the tax laws, these individuals can end up providing housing and jobs for people. In some cases, they can do a much better job of providing these necessities than the government can because they can do so in a more cost-effective way.

FINANCIAL INDEPENDENCE

In the very first line of the preface of this book, I told you that I would show you how to become financially independent by owning as few as four single family homes. Although it may sound impossible, it is nonetheless quite feasible. It works out on paper, and if it works out on paper, you can make it work out for you in your life.

Most homebuyers and renters spend approximately twenty-five percent of their gross income for housing. Most lenders use this figure as a guideline when determining how expensive a house a person can afford. If you are a recent homebuyer or someone who is currently renting, your housing expenditures are probably very close to this amount. If you figure out your housing cost and it comes to a higher percentage, don't worry. Many lenders think that expenditures of up to thirty-eight percent of a person's gross income are still in the safety zone.

Using the conservative twenty-five percent figure, what do you think would happen if you went out and purchased four homes (or rented four apartments) similar to your present living accommodations? In all likelihood, you would find that you have one hundred percent of your gross income going out (4 × 25% = 100%). Now suppose that you owned those four units free and clear and rented them out to someone else. Wouldn't you then find that you have one hundred percent of your gross income coming in? Yes, you would—and that position, ladies and gentlemen, is called financial independence.

"But what about my expenses?" you say. Expenses usually run about thirty percent of the gross rental income if the property is in good condition and the tenant pays all his own utilities. (Expenses include property taxes, insurance, maintenance, and repairs.) Deducting the expenses leaves a net rental income seventy percent of the gross income. In most cases, this income is and will remain completely tax free because of the incentives written into the tax laws by your good Uncle Sam. Considering that you will be lucky to be left with seventy percent of your earned income (wages or salary) after tax, your net income from renting out just four units will be as good as, if not better than, your net income from working for a living.

"But there's a catch," you say. "This only works if you own the properties free and clear." You're absolutely right. If the titles to the properties are not free and clear, the debt payments will probably use up a good portion of that rental income. This position isn't called financial independence, but all is not lost. All is not lost even if you don't have any money to start off with. All you really need is my formula for financial freedom (which I will explain in a minute) and the desire to put it to work for you.

BUYING IT RIGHT

One of the most important aspects, if not the most important aspect, of any investment is the ability to buy it right. If you do not purchase for the right price and in the right way, it may take you years to realize a profit, if you do so at all. You can even create a substantial loss by not buying right, a loss that you may never recover.

Many people think that how you sell an investment is more important than how you buy it. If you figure your profit as the difference between the two, these people are wrong; how you buy it is more important. Since it is infinitely easier and more profitable to negotiate what you want when you are buying rather than when you are selling, that is when you will want to work to lock in your gain. If you are going to be holding on to your investments and not turning right around and selling them, buying them right is even more important.

All successful real estate investors operate using one of two fundamental principles of investing. Either they buy at their *price* or they buy on their *terms*. They may concede on one of these points in order to gain on the other, but they never concede on both. The phrase "My price your terms, your price my terms," is their watchword. Even the most successful investors use these two principles, although they use them a little differently. They don't buy unless they get both their price and their terms.

These two principles of successful investing are the backbone of two different methods you can use to become financially independent in a relatively short time. Both these methods are easy to understand and easy to use, and they work no matter how much or how little money you have to work with. Either of these methods will work for you as they have both worked for me and for others. Nor is it uncommon for either one, used just once, to make you more money than most people earn by working for an entire year.

The two methods of becoming financially independent that we are about to discuss have one thing in common: they enable you to create wealth by buying a home for less than it is worth and then to create even more wealth by improving the home. They differ chiefly in that method one places more emphasis on the price of the home, while method two places more emphasis on the terms of the purchase. Using method one, you buy and improve a home in such a way that you achieve fifty percent equity (equity is the interest or value that you have in real estate over and above the liens against it). Using method two, you buy and improve a home in such a way that only fifty percent of the rental income goes to support the home and its indebtedness, so that the remaining fifty percent can go into your pocket.

FORMULA FOR FINANCIAL FREEDOM

It is now time for me to share with you my formula for financial freedom that I mentioned earlier. You remember that I showed you how you could be financially independent by owning as few as four single family homes. If you recall, there was a catch: you had to have enough money to go out and pay cash for those homes. But I told you that even if you didn't have any money you could still become financially independent if you had and used my formula for financial freedom. The formula is this:

$$8 \times M = FI$$

"M" stands for the method, and "FI" stands for financial independence.

If you use method one eight times in this formula so that you end up owning eight homes with at least fifty percent equity in each, you will be financially independent. Once you have these eight homes, you could choose to sell off four of them and use the proceeds (equity) to pay off the remaining four homes. At that point you would have four homes free and clear, and you would have acquired them all with little or none of your own money.

By the time you are finished with this book, you will know of a number of ways to purchase the homes, even if you don't have any money to start with. You should also come to realize that owning eight homes with fifty percent equity is a better way of getting wealthy than owning four homes that are completely paid for.

Method two can make you financially independent just as well as method one. Although method one may inadvertently produce a fifty percent cash flow, it is not the chief aim (creating fifty percent equity is). The chief aim of method two, however, *is* to produce cash flow. Since this is the case, the *terms* of purchase are very important, and you will negotiate for these more than you will for the price alone.

It should be noted that the percentage of the rental amount needed as cash flow decreases from fifty percent to twenty-five percent as your tax bracket increases. To find the amount of cash flow required to have your rental income approximate your current earned income (net income), use the table below.

Current Tax Bracket	Present Net Income	Required Cash Flow
0%	100%	50% of rental income
10%	90%	45% of rental income
20%	80%	40% of rental income
30%	70%	35% of rental income
40%	60%	30% of rental income
50%	50%	25% of rental income

A number of creative financing techniques we will be discussing when we get into financing will allow you to create a cash flow of fifty percent of your rental income and even better. Having eight homes producing at this rate is as good as having four homes "free and clear" and, just like purchasing eight homes according to method one, can make you financially independent too.

It doesn't matter whether you choose to use method one, method two, or a combination of the two; the formula for financial freedom can make you financially independent. Although eight homes may be considered a minimum when you are starting out with little or no money, remember, financial independence can be achieved with fewer—I did it with just six homes, and I had a disastrous start.

I should mention that if you have a very high income, you may not want to invest in homes as expensive as your own residence. Besides the fact that most high-income individuals can afford to buy their own home, those that do rent aren't always the most desirable tenants. Because of this, you will probably want to invest in middle-income properties and get whatever number it takes to equal the value of four of your homes.

At this point, some of you are probably saying, "It sure sounds simple enough, and it does work out on paper, but it just can't be that easy to do." The truth is, it *is* simple and it *is* easy to do. Many people never try simple, easy things. They think that the only things that work are complicated, hard things. Most of these people come to this conclusion because they are already working as hard as they can, or as hard as they care to, and still not getting anywhere. Thinking success must involve even more effort, they don't try. They never seem to realize that the successful people aren't always those who work harder, but those who work more intelligently.

Many people don't believe that you can buy real estate using either of the two methods I have described. Most of these people have never even attempted to do so, but they will attempt to impose their beliefs and limitations on you. Some of these people may even be realtors or investors. No matter who they are or what they do for a living, don't listen to them. I have met too many people like that in my career, and every one of them has been wrong.

These two methods and the formula for financial freedom will work for you just as they have for me and other successful investors. All you have to do is use them. Once you do that, you will find that they will more than make up for all the special knowledge, unlimited income, inside connections, and luck other investors have or claim to have. Life truly is more logical than lucky, and the formula for financial freedom has a mathematical logic and a success rate you just can't argue with.

FIVE STEPS TO SUCCESS

Using either one of the two methods and the formula we just discussed can start you out investing on the right foot (buying right). If you want to end up at your final destination (goal) in the least amount of time and with the least amount of wasted effort, it would help to know the shortest and most direct route.

As trips go, the one I am about to give you is a very short one—it takes only five steps. Many people spend a lifetime wandering around and never seem to get anywhere. Many investors do the same thing, because they don't know where they are going. Without a destination and without a track to run on, it's easy to get distracted. Remember, too, that even if you are on the right track, you can get run over if you just sit there. Are you ready to move? Here are the steps you will want to take:

Step 1—Find a home owned by a motivated seller, in need of repairs and/or improvements, with no major structural problems.

Step 2—Purchase the home at least twenty percent below value using little or no money down.

Step 3—Make the maximum number of improvements with a return ratio of 4:1, without going over budget.

Step 4—Refinance your profits out at the earliest or the most financially satisfactory time.

Step 5—Have your home start producing income as soon as possible by renting it out to good, qualified tenants.

If any of these steps aren't perfectly clear at this point, don't let that bother you. By the time you get to the end of this book, you should have a clear understanding of them all and know how to take each step yourself. Once you are able to do that, your working days should be over. Financial independence won't be a dream; it will be reality. You will know how to get the properties you will need, and you will know how to work them so that *you* never have to work again.

$OP + OPM = \$UCCESS$

I'm going to close this chapter with an equation. I like this equation because it sums up everything we have been talking about on the subject of success, especially financial success. Success, if you recall, is an individual thing, but even though each individual may have his own definition of success, there isn't a person alive who ever became successful strictly on his own. All successful people owe their success to at least one other person. All financially successful people owe their success to both other people and other people's money.

If you are married, your spouse can be a tremendous help in your quest for financial independence. At the very least, you will want your marriage partner to understand what you are doing and why. If you don't, he or she will probably get scared and try to stop you. If you are fortunate enough to have a marriage partner who wants to be your business partner too, you've definitely got a winning combination. Not only will your journey on the road to success be faster and more enjoyable, but it will also bring the two of you even closer together.

Aside from your spouse, there are a lot of people out there you will need to depend on in order to reach your goal. Lawyers, lenders, contractors, accountants, insurance agents, and realtors are among the first to come to mind. Your success will depend on your knowing how to find the most qualified people in each of these professions and how to make the best use of their services. Your success will also depend on your knowing how to find the financing you will need and how to make the best use of it. This book doesn't skip either of these two important areas.

The Chinese have a proverb that if you invite a man over for dinner, you feed him for a day, but if you teach him to fish, you feed him for a lifetime. I would like to be your teacher and guide and take you on an exciting and profitable fishing expedition. I'll show you where the big ones can be found and how you can catch them. As much as I would like to do more than that, I can't. It stands to reason that I can't make you use the information I am giving you, nor do I have any control over how you use it. You, and only you, exercise that control. It's up to you to cast your lines into the water and reel them in when you get a bite. Then and only then will you attain financial freedom and true financial security.

If success is what you want, then it's up to you to go out and get it. Not everyone can become as wealthy as the Rockefellers, but everyone who reads this book has the ability to become financially independent. Remember this point as you go through the remaining pages and as you go out to realize your financial goals.

CHAPTER THREE

A CASE FOR SINGLE FAMILY HOMES

When you do the common things in life
in an uncommon way, you will command
the attention of the world.

GEORGE WASHINGTON CARVER

I don't have any guts. I never did, and I probably never will. Because of this affliction and my desire to become financially independent, I had to find an investment that would not only afford me unlimited opportunity but would guarantee a high degree of security for my money as well. Single family homes are such an investment.

When it comes to real estate, many people think that in order to be successful they have to go out and get into the big deals, the big investments. All the success stories they read or hear of are about the big boys and the big deals they pulled off. Rarely if ever do they read or hear anything about the thousands of successful investors who didn't make the headlines just because they didn't pull off one of the biggest deals of the century.

I used to think that investing in single family homes was a go-nowhere Mickey Mouse investment. I used to think I could never do as well as the big boys by playing for such small stakes. It took me a long time, but now I know I was wrong. As in the fable of the tortoise and the hare, I know a person can win, and win big, by taking the slower and surer route.

I don't envy the high rollers anymore, because I have seen too many of them lose everything they have because of an oversight or a miscalculation. I don't look at the big deals anymore either and feel bad because I'm not in them. My single family homes provide me with everything I could want out of an investment, including a good night's

41

sleep. A number of high rollers may show little or no interest in this area of the real estate market, simply because it doesn't have the sizzle of a steak. All I have to say is, "Hamburgers sizzle too."

These observations have led me to develop an investment philosophy over the years. This philosophy deals with hamburgers and the hamburger business, but the hamburger business has a lot in common with real estate investments in single family homes. Before I get into all the reasons why single family homes are the best real estate investment for those seeking financial independence, I want to tell you about this investment philosophy, because I believe it can help you develop good business sense and good investment sense. The parallels between investing in hamburgers and investing in single family homes can be signposts to the road to financial success.

GRZESIEK'S HAMBURGER PHILOSOPHY

More fortunes have been made in hamburgers than in steaks. Not only have the people who pioneered a number of the national hamburger franchises made a fortune, but so have many of the people who own and operate those franchise operations. You can bet that when any of these people eat out, they eat steak and not hamburger. I have even noticed with a certain degree of humor the eating habits of a well-known clown who is the spokesperson for one of the national chains. In all of the television commercials I have seen, I have never seen him eat a hamburger. In fact, I have never even seen a hamburger touch his lips. You can bet again that when this clown goes out to eat, he doesn't order hamburger; he orders a great big juicy steak.

When it comes to real estate, single family homes are looked upon as the hamburgers of the business. As an investment, they may not be very glorious, but they can make you a fortune nonetheless. A fortune amassed this way may take a little longer to make, but all things considered, it's well worth the wait.

You don't have to have the best hamburgers in the world to be successful. You won't find very many people who will say that any one of the national franchises has the best hamburger in the whole wide world. Yet despite this apparently major obstacle, each one can be very successful. The secret of this success is that each has a decent product and that it's at a price the average person can afford.

When it comes to single family homes, you will be successful if you follow this example. You won't want to have the best or the most expensive homes in the world. You will want to have decent homes, and you will want to rent them out at an amount that the average family can afford.

There is more than one way to fix a hamburger. There is a national franchise that offers its hamburger with the option of any or all of eight different condiments (mustard, catsup, lettuce, pickle, etc.). With just these eight different items it is possible for this chain to offer its hamburger in any of 256 different combinations.

When it comes to single family homes, there is an unlimited number of ways to fix up a house. Add to that the number of different ways to finance your purchase, and you will come up with a number hundreds or thousands of times greater than eight. The actual number of combinations or deals you can put together is boundless. In fact, you will be limited only by your ingenuity and your determination. You can put together deals that are as individual as you are. You can, in effect, create a deal that appeals to your financial appetite as easily as you can create a hamburger that appeals to your own particular appetite for food.

Competition means more business and more profits. If a new hamburger stand were to move into your town, where do you think the owners' first choice for a location would be? More often than not, their first choice would be right next door to their competition. If they couldn't get that location, they would probably try for one right across the street. Your first impression may be one of wonderment, but they really know what they are doing. They know that they are more likely to do more business in that location than they could anywhere else, even if that anywhere else were the other side of town where there isn't any competition at all.

When it comes to single family homes, you will get more and better buys because of the competition than you ever could without it. For example, if you are the only person to put in a ridiculously low offer on a house, the seller may doubt your judgment and turn you and your offer down. On the other hand, if your offer is one of many such offers, the seller will start to doubt his own judgment and may accept your offer.

WHY INVEST IN SINGLE FAMILY HOMES

It's no secret that real estate is one of the best investments around. What isn't very well known is that single family homes have outperformed all the other types of real estate investments for years. The American dream of home ownership may be the biggest factor in explaining this performance, but there are many other reasons for it too.

Man's most desirable form of housing. Housing, or shelter, is one of the basic necessities of life. Everybody needs a place to live. Most people, not all people, would like to have a home of their own. Those that can't afford to buy a home of their own at least would like to be able to rent a home. Those that can't do either have to settle for what is left. Apartments are what is left, and for most people apartments are the least desirable form of housing.

Easy to control, easy to understand. That they are man's most desirable form of housing may be the biggest advantage of investing in single family homes, but it isn't the only one. If you are a beginning investor, the importance of an investment's being easy to control and easy to understand can't be overstated. If you are a seasoned investor, you are probably already aware of the importance of these two crucial requirements.

The stock market is a good example, but not the only one, of an investment from which these two requirements of a good investment are missing. When you buy stock in a certain company, what control do you have? Beyond being able to tell your broker, "Buy this," or "Sell that," you have none. In most cases, you can't direct the company, you aren't consulted when there is a decision to be made, and you don't even know the people who run the company or their qualifications.

When it comes to understanding the stock market, things aren't much better. I don't know about you, but I find all the charts, graphs, analyses, and reports are confusing. Even the terminology is like a foreign language. When you are faced with this kind of situation, the only thing to do is abdicate and rely on someone else.

I have found that nobody cares about me and my money more than I do. If a broker makes a few bad calls and I end up losing a lot of money, all he stands to lose is a client. He might feel bad about it (he will probably feel worse about losing a client than about losing my money), but I'm the one who suffers the greatest loss.

Since nobody cares about you, your money, your family, and your future as much as you do, why not find an investment you can control and understand? If ever an investment was created that allows you to do this, it is single family homes. Just about anybody can buy a home. It doesn't take any special training, any special knowledge, or any special degrees or diplomas.

Buying a home for investment purposes isn't any more difficult than buying a home to live in. When it comes to controlling your investment, there really aren't any big problems. You control the purchase price, the rental rate, the improvements you put in, and just about everything else. When it comes to understanding your investment, there really aren't any big problems either. Your cost, your returns, and anything that may affect them aren't any great big, unexplainable mysteries.

Low vacancies. Again, because single family homes are man's most desirable form of housing, they have the lowest vacancy rate of any type of residential real estate. This may not appear to be that important an issue in good times, but let a recession come along, and it's a whole different picture.

Recessions cause people to cut their spending and their expenses. One of the things they do during these times is move back home with Mom and Dad, or bunch up and move in with someone else. This movement causes vacancies, and the market that suffers the least, if it suffers at all, is the single family home market. Even in good times apartment owners have to figure on a vacancy factor of seven to ten percent. People who invest in single family homes don't see those kinds of losses even in the bad times.

No rent controls. Many times in a troubled economy politicians will turn to rent controls to pacify the populace. These rent controls usually affect only buildings that have four or more units in them. Because of this, single family homes are usually immune to this highly undesirable regulation.

If rent controls are ever put into effect, and they do affect single rental units and make them unprofitable, you have a very desirable option—you can sell your homes. Not only can you sell them, you can probably sell them at a profit. Owners of other income-producing property (duplexes, multi-units, apartment buildings) may not be so lucky. The only way they will be able to unload their "alligators" is to sell them at a loss or try giving them away. A look at all the abandoned apartment buildings in some cities will show you how many investors couldn't even do that, so they just upped and walked away.

Statistically, only five percent of all buyers of real estate are buyers of income properties, and ninety-five percent are buyers of personal residences. Although the number of units investors buy is a much higher percentage (because they usually buy hundreds of units at a time and not just one unit as do people who are buying their own place), the numbers are very much more on your side if you are selling a home rather than other kinds of income-producing property. When you are selling a home ninety-five out of every one hundred buyers could knock on your door. Those are darn good odds, and ones I don't mind having on my side.

Good place to learn the basics. If you are just starting out, investing in single family homes is a good place to learn how to play this game of real estate. For a starter, you will learn about negotiating, buying, financing, improving, and managing income property.

One of the best reasons I can think of for investing in homes is that if you make a mistake, *it won't kill you.* Buyers of larger properties can't say that. There are even many consumer protection laws that watch out for home buyers, but not for investors in larger properties.

When you get into the big leagues, the rule is "buyer beware." You have to know what you are doing, and you have to know it well. No one is there to watch out for you. It is better to get your education buying and investing in homes before you decide to take your chances out in the world of high finance and high risk. Besides that, homes are such a good investment, you almost have to try to lose money (and even then it's hard to do).

Availability. Just about everywhere you find people you find single family homes of one kind or another. Not so with apartment buildings. Some small communities don't even have one good-sized multiple unit or apartment complex. Even in those communities that have a number of these buildings, the right ones at the right price and terms may not be available.

When you invest in single family homes, you will always have a choice of homes to buy. It doesn't matter if you live in the smallest town in the state or if you live in the state capital. There will always be more than one property in the price range, size, style, condition, and location that you are interested in. This kind of availability means that whenever you are ready to invest, the properties you need will be there. This kind of availability also means that you can shop and compare. This alone will allow you to get better buys and keep from making a mistake.

Investment flexibility. If all you have are eight rental units, it's far more desirable to have eight single family homes than it is to have all your holdings tied up in one eight-unit apartment building.

If you own an apartment complex, a new apartment building across the street or even across town could cause your building to have vacancies. The opening of a new highway or the closing of one of the area's major employers could also cause vacancies. Even the possibility of the neighborhood changing for the worse overnight could cause vacancies. Vacancies like this mean only one thing—loss of income and loss of the property's value.

The problem of having all your eggs in one basket should be apparent. Although single family homes are not as vulnerable to vacancies as apartment buildings (for reasons already discussed), they are subject to the effects of a neighborhood deteriorating. In areas where most of the units are homes, changes are slower, easier to detect, and therefore, easier to get out of before it's too late. Even if you do get caught and one or two of your homes are affected, it's nice to know that your other homes will help soften the blow.

When it comes to financing, refinancing, or selling, the flexibility of eight homes over one apartment building is even more compelling. If you want, you could transfer all your debt onto some of your homes and own the rest "free and clear." If you wanted to refinance some money out of any particular home, you could do so without disturbing the financing you have on the other homes. (This is important especially if some of that financing is at low rates and on nice, easy terms.) Finally, if you ever want to sell, you can sell only the homes you want to sell, when you want to sell them.

Estate flexibility. Dividing your estate up is a lot easier to do when it already is divided up. Willing or giving eight homes (rather than one apartment building) to eight different people will probably work out much better for everyone involved. Too many cooks can spoil the broth, and too many people involved in one property can put a strain on the investment and their relationships.

Active to passive involvement. Many investors aren't interested in single family homes because they think they are too hard or too time-consuming to manage. One of the advantages real estate has over any other investment is its ability to offer the investor any type and amount of involvement he chooses. If a person wants to run a "ma and pa" operation and do everything himself, he can. If he wants to delegate any or all the responsibilities, he can do that too.

Managing single family homes can be as involved or as removed as you want it to be. I used to swing a pretty mean hammer at one time. Back then, I did practically everything myself. As time went by, I started delegating more and more of the things I didn't enjoy or didn't enjoy anymore. I finally turned everything over to other people and moved 300 miles away from my properties. That's about as passive an investment as you can get, and I arranged it by investing in single family homes.

Great insurance. My investments offer me and my family better insurance than any life insurance policy I have ever seen. If I were to die tomorrow, my family would continue to live in the style to which they have become accustomed. There would be no lump sum that could be all used up and gone someday. There would be no monthly stipends that would end after so many years. There would be no set payments that may be great today, but totally inadequate for to-morrow's economy. They would have an income that would keep pace with the economy, and they would have it to the day they died.

Great assurance. Because my wife and my family worked with me, and because they have an understanding of how to manage real estate, I have no doubt that they could continue to manage it effectively if I did die tomorrow. With that kind of assurance, and the insurance provided by my properties, I know my family will always be taken care of.

Historical evidence. History is a great teacher. When it comes to real estate, it teaches us an awful lot (no pun intended). Since housing is one of the necessities of life, it has been, and will continue to be, a secure investment.

It's a fact that in the past single family homes have increased in value more than any other form of real estate. Real estate in general is a darn good investment because it keeps pace with the economy, but this fact proves that a good thing can be made even better.

As long as we are on the subject of history, I would like to tell you about my grandmother. I'll never forget the impression she made on me the day she happened to mention that she had paid $3,000 for her home. I was just a youngster at the time, and my idea of a lot of money was a nickel, because it could buy everything I wanted in life. The fact that my grandma had paid $3,000 for her home led me to believe she was just about the richest woman in the world.

As much as all this impressed me, I was even more impressed the day she sold her home for around $30,000. During the years my grandmother owned her home, its value had gone up and down with the economy, but in the end her house increased in value. It didn't increase just a little, and it didn't just double in value either. It increased in value a whopping tenfold.

Today, Grandma's house is worth much more than she sold it for. In reality, her house didn't increase in value at all. The value of the dollar just went down, and now it takes many more of them to buy what fewer dollars could buy back then. There are two lessons to be found in all of this. One is that real estate, especially single family homes, is an excellent storehouse of value. The other lesson is: Don't hold today's dollars for tomorrow's economy.

WHY INVEST IN EXISTING SINGLE FAMILY HOMES

There are two very important reasons for investing in existing homes rather than building new ones: cash flow and your ability to choose the conditions. Although cash flow is covered first, the ability to choose conditions is the more important.

Immediate cash flow. With an existing home, as soon as you purchase it you can turn around and rent it out. If you are going to build, you don't have that advantage. Building takes time, and time is money. It takes time to find a lot, decide on plans, choose a builder, and get a construction loan. Labor problems and material shortages can also use up more valuable time and cut further into your eventual profits.

Ability to choose the conditions. By investing in homes and areas that have already proven themselves, you are making one of the most secure real estate investments even more secure. All older and existing homes have a record of past performance. You will know by looking at their past if they are in an area that will be going up, going down, or going nowhere at all. Knowing this, you will have a pretty good chance of predicting their future and yours.

When you are building, you are usually trying to create conditions that didn't exist before. I'm sure you have all seen subdivisions that have died on the vine. Someone put a road through a field, and someone else was unfortunate enough to buy and build there. The people who developed these miniature ghost towns may have been professional developers, experienced builders, and seasoned financiers. These people may even have had feasibility studies done which backed them up. Everything pointed to success, and yet the venture failed. It failed because they were trying to create conditions that didn't exist before.

WHY NOT OTHER REAL ESTATE INVESTMENTS

Single family homes are not the only avenue open to you in the land of real estate. You can invest in vacant land, commercial properties, apartments, and condominiums. Each of these has its own advantages and disadvantages. Although these other alternatives usually involve a higher risk, they can produce higher returns. You can get rich virtually overnight in some of these investments, but you can also lose your fortune that quickly too.

Vacant land. By far the biggest disadvantage to investing in vacant land is that it is not self-supporting. You make the down payment, you make the payments, you pay the taxes, and you pay the insurance. If there are weeds to be cut, you end up paying for that too. You might even have to pay for all or part of the improvements that run past your property while you are the owner (roads, sewers, water, etc.). Buying vacant land in the hope of selling it at a later date for a profit really isn't investing at all; it is speculating. You are betting that conditions that you can't control will cause your land to increase in value more than the cost you incur while holding it.

Buying vacant land with the intent of developing it is not really investing either. It is more of a business than an investment, and should be treated as such. It is a business that is dependent on creating conditions that didn't exist before. Many developers, both large and small, have gone out of business trying to do just that. Investing in vacant land takes money, guts, and luck. Developing a piece of land takes a lot of money, guts, luck, and business sense.

Commercial properties. Investing in commercial properties can be a very lucrative and trouble-free investment. Most commercial property is leased out for terms that can run from a year all the way up to ninety-nine years. Many commercial leases leave the tenant responsible for maintenance, repairs, improvements, remodeling, taxes, insurance, and anything else the owner wants to delegate to him. This kind of situation relieves the investor of all management responsibilities for his property. All the investor has to do is sit back and cash the rent checks when they come in. It is possible for investors in situations like this to buy properties they will never see or visit. It doesn't even matter if the properties are located in other states or on the other side of the country.

Anything this good has to have a catch, and commercial properties do have a catch. When commercial properties become vacant, they can remain vacant for some time. This can be very expensive, and if the vacancy is too long, it can be downright devastating. Getting a new tenant to move in can also be expensive. He may require that you remodel and update the building before he signs the lease. Even if you get him to sign a ninety-nine-year lease, he could go out of business six months later. If you had put a lot of money into the building, you could find yourself in a lot of trouble. If you are able to survive something like this, and are lucky enough to find another tenant, you may have to put more money into the property to get him to sign a lease.

Besides the high cost of vacancies and improvements, commercial properties also have another major drawback: they are very vulnerable to the economy. When times are tough, many businesses close their doors. A vacancy at a time like this can be awfully hard to fill. Existing businesses usually aren't expanding and will not be interested in leasing more space. People wanting to go into business will want to wait until things pick up before they open shop. By the time the economy turns around, you could also be out of business.

Apartment buildings. Apartment buildings can be great investments if you have a good building, a good location, and a good
manager. Finding all three of these things may be a problem, but not
your only problem. As mentioned earlier, when the economy goes
down, the number of vacancies in apartments goes up. The opening of
a new apartment building and the closing of a business cause
vacancies to increase, too. A change for the worse in the neighborhood
surrounding the apartment building and the implementation of rent
controls can also increase vacancies, reduce rental income, and
reduce the value of the property itself.

If you live in an area where there is a good selection of apartment
buildings and you think you may want to try investing in them, invest
in a few single family homes first. By getting your feet wet this way, you
will be less apt to make any big mistakes. You will also want to read a
couple of books by Albert J. Lowry before you start. One is *How You
Can Become Financially Independent by Investing in Real Estate,* and the
other is *How to Successfully Manage Real Estate in Your Spare Time.*

Condominiums. To my way of thinking, many condominiums are
just overpriced apartments. They allow you the chance to buy an
apartment which would rent for $300 a month for a "mere" $500 a
month, plus a "small" maintenance fee of about $50 a month. As
resistible as this proposition may sound, many people are finding it
hard to say "No."

Many shrewd speculators and apartment owners are taking advantage of this latest real estate kick. It's not uncommon for a speculator to
buy a condominium before the ground is even broken, just so he can
turn around and sell it for a quick profit once the place is built. Usually
it's another speculator who buys the condominium from him so that
he can turn around and sell it for a profit. Many apartment owners,
wanting to get in on the act, have started converting their apartments
to condominiums. It wasn't any surprise to them when they found
they could sell the parts for more money than they can get out of the
whole building. Many other apartment owners, with undesirable or
unsalable properties, have found that they could get rid of their
"alligators" at a profit by converting them to condominiums.

Investing in condominiums can be risky even without the problems
just covered. Restrictions and conditions that go along with most units
may not allow you the freedom to do what you want with your invest-

ment. Even under the best of circumstances, you will never have total control over what happens to the building that your unit or units are in. A deteriorating building, a defunct project or developer, legal problems, management disputes, or undesirable neighbors can render your investment unsalable, even at a substantial loss. On the whole, condominiums seem to have all the disadvantages of apartments but none of their advantages. Investing in condominiums gives a whole new dimension to the ancient adage, "Let the buyer beware."

IN CONCLUSION

I don't believe that there is a better all-around all-time investment than real estate. Since people are always making more people but nobody is making any more land, the future for real estate is a good one. Of course, most large institutional investors have known this for years. That's why most insurance companies and banks take your money and invest it in real estate. Most of them do give you a little something for the use of your money, but they keep the lion's share for themselves. After I show you how to compute the returns you can get by investing in real estate and you see how high they can be, you will never again be willing to accept the paltry sum these middlemen pay you for the use of your money.

Yes, investing in real estate can make you wealthy. I believe that the easiest and the safest road to wealth you can take is the one that leads you up a street lined with single family homes. I hope this chapter has shown you why I feel the way I do. What you are about to learn in the remaining chapters is how to complete the rest of the journey. The way I have mapped it out is not new or untried; it is proven. It has been traveled by many successful investors before and since I traveled it. If your journey proves to be anything like mine (and I'm sure it will), it will be short and sweet. It may even end up being one of the most enjoyable and memorable trips of your life.

CHAPTER FOUR
WHY PEOPLE INVEST

*Unhappiness is not knowing what we want
and killing ourselves to get it.*

ANONYMOUS

Before you put your first dollar into any investment, you should know what kind or kinds of returns you want. Once you know that, it is fairly easy to decide what you are going to invest in and how you are going to finance your investment. Since no two people are alike, no two investment programs will be alike. Although you may share the same financial goal as thousands of other people, each one of you will probably have to go about attaining it in a different manner, using different means.

Most investments offer you what I call the abc's (appreciation, beneficial tax treatment, and cash flow). Investing in real estate offers you a fourth return that many other investments don't—debt retirement. These four investment objectives or returns can be mixed to any degree, in any amount, to create an investment that is as individual as you are. For those of you who are still worried about competition, this one fact alone should put your fears to rest. The possibility that a certain investment (house) can be purchased in such a way as to give you exactly what you want also creates the possibility that the same investment won't produce what another investor wants. In effect, one man's meat is another man's poison.

If you don't want to end up accidentally poisoning yourself, you are going to have to know what these four returns are and how they can affect you.

55

APPRECIATION

If you are looking for an investment that can make you wealthy or even a millionaire, you should be interested in an investment that appreciates. Appreciation is the increase in value that occurs while you are holding an asset. Appreciation is what happens when you purchase some real estate and ten years later wake up to find it has doubled or tripled in value. There are basically two types of appreciation, uncontrollable appreciation and controllable appreciation. Each type can be caused by a number of factors.

UNCONTROLLABLE APPRECIATION

You as an individual and an investor can't control this type of appreciation. It is caused by the government, business, or other large groups. You can take advantage of this type of appreciation when it exists, but you should never base your entire investment on such fickle ground. Remember, the same sword that makes can take away, and sometimes very fast. Here are the three basic causes of uncontrollable appreciation:

Inflation. When the government allows the value of the dollar to drop, it takes more and more dollars to buy the same piece of property. In this case the property doesn't actually increase in value, only in price. Borrowing money to buy an asset that appreciates because of inflation and then paying off the loan using cheaper dollars is a great way to make money as long as inflation continues at a certain pace. If inflation slows down or if it is reversed, doing this can spell disaster.

Supply and demand. When the supply of housing in an area goes down or when the demand for it goes up, the price can increase dramatically. This higher price means that the intrinsic value of the property has increased and that whoever owns it has really made some money. Of course, if things go the other way, the owner can end up really taking a loss.

Speculation. When speculators (not investors) get into a market, prices may go smashing through the roof one day and come crashing to the ground the next. Here emotions rule, not common sense.

Neither the rest of the economy nor normal supply and demand makes any difference.

This seems like a good place to bring up something called the "greater fool theory." Simply stated, this theory says, "Anybody will pay any price for anything if he feels a greater fool will come along and offer him a greater price." Many investors—and people who aren't investors—throw common sense out of the window when they begin speculating. Many of these people never even realize that the fact that everybody is doing something is a good reason not to do it. "Gold fever" and greed blind them to the fact that money is made not by selling investments, but by having and holding on to them.

Any appreciation that occurs because of speculation is very uncontrollable and very volatile. In a matter of minutes the savings of an entire lifetime can be wiped out. When it comes right down to it, speculating is gambling and not investing. Speculating means one person is betting that something is going up and another person is betting that it won't. Somebody always loses, and if that somebody is the last one in line, he loses big.

CONTROLLABLE APPRECIATION

This type of appreciation is caused entirely by actions you as an individual and an investor take and direct. Because of this, I like to refer to this type of appreciation as forced appreciation. The limit to the amount of appreciation you can cause is set only by you and your abilities. You can force appreciation in any of the following ways:

Buy below value. The first, the best, the fastest, the easiest, and the most economical way to force appreciation is to buy property for less than it's worth. There are no waiting, no confusing calculations, and no need for additional hard work or investment in improvements to get this easy instant return.

Buy the worst house in the neighborhood. The next best way to force appreciation is to buy the worst house in the neighborhood. Any improvements put into this property will produce a higher than normal return than similar improvements put into any other property because of the value and condition of the surrounding properties. Buying the worst house in the neighborhood below value can make you a double winner.

Buy properties that need repairs and/or improvements. Renovating properties isn't the easiest way to make money in real estate. It's going to take time, money, and work (yours or someone else's), but the rewards can be great. When buying these kinds of properties, remember these two points: improvements should always make you money, while repairs will always cost you money. You make your profit from repairs by buying the property at a discount far greater than the cost of doing the repairs. Remember that buying the house below its "as is" value can make you a double winner, too.

Improve the management. Improving the management is usually the most overlooked method of controlling inflation. Increasing the income without increasing the vacancy factor or cutting the expenses without decreasing the value by foregoing necessary maintenance and repairs can increase your cash flow and the value of your property. As a rule of thumb, every hundred dollars you can make or save here will increase the value of your property by a thousand dollars.

BENEFICIAL TAX TREATMENT

If you have a large income or any other circumstances that render a sizable portion of your income taxable, you should be interested in an investment that eliminates all or most of your tax liability. Even if your taxes are not all that consuming, you may be interested in finding a way to cut them legally down to zero. Not only is this possible, but it also has Uncle Sam's approval and blessing. A zero tax situation is possible when you have enough paper losses to offset your other income. Paper losses are not actual losses like the loss that would occur if one of your houses were destroyed. These losses are losses that occur on paper (in your books) only.

There are many ways to create paper losses. When it comes to investing in real estate, most of them revolve around the word *depreciation.* Basically, depreciation is the opposite of appreciation. Appreciation is an increase in value, and depreciation is a decrease in value. Even though your houses are increasing in value every year, Uncle Sam allows you to treat them as though they are decreasing in value. Every year, when you fill out your taxes, you are allowed to write off a portion of that artificial loss. You can continue to do this as long as you own the houses. Besides being able to write off the entire cost of your houses, you can write off all the improvements, maintenance, repairs, taxes, and insurance, and just about every other expense associated with the property. The only things you can't write off are the cost of the land and your own labor.

Tax benefits can make the difference between a good investment and a great investment. What you make is not nearly as important as how much you actually get to keep after taxes. This is the bottom line. This is the figure that you should always be concerned with. Many times a smaller, tax-free income or an investment that produces a tax loss (paper loss) is better and more desirable than a larger, taxable income or gain.

CASH FLOW

If you are looking for an investment that will give you an income, you are looking for an investment that produces a cash flow. Cash flow is the spendable income that remains after deducting the operating expenses (taxes, insurance, maintenance, and repairs) and the debt service (mortgage payments) from the gross rental income. You can create an investment that produces a negative cash flow, or you can create one that produces a positive cash flow. You can even create conditions which make that cash flow taxable or non-taxable. You can create just about any amount and any kind of cash flow you need or want. All you have to do is purchase, improve, and manage your houses with that purpose in mind.

When I set out to become financially independent, I set out to find six houses that could produce a combined cash flow equal to my salary at that time. Whenever I found a house that could produce the cash flow I demanded, I bought it. If any of the houses I looked at couldn't be purchased and improved in such a way as to meet my investment objectives, I didn't buy them. If you want to reach your objectives, I encourage you to operate using the same principle. Such decisions are easy to make, and you will never be disappointed with the results.

Although it is nearly impossible to achieve great wealth through cash flow alone, it is very possible to achieve financial independence. The secret to getting the cash flow you want out of your investments is heavily dependent upon the way you buy, improve, and manage your property. The secret to getting the appreciation or the tax benefits you want out of your investments is also dependent upon these three factors.

DEBT RETIREMENT

If you are looking for an investment that has more advantages and fewer disadvantages than a life insurance policy, you should look into an investment that carries a mortgage. Most life insurance policies are nothing more than forced savings plans with a death benefit. Should you die before you have put aside enough money to cover the face value of the policy, the insurance company makes up the difference. A mortgage is basically a forced savings plan too, and you can even have the death benefit added (mortgage insurance or declining term insurance) if you so desire.

One of the biggest advantages of a mortgage payment on an income property over a premium on an insurance policy is the fact that the tenant makes your mortgage payment for you. Add to this the fact that the mortgage payment is made with before-tax dollars and the insurance premium is made with after-tax dollars, and you have a nice way to have your cake and eat it too.

Another big advantage of an income property with a mortgage on it is that your equity builds up faster than the cash value of an insurance policy ever could. If at the same time as you purchased a home you purchased a life insurance policy with a death benefit of an amount identical to the cost of the house, here's what would happen. Starting with the first payment and continuing with every one after that, the equity in the property would increase because the debt would be decreasing. It usually takes years on an insurance policy before any cash value even starts to appear.

Inflation is another point to consider. Inflation causes the actual value of the insurance coverage to decline. A policy that originally provided more than adequate coverage can be totally inadequate a few years down the road. In a case like this, the insurance company becomes a net winner. You're the one who goes in paying the company's premium using expensive dollars, and the company is the one that comes out paying you off in cheaper and cheaper dollars. On the other hand, inflation causes the value of the house to increase.

Inflation also causes the rent to increase. Both of these results of inflation make you, the investor, the net winner.

When it comes to borrowing that money (equity or cash value), the house beats the insurance policy again. Because of inflation and the monthly mortgage payments alone, the equity in a house could increase dramatically. If, in a few years, a person wanted to finance that equity out, a new mortgage may well yield more money than the original purchase price of the house or the face amount of the insurance policy. It doesn't matter how long you live or how much you eventually pay in insurance premiums, you could never borrow that kind of money from an insurance policy.

There is one area in which an insurance policy is generally better than a mortgage. That area involves the interest rates you would have to pay on a mortgage compared to the interest rates you would have to pay on money borrowed from your life insurance policy. Although the interest rates on your policy may be lower, they may not be deductible if you don't or can't itemize your deductions. This will never be a problem with the interest you pay on a mortgage for one of your income properties. If this little plus isn't enough to stop you worrying about the higher interest rate you may have to pay on a mortgage, remember this. You have to pay back your loan to the insurance company, but you don't have to pay back your mortgage. Your tenant does that for you.

There you have the four different returns you can expect to get from real estate. Every one of these returns will affect every investment you make. You can't eliminate any one of them, but you can control to what extent each one of them affects you. Later on I will be showing you what you can do to control and change these returns and how you can compute them. For now all you have to remember is

> **appreciation** creates wealth,
> **beneficial tax treatment** protects it,
> **cash flow** lets you enjoy it, and
> **debt retirement** insures that you do.

CHAPTER FIVE

FINDING BARGAINS

A penny saved is a penny earned.

BENJAMIN FRANKLIN

Finding bargains is the name of the game. In order to be a winner, an investor has to know where to look, what to look for, and what to look out for. We have already discussed the importance of buying a property right, getting it at either your price or your terms, or both. The upcoming chapters, "Offers and Negotiations" and "Financing," will help you do just that. Still, the fact remains that every property for sale isn't, or can't be, a bargain property. This chapter will show you how to recognize those that are potential bargains and the motivated sellers who own them.

THE BEST RENTAL MARKET

Before I get into all the things that can and cannot make a bargain, you should have some idea of what rental market you want to invest in. In order to determine that, it would help to have some understanding of the alternatives open to you.

The best type of tenant. For investment purposes, tenants can be divided into three groups: low-income, middle-income, and high-income. Low-income tenants and high-income tenants have a couple of important similarities. Both have a tendency to be late in paying their rents, and both have a tendency to damage your property. Low-income tenants who do one or both of these things seem to do it because it's just part of their nature. High-income tenants are generally late because they reason that they are able to pay, so you won't have any problem in waiting until they are ready to pay. High-income tenants who damage your property probably do so because they figure with the rents they are paying you, you can afford to fix the things they destroy.

Aside from these similarities, there is a difference between low-income and high-income tenants. Low-income tenants generally have a tendency to demand all kinds of real and imaginary "rights." High-income tenants generally have a tendency to demand all kinds of extra and special "services." Both of these kinds of tenants and their demands can make being a landlord anything but enjoyable.

I have found middle-income tenants to be the most desirable type. Because they are usually living for the American Dream (to own their own home someday), they take care of your property with the same pride they will someday take care of their own. Since they are usually saving for the day they will buy their own home, they don't have any problem coming up with the rent and paying it on time.

The best type of house. If you are going to be renting out property to the people who are living the American Dream, you will be better off investing in either large two-bedroom or small three-bedroom homes. Anything smaller than this eliminates your market, and anything larger will get you professional tenants who probably can't afford the house or its utilities. Professional tenants are people who for one reason or another will never own their own home.

If you recall the second point of my hamburger philosophy, you will know that you don't have to have the best homes in the world to be successful. Decent and affordable homes with only average amenities are all you need. Family rooms, fireplaces, garages, fenced yards, and all the other extras are nice to have, but they aren't necessary.

The best locations. Again, if you are going to be investing in the middle-income market, you will generally want to buy homes in good middle-income neighborhoods. As a rule, you will want to be in or near town. The lure of living in the country or out in the woods has lost a lot of its original appeal. People are now more aware of the high cost of transportation and the added inconvenience involved in getting to work, going shopping, and getting the kids to and from school. Finally, you will probably want to stay out of and away from "one horse towns." These are towns that are totally dependent on any one industry or company. If anything were to happen to this key employer, you could find yourself owning a very nice but worthless piece of property in a modern-day ghost town. One only has to watch the major news programs to realize that ghost towns aren't just things from the past; they can and do exist in today's world.

WHERE TO LOOK FOR PROPERTY

Knowing where to look for bargains is as important to a successful investor as knowing where to fish is to an experienced angler. In fact, fishing and finding bargains have a lot in common. In this section I am going to cover those similarities and show you how to use them to your advantage.

NEWSPAPERS

Newspapers are like public fishing sites, because they are open to everybody. One of the best places to start your search is the classified ad section of your local newspaper. Under the "homes for sale" heading, you will find a variety of ads placed by private owners and realtors alike. Reading through these ads will give you a good, basic feeling of the homes and the prices in your area. Make it a daily habit of turning to this section of the paper as soon as it arrives at your door. Not only will this habit give you a feel for the market; it will give you a jump on any other buyer who may be out there looking for bargains in the paper too.

This habit has paid off for me many times in the past. The first time, though, was the most memorable. It was an extremely hot summer day, and my wife and I had gone over to my parents' house to cool off in their pool. As soon as the paper came, I had my brother bring it to me (I was too lazy to get it myself). Hanging over the edge of the pool, I proceeded to go through the "homes for sale" section. Noticing a new ad for a house that seemed to be exactly what I was looking for, I immediately jumped out of the pool and ran into the house to call the realtor (I wasn't too lazy to do this!). I told her that I was very interested in the house and that I wanted to see it right away. She agreed. Not fully dressed and still wringing wet, I jumped into the car and left. The house was an exceptional buy, and I told her then and there that I wanted it. After we got back to her office and filled out the offer-to-purchase forms, she told me that she had one other committed buyer, who had called right after I did. I respected her for not having mentioned this earlier, and I believed her because I knew the value of the property. I also knew that two other serious buyers had called while I was there.

Before leaving the subject of the newspaper, I should mention a word or two about the type of ads you will see there: "for sale by owner" ads and realtor ads. I also want to mention another source of information about homes for sale in your paper: the legal notices.

For sale by owner. Many people try to sell their homes or their investment properties themselves. Many of these sellers have an over-sized ego or an inflated idea of what their property is worth. Just because the guy down the street sold his mansion for a certain price, they think their tumbledown shack is worth the same amount or even more. Sellers who are this unrealistic are usually difficult, if not impossible, to deal with even under the best of circumstances. Time spent in direct negotiations with these people is usually time wasted.

One of the biggest misconceptions, when it comes to buying a house, is that you can buy it for less by dealing with the owner rather than going through a realtor. This myth is propagated by the owners, who are trying to get you to pay their price. At first, the logic is convincing. The owner leads you to believe that he can sell you his house for less. He tells you that, since he won't have to pay a realtor's commission, he can pass those savings along to you. House feathers! Most sellers are not good Samaritans; they are not interested in passing along any savings whatsoever to you. They want all they can get. If seller would really end up netting the same whether he sold his property himself or had a realtor sell it, he would have a realtor sell it. Only a complete idiot would put himself through all the time, energy, and bother involved in selling a house himself, especially if he could find someone else willing to do it for him. Most sellers are not complete idiots, but *you* could qualify as one if you buy their line and their houses.

I must confess that I bought this line, and my first three homes, from private owners. Back then I refused to buy any home listed with a realtor since I felt the commission only increased the price of the home. My logic would have been excellent, had not my perception of the owner's real motive and the realtor's real usefulness been far from accurate. Once I learned where these owners were coming from and where the realtors could take me, my career as an investor really took off.

Realtor ads. Most realtors use the newspaper as their main advertising medium. They do this because they know that seventy-two percent of all buyers start looking for a home by looking in the paper. Although realtors may advertise any number of homes in the paper, many of the homes they have available never appear. As a rule, they advertise only those homes they feel are enticing enough to get you to pick up the phone and call them. Once you do that, they can get your name and find out what kind of property you are really looking for. Armed with that information, they then start to work to find a home for you and a sale for themselves.

Legal notices. Mortgage foreclosures are published in many papers. People who are losing their homes in this way can be spared a lot of agony if they are able to sell their home before it is auctioned off on the courthouse steps. If there is a way you can help them and yourself at the same time, you might want to consider this source.

Personally, I don't feel good about profiting from someone else's misfortune. Because I feel this way, I have never approached anyone who was in the process of a foreclosure. If you feel all right utilizing this source, then by all means do so. I have only mentioned my own feelings because there are so many ways to make money and feel good about it that you don't have to resort to anything that doesn't appeal to you.

REALTORS

Using a realtor is like using a professional guide when you're on a fishing trip. You aren't guaranteed that you will make a big catch, but your chances sure are a lot better than if you went off on your own.

Multiple listing service. Many realtors belong to some type of multiple listing service (M.L.S.). Every realtor who is a member of that service provides it with a record of all his current listings. All these listings are then compiled, printed, and distributed (usually every week) to every realtor member.

These M.L.S. books can be very helpful when you are looking for property to invest in. In the M.L.S. book, you will find a picture and a copy of the listing information for each property listed. To make matters even simpler, all the properties are arranged first according to area and then again according to price (from lowest to highest). All you have to do is open this book to the areas or the price range you are interested in and start shopping. It's a regular investor's smorgasbord!

I should mention that not all of the listings a realtor has end up in the M.L.S. book. Even though the book may be published weekly, some listings never appear between its covers. These listings are the ones that come in after the book went to print and are sold before the next issue hits the press. These best sellers (houses) are snapped up, either by those buyers who are in constant contact with their realtors or by those investors who have let their realtor know exactly what they are interested in.

"Looking for" list. It doesn't take a realtor long to find a buyer for a real bargain. All he has to do is call a few of the investors on his "looking for" list. If you want to get on that list, it's not a bad idea to sit down and make up a "looking for" list of your own. On your list you will want to write down the size, location, condition, price range, and financing of the type of property you are looking for and anything else that helps describe it. Once you have your list complete, give it to your realtor.

If you don't have a realtor already, get one as soon as possible. If you don't know of a good one, or if you don't know how to find a good one, here is a way to find one in a relatively short time. Take your "looking for" list and give it to a number of realtors, and then sit back and see what happens. Some realtors will start calling you every day with properties that have no similarity whatsoever to what's on your list. Your lack of interest will become apparent, and pretty soon they will be calling every other day, then every other week, and then every other month. Don't waste your time with these people. The realtor you are looking for is the one who may not call for a while, but when he does, he has something.

If you are going to use this method for finding a realtor, don't try it on just one at a time. It could take you forever to find that special one if you go at it like that. Take your list and give it to ten or more realtors at the same time, and let the law of averages work for you.

LENDING INSTITUTIONS

Going into lending institutions is like going into restricted areas to do your fishing. In order to fish these areas, you are going to need special permission.

Any lending institution that makes home mortgages has an occasional one that goes bad. No one likes to publicize the fact that this sort of thing happens, so the problem properties are disposed of as quietly and as quickly as possible.

The primary reason these institutions end up with repossessed properties isn't that they want them. They want their money, and foreclosure is the only alternative. Lending institutions are not in the housing or real estate business. There are certain laws and regulations that limit what and how much property they can hold. When they find themselves approaching their limit, they will make some unbelievable deals. In order to get in on these bargains, all you have to do is introduce yourself to the mortgage loan officers at the lending institutions in your area. Let them know that you would like and are able to assume some of their repossessed properties (problems).

Don't expect to be welcomed with open arms or treated like a hero on your first visit, especially if the institution's officers don't know you. They probably already have a number of regulars who are willing and able to assume their foreclosed properties. All you want to do this very first visit is let the right people know you are interested and give them a chance to get to know you. You should conclude your meeting by asking them please to keep you in mind and asking them if it would be all right to check back with them every once in a while. If you get a positive response, by all means follow up. If you are contacted by them, don't waste any time in replying or you may find the door closed again for good.

YOU

You may never have thought of it, but you are an excellent source of bargain properties. Stop and think for a minute of all the people that you know. No doubt there are quite a few. There are your friends and relatives, the people you work with, and the people you know through your church, clubs, and other organizations. Don't forget all the people you know where you shop, bank, eat out, and go out. And don't forget the people who are usually the first to know when a property is going to be available: the mailmen and the meter readers in your community. All of these people will be more than happy to keep their eyes and their ears open for you. All you have to do is ask them to let you know whenever they see or hear of anything that may be of interest to you.

Finder's fee. You could offer a finder's fee to anyone who finds a property which you eventually purchase. You may not necessarily want to offer this fee to everyone, because most people like to be helpful and bringing money into the arrangement just causes problems. If you choose to do so, make sure you keep a written record of who found what property and when. Give the finder a copy, and date it. This will avoid any confusion as to who was the first to find that particular property.

Since months may lapse between the time you first hear of a property and the time you actually buy it, the need for good records can't be overstated. You will also want to make it perfectly clear that only the first person on record receives the fee. If you don't do any of this, the whole thing can backfire, and you could find yourself running a campaign to clear your name or paying out money to a lot of people who really shouldn't get it in the first place. Last but not least, you should set the fee at a reasonable amount. About $100 should do it.

If you are looking for a good way to get your children interested in real estate, offering them a finder's fee is one of the best ways I know. It doesn't matter how young they may be, their contacts in the neighborhood and in the school-yard make them some of the most knowledgeable people about what's going on in the area. Besides getting them interested in real estate and making use of their communication network, offering a finder's fee only to your children is an excellent way to keep the money in the family.

Sunday safari. Offering a finder's fee to your children is a good way to get an army of scouts out in the housing jungle looking for big game. Another way is to do something as a family, and that something is to take a Sunday safari. A Sunday safari is nothing more than a ride in the family car; you pack up the wife and kids and take off for a couple of hours. What makes this a safari is the fact that you are going out with the purpose of beating a few bushes and possibly flushing out a prize-winning catch or two. You should confine your safari to the area or areas that you want to invest in, and you should include a number of stops to talk to some of the natives (neighbors) and some of the chiefs (owners of the houses you are interested in buying).

The Sunday safari also gives you the chance to check out some of the houses you noticed in your travels during the week. Instead of taking the same old way to work every day, vary your route to take you up and down different streets. Make a note of which houses look vacant, neglected, run down, for sale, or for rent. You can do the same thing every time you go shopping, go out to eat, or go over to Grandma's house. This exercise in finding potential bargains takes very little extra time and effort. You may even find yourself enjoying the hunt and the little side trips that go along with it. Come the weekend, you will have plenty of places to check out and the time to do it. You will also have a better chance of finding more natives and chiefs at home.

Someone once jokingly said, "Two heads are thicker than one." Although that may be true, the original axiom, "Two heads are better than one," is also true. If you are married, don't forget that your spouse can play an important part in the hunt. If you both work, you can both vary your routes. If you drive to work together, one of you can write down the addresses as the other drives. If one of you spends the days at home, that person could take a few minutes each day to check on various houses and to set up appointments to see them together. As you can see, two heads or two people are better than one, especially when they are working towards the same goal.

WHAT TO LOOK FOR IN A PROPERTY

A MOTIVATED SELLER

The very first thing you should look at before looking at a piece of property is the seller. Most people never seem to realize how important the seller really is, and so they waste a lot of precious time looking at problem properties that can never be turned into bargain properties. Remember, it doesn't matter how many problems the property may have; if the seller doesn't have any, the property may not have the main ingredient necessary in order for it to be a bargain property—a motivated seller.

Every seller who has a problem may have a bargain property, but every property that has a problem may not have a motivated seller.

Learning how to spot a motivated seller won't improve your eyesight, but it will improve your foresight and, therefore, your profits. Someone once referred to these motivated sellers as "don't wanters," and that's exactly what they are. They are people who will do virtually anything to get rid of their property. On any given day, it is estimated that at least ten percent of all sellers are "don't wanters." In many cases, these people will sell their property for twenty percent or more under its current market value.

Here are some of the major reasons a seller can become motivated to get rid of his property.

Tenant problems. If anything can make an owner a "don't wanter," nothing can do it quite as fast, and quite as well, as tenant problems. The tenants could be delinquent in their rents, they could be damaging the property, or they could be doing both. There could also be a high turnover rate or a high vacancy factor, because of either poor management or poor property conditions.

High expenses. Because of an inadequate or non-existent maintenance program, the property could be in such poor shape that it now requires a major outlay of funds to get it back in good condition. If this need doesn't exist at present, maybe a financial commitment will be required in the near future. It could be in the form of assessments for paving, underground utilities, utility hook-ups, or some other major expense.

Absentee owner. If the owner is about to move out of town, or be transferred, he could become more and more motivated to sell as the moving date approaches. If the owner is already out of town and unsuccessfully trying to manage the property from afar, he could be a very motivated seller.

Disappointed investor. There aren't very many jobs or professions a person can be successful at with little or no education. You don't need any special training to invest in real estate, but you do need to know what you are doing if you want to be successful. Yet many people invest in real estate without as much as an hour's worth of training and then find themselves at a loss for words (and money) when they fail. The disappointed investor may be sitting on a bargain property, or one you can turn into a bargain by virtue of the knowledge and expertise you have gained by reading this book.

Tired investor. Most tired investors are those who try to do everything themselves; they run what is called a "ma and pa" operation. They never seem to realize that there is a limit to how much any one person can do. Being a "ma and pa" operator may be a great way to start, but it's a lousy way to grow. Commitments to the property, an outside job or vocation, and other interests can soon become overwhelming. When this happens, a person becomes a motivated seller, and his property a bargain property.

Person who doesn't want the property. It's not unusual for a person to inherit some property and then want to sell it and convert it to cash. The sooner he wants his money, the more motivated he is. It's also not unusual for someone with investment property to want to sell it and get into something bigger and better. The faster he has to move, the more motivated he will be.

Person who wants or needs money. Many times the lure of all that equity just sitting there in a piece of property is too much for a person. He starts thinking of all the toys and trips he could have if he sold his property. He is motivated from within. Many times a person's personal or business debts will force him to sell and use the equity in his property to erase his debts. He is motivated from without.

Person who has personal problems. Poor health or a personal tragedy, like a divorce or the death of a spouse, can cause a person to want to get rid of his property. These and other personal problems can make anyone a motivated seller.

Person who is scared. People get scared for any number of reasons, some good and some not so good. When the economy and the future don't look very promising, many people (including investors) will sell everything they have at a discount. Many people (including investors) will also sell at a substantial discount if their property, the neighborhood, or their tenants scare them.

Person with an old listing. Last but not least, any owner whose property has been on the market for some time is very likely to be a motivated seller. It doesn't matter if the seller, the realtor, the property, or the price is at fault. Time has a way of eroding expectations, and therefore time is on your side. Use it, but use it wisely.

There are probably as many reasons for a seller being a motivated seller as there are people. This list isn't all-inclusive, but it does include the major reasons. Whatever the real reason, you will want to keep looking until you find it. It is your assurance of a good buy, and your insurance against making a not-so-good buy. The only word of caution I can give you is this: Make sure the seller isn't a "don't wanter" because the property has some incurable deficiency or fatal illness. If it does, make sure *you* are the one who is the "don't wanter."

CURABLE DEFICIENCIES IN A PROPERTY

Curable deficiencies are minor illnesses you can cure. Sometimes these deficiencies can be taken care of with just a little time and money. Many buyers treat a sick house much like a person with the bubonic plague. They go out of their way to avoid contact, and therefore pass up many of the bargain properties that come their way. As a smart bargain hunter, you will want to be able to tell the difference between a house with curable deficiencies and one that has a fatal disease and is dying. As a smart buyer, you will only be interested in properties that can be nursed back to health. As a smart investor, you will want to reap the rewards that come from curing the patient and having that patient lead a long and productive life.

A house that has curable deficiencies is a house with the right things wrong with it. You may feel that no deficiencies are too big or too many, or you may want to become a specialist and buy only houses that have one or two of your favorite deficiencies. The choice is yours. All you have to do is learn how to spot opportunities in disguise. These opportunities (deficiencies) are listed below. Not only will they provide you with ways to make money by making the improvements, but they will also provide you with the ammunition you need to shoot for, and negotiate, a lower purchase price.

Please note: the return ratios given for each of these items below indicate the return you can expect if you do the work yourself. If you hire the work out, you can expect to cut these returns in half. Also note that there is a limit to how much money you can put into an improvement to get these returns. For example, $100 in landscaping may raise

the value of the property $1,000 (a ten to one return on your improve-
ment dollar). $500 in landscaping may still only raise the value of the
property $1,000. There is a point of diminishing returns on all
improvements; don't go beyond it.

Dirt. (Return is unlimited) Dirt is the bargain hunter's first sign of a
potential bargain. The amazing thing about dirt is that it can take on so
many different forms, and all of them have the same effect: they turn
off most buyers. Dirt can be found outside the house, and it can be
found inside the house. It can be litter and trash strewn all over the
yard, or it can be fingerprints and filth spread throughout the house. It
can be offensive to the nose as well as the eye. It can be caused by
people who live like animals or by animals that live with the people.

One of the nicest things about dirt is that it can be cleaned up dirt
cheap. A few dollars' worth of cleaning supplies and a little elbow
grease can earn you an unbelievable amount of money for your time
and effort invested. Don't ever let the presence of dirt turn you off. Let
it turn you onto and into a potential money maker.

Poor landscaping. (Return ratio of 10:1 means $1,000 increase in
value for $100 invested) Have you ever driven through a subdivision
where all the homes are the same? Have you ever noticed what a big
difference landscaping, or lack of it, makes in the appearance and
appeal of those homes? Worn out grass, overgrown shrubs, and dead
trees are just about as bad as no grass, no shrubs, and no trees. These
are conditions that you will want to be on the lookout for. They offer
you the chance to see your investment grow as the plants themselves
grow. Professional landscapers will tell you that as little as $100 of well-
chosen landscaping can add as much as $1,000 or more to the value of
a house. That's a good return and one well worth digging for.

Need of exterior and interior painting. (Return ratio of 10:1
means $1,000 increase in value for $100 invested) Remember, the
worse a house looks on the outside, the more buyers and renters it
scares away. A new coat of paint can make a world of difference. Old,
weather-beaten, worn, or peeling paint on the outside really detracts
from a house's "curb appeal." Equally detracting is faded and
chalking siding. No matter what kind and condition of exterior, it can
be made to look like new with a fresh coat of paint or stain. It doesn't

take a lot of money or a great deal of skill to paint a house; it takes only time, an extension ladder, and a few nice days.

The outside appearance of a house is very important. The inside of a house is important too. An interior that needs a major painting or decorating job can turn away many potential buyers and renters (though not as many as an exterior that needs work). If both the exterior and the interior need painting, you may be looking at a bargain that most people would pass up.

There isn't any surface, inside or outside a house, that can't be made to look better with a new coat of paint or stain. If in doubt as to what to use or how to apply it, contact an established paint store or a qualified contractor. Remember, too, that ten dollars' worth of paint in the bucket is worth a hundred dollars on the walls.

Outdated kitchens and baths. (Return ratio of 4:1 means $1,000 increase in value for $250 invested) There are no rooms in a house that will date it and make it unattractive more than these two rooms. These two rooms also turn off and turn away more buyers than any other feature of a house. Because these two rooms are so important, they also hold the most potential of any rooms for increasing the value of a home. Improving or remodeling these two rooms need not be expensive or as big a project as most people envision. Later on, I will show you how to use ideas to do so, rather than a lot of time and money.

Poor wall and ceiling surfaces. (Return ratio of 4:1 means $1,000 increase in value for $250 invested) Small cracks and holes are easy to repair and tend to scare very few buyers. On the other hand, large cracks and holes and crumbling or fallen plaster scare even the most courageous buyers. With all the products on the market today, you are not faced with the work or expense associated with these problems in the past. All you have to do is choose how you wish to repair or cover the problem. New patching materials, texture paint, drywall, paneling, wallcoverings, ceiling tile, and suspended ceilings are but a few of the choices. And don't forget, all these things come with instructions for the do-it-yourselfer.

Poor floor surfaces. (Return ratio of 4:1 means $1,000 in value for $250 invested) A new floor covering can do as much for a room and a house as everything you can do to the walls and the ceilings combined. Unless you have had the chance to see a room before and after new flooring has been installed, you can't imagine the difference and the effectiveness. Linoleum and tile have some advantages over carpeting, but their biggest drawback is that they have to be installed over a fairly good surface. Carpet, on the other hand, can be installed over just about any surface regardless of its condition. This one advantage can save you a lot of time, money, and hard work.

Old, broken, or non-existent lighting fixtures. (Return ratio of 10:1 means $250 increase in value for $25 invested) Installing one nice, not expensive, light fixture is your best limited investment item. You can add more appeal and value to a house by putting a fancy light fixture in one of the focal rooms (foyer, living room, dining room, kitchen) than you can by putting that money anywhere else. Homes with broken and outdated fixtures generally have a profit potential because they can easily and inexpensively be replaced. Homes without lighting in any rooms can also produce profits, but only if the price of the electrical work is negotiated off the purchase price.

Please note: The next three items usually don't make you money by your fixing them; they make you money because you buy the house for less money because they exist. The return ratios stated for the first two are optimistic, to say the least.

High energy cost. (Return ratio of 1:1 means $1,000 increase in value for $1,000 invested) Buyers and tenants alike are becoming more and more energy-conscious. The cost of heating and cooling a home is becoming a primary concern, and it should become one of yours also. If energy costs are high, can they be lowered by the addition of insulation or storm doors and windows? Can the house be insulated easily, or will it take an insulation contractor and special equipment? Will you be able to retrieve your cost in a few years, or will it take longer than that?

Aging heating, plumbing, and electrical systems. (Return ratio of 1:1 means $1,000 increase in value for $1,000 invested) If any of these systems is twenty-five years old, they could probably use some updating or complete replacement. These kinds of improvements are usually expensive and require the services of a licensed tradesman.

The cost that you incur when attempting these projects may take years to recoup. It's not a bad idea, before buying, to estimate the remaining useful life of these systems and their eventual replacement cost. You don't need any big unexpected expenses upsetting your program, and these items can do it. If you have any doubts about any of these systems, have them checked out. If there are any problems, either have the seller correct them before you buy, or use them to negotiate a lower price.

Emergency repairs. (Return is usually negative) A leaking roof, broken doors and windows, unworkable switches and outlets, defective locks, and dripping faucets are a few of the things that qualify as emergency repairs. Fixing these things around your own house doesn't increase its value, and fixing them on one of your investments doesn't increase its value either. Although you can't make money by doing any of these things, you can make money by buying a house at a great discount because of their existence.

WHAT TO LOOK OUT FOR IN A PROPERTY

Again, the seller and not the property is your first and most important consideration. Once you are satisfied that the seller is not out to get you, you can turn your attention toward the property. Aside from these two things, the only other thing you have to look out for is hurting yourself. The chapter on offers and negotiations will help you to avoid this, by showing you ways to keep yourself and your emotions in check.

SELLERS LOOKING FOR SUCKERS

Mr. For Sale By Owner. Many people who attempt to sell their property themselves have a very inflated idea of its true value. They also have the idea that using a realtor is ridiculous, because it will take away some of their profits. Because of these two beliefs, sellers who use the "for sale by owner" approach are difficult to deal with, to say the least. If you are going to deal with these sellers, it is best to have your attorney or your realtor negotiate for you.

Mr. Professional Investor. If an experienced investor is going to unload any of his properties, the first ones to go will usually be his "dogs." Add to that the fact that his experience may allow him to negotiate *his* price and terms, and you don't stand much of a chance for getting a good deal.

Mr. Pay-For-Potential. This is the guy who tells you that once you make all the necessary improvements, the property will be worth at least what he is asking. If he is so positive, ask him to prove it by fixing the place up using his time and money, and not yours. Tell him that once the improvements are finished, you might consider buying, but then only at your price and terms.

Mr. Complexity. This is the seller, or his agent, who dazzles you with figures and formulas that you can't understand. The outcome of all these complicated computations is that you are going to make a bundle and you really don't have to understand how. Remember, if you can't understand it and control it, you don't want to own it.

Mr. Faulty Logic. This is the person who projects that great things will happen to you if you buy. Unfortunately, all his assumptions are based on conditions that can and do change. Many times he proves his point by using successful examples from the past. He fails to mention that for every success there may have been a thousand or more disasters.

Mr. Pressure. This is the person who tells you that if you don't act right now, there is someone else waiting in the wings to scoop up this fabulous buy. Your best response to these tactics is to get up and walk away. Of all the times I have had this used on me, only once was there someone else really there, and he didn't end up buying it either.

INCURABLE DEFICIENCIES IN A PROPERTY

Incurable deficiencies are those problems that can eventually kill off a house and your investment program in the process. It can be a fast death, like the one that overtook my first house (condemnation), or it can be a slow, agonizing process that keeps requiring more and more transfusions of money to keep the patient alive for just another day.

Regardless of the fatal disease a house has contracted, you will want to avoid it at all cost, because that's exactly what it will end up being—

all cost and no profit. Yes, you can bury your mistakes, but the funeral (demolition) can be rather expensive. Undertaking a property with incurable deficiencies is a sure way to end up in front of the undertaker. Don't do it.

Problems with the lot. There is an old axiom in real estate that the three most important things about any piece of real estate are location, location, and location. Location is important. A house can vary in value thousands and thousands of dollars just by virtue of its location. In such a case, the location of the lot affects the value of the house that sits on it.

If the lot happens to be substandard (smaller than the minimum size required today in a given area to build on), there could be problems. You may not be able to get building permits to improve the property. You also may not be able to get building permits to repair the property if there is damage to it. In such a case, you may have to tear it down and haul it away.

If the lot happens to be the lowest lot in the area, it could become the community reservoir every time it rains. Owning lake front property may be profitable, but owning the lake is not. Stay away from these kinds of lots unless the problem can be solved permanently.

Problems with the structure. Homes with structural problems should be avoided like the plague. If it is possible to correct the problems, it usually takes so much money that it isn't profitable to do so. Carry a flashlight and a screwdriver with you whenever you look at a house. Go into the basement (or the crawl space) and attic, and poke all the joists and rafters. If the screwdriver goes in, you'd better get out! The home has structural problems, and you don't want to own it.

Problems with the floor plan. Many times a house grew as the families in it grew. Each new addition added more space, but at a sacrifice; the home in its present condition may have a terrible floor plan. Changing it isn't just a simple matter of blocking off one door and cutting a hole for a new one. The wall where the new door is to go may be a load-bearing wall, or it may have utility lines running through it. If you are contemplating a change, have a contractor give you a *free* estimate before buying, to determine if it is physically and financially possible.

Problems with the closet and storage space. Many older homes were built with little or no closet space. Back then everything a person owned could be put in a foot locker or a free-standing closet. Today such methods of storage are totally inadequate. If a home doesn't have ample storage space or if closets can't be added, it has a definite drawback. It will turn off both buyers and renters.

Problems with the deed, zoning, ordinances, easements, and existing financing. If there are any unsurmountable problems in any of these areas, it's nice to know about them before you waste too much time looking at a property. Usually the seller's realtor, or your realtor, will know of these problems if any exist. The people at your local title companies can help you too. They can show you how and where to do your own research. Once you get to the point at which you are ready to put in an offer or going to set up a closing, your attorney can give everything a final once-over. If he finds anything that isn't in your best interest at that point, let him take over.

HOUSECHECK

The housecheck form (found at the end of this chapter) that we are about to go over is one of the most valuable and useful tools any investor can have in his bag. I encourage you to use it every time you look at a piece of property. Not only will it save you thousands of dollars in oversights, but it will also make you thousands of dollars when it comes time to negotiate the price.

The best time to use this form is on your first trip through a property. You will find that by filling it out at that time and noting all the deficiencies, you tend to destroy completely the seller's expectations of getting a high price.

The left hand side of the page. The housecheck form is laid out so you can easily file it and find it. When the form is placed on its side in a file or in a folder, the property address is the first item you will see. This will make it easy to find the form for a given property if and when you go back later to look it up. Depending on the size of your town and the number of forms that you fill out, you may want to file them alphabetically by street or by area. It doesn't matter what kind of filing system you use as long as it works for you. Just make sure that you use and file your forms.

Sometimes it happens that a couple of months or even a couple of years after you look at a house, the seller may contact you. He may want to know if you are still interested because he is now interested in bargaining. It sure is nice to be able to go to your file when this happens and pull out your forms. You will be getting calls like this every now and then if you are out there looking at enough homes, so it is wise to be prepared. Also if you are out looking at and considering a lot of different homes, it becomes a necessity for you to keep records. Without a file and a record like this, it will be impossible to keep all the houses separate. It will also be impossible to remember what you saw and what needed to be done to each different home.

All the information along the left side of the page should be filled in. Make sure you get the owner's name and the date you looked at the property. Although there is not enough space provided to describe completely the landscaping, driveway and walks, exterior painting, interior painting, emergency repairs, walls, ceilings, floors, floor plan, kitchen, bath, plumbing fixtures, and electrical fixtures, you may want to put down one or two key words that will jog your memory. If you need more space, use the back of the page or attach separate pages or lists to this form.

Lot elevation. Buying a house that sits on the lowest lot in the area can create "a lot" of problems. Having a muddy yard is the least of them. If the house has a septic tank, the sewage system may fail to work for a day or two after every good rain. If there is a basement or crawl space, it may be continually damp and musty or be open to an occasional flooding. Furnaces and water heaters on lots like this have a tendency to go out, wear out, and rust out much more often. If rainwater is not diverted from the house, these problems can also exist regardless of the lot elevation.

I once bought a house that sat on the lowest lot in the area. I knew better at the time, but I figured that I was pretty smart. I figured that I could bring in a couple of loads of dirt and solve the problem. Well, I did, and it solved the problem for about a month. The neighbors missed my low lot so much that they brought in some dirt to raise the level of their yards. I was back to square one.

Foundation, crawl space, basement. Are the walls, the footings (if they are visible), and the basement floor (if there is one) sound?

Are there any signs of flooding or water problems? Water stains and discoloration are usually good indicators of a problem; so is a musty smell and the presence of mold. If there is a problem, is it caused by rain water not being directed away from the house, or is it a more serious problem than that?

Structure. If any of the floors or walls are not square or sound, it is a pretty good indication that the house has structural problems. Structural problems are expensive to correct, if they can be corrected at all. Homes with major structural problems should definitely be crossed off your list of prospective homes. Remember, you want to buy possibilities, not problems. Structural problems are real problems. Avoid them at all cost.

Many times the windows, doors, or sills in a home may be rotten. This condition doesn't necessarily mean the whole house is rotten or structurally unsound. If the damage is limited to these items, it is worth replacing them, but make sure you negotiate the cost off your purchase price. If the damage has gone beyond these areas, don't even consider the place.

Dry rot and termites are major problems. Dry rot can be found by poking at the boards, joists, and rafters in the basement and in the attic. Use a screwdriver; if it sinks easily into the wood, you know the wood has dry rot. There is no cure for this other than replacing all the wood or, in other words, replacing the house. Moisture and poor ventilation usually cause this problem. Termites are just as great, if not a greater, problem. If you live in an area where they are known to exist, learn to recognize their presence. If you have any questions, check out your local library or consult your local pest control man. If you are still in doubt, have the seller furnish you with an inspection report. If there is a problem, have the seller correct it before you buy.

Falling porches, awnings, and shutters do not necessarily denote any structural problem, but they just may provide a house with enough earmarks to make it a real eyesore. If these things exist, you just might be looking at a real bargain, as long as the problems can be corrected without a great deal of expense.

Roof. Most roofs have a twenty to twenty-five year life. If a roof is approaching that age, it won't be too long before it needs replacement. A lot of sun, extreme temperatures, and constant moisture can hasten the aging process. If there are two layers of roofing on already, many building codes require that they be torn off before a new roof can be installed. This can add a great deal of expense to the job by almost doubling your cost.

Are there any eaves on the house? Some areas of the country do not use them and other areas do. Are they needed in your area or on the particular house you are looking at? If there are eaves on the house, are they in good condition, and do they carry the water away from the house? Have they gotten blocked up and caused the edge of the roof or the trim boards to deteriorate or rot?

What shape is the chimney in? If the mortar is powdery or washing away or if there are bricks or blocks missing, it will have to be rebuilt. Rebuilding a chimney is not fun and can end up costing hundreds of dollars if you have to hire somebody to climb way up there to rebuild even the top couple of feet. Another thing you will want to check is the height and placement of the chimney. If the chimney is not at least three feet higher than the peak of the roof, there may be a tendency for backdrafts to blow down the chimney. These backdrafts can blow out pilot lights on furnaces and water heaters. They can also blow lots of soot, dirt, and fumes into the house. If there are backdrafts, there is usually evidence of dirt or soot around the draft control mechanism. This device is a special type of vent or damper inserted somewhere in the line that carries the exhaust from the furnace to the chimney.

Insulation. The type and the amount of insulation that a house has or doesn't have are becoming more and more important. So is the existence of storm doors and windows. Last year's heating bill should give you a good idea of just how well the house is insulated and if it needs more insulation or not. If the house is going to require more insulation, can it be easily installed? Will it be cost-effective? Can you have the seller do it?

Heating system. How old is the system? If it is over twenty-five years old, it will probably need replacing in the near future. Is it an old furnace that was converted? Will the ducts have to be replaced or re-run when a new furnace is installed? If there is a supplemental heating system, is it properly installed to prevent asphyxiation or fire?

I once bought a house that had an old coal furnace and no hot water heater. If you wanted hot water, you had to fire up the furnace because the hot water lines ran through the furnace. No fire, no hot water. Because this was such an undesirable situation, I was able to buy the house right. Normally, though, replacing a heating and plumbing system will not net a profit like this one did. That is why you will want to negotiate these costs off the purchase price of a home, especially if they are expenses that will be coming up in the near or immediate future.

Plumbing system. If a house has city water and sewers, you will want to know if they are hooked up and if the assessments are paid. If a house has a well, you will want to know its age and if it is a shallow or a deep well. You will also want to know where the well and the water pump are located. Most important, you will want to know if the water is safe and make sure the well is not contaminated. You will always want to make sure that the health department has checked and approved a sample of the water before you buy a house. Unknowingly I once bought a house with a contaminated well. By the time I got it back in order, I was out almost $1,000 in lost rents and the cost for a chlorinator.

If a house has a septic system, you will want to know the size of the tank (number of gallons), its location, and the location of its cleanout. Nothing is worse than digging up the whole yard trying to find the tank and its cleanout the first time you have a problem. If nobody seems to know the answers, you can and should check with your local health department. If their records go back far enough, they will have all the information you need. They may also have the information on a well.

If a well or a septic system is over twenty years old, it may be inadequate. They may also start having problems and need replacement. In order to be prepared for that day, ask the friendly people at your local health department what the new requirements are for wells and septic systems (size and depth) and what the estimated cost may be. They will be glad to help, and you will want to know that information before you get into the house.

After checking the type of systems (well, septic, city water, city sewers), you will want to check the systems themselves. Your first step will be to check the water pressure. This is done by turning on both the hot and cold water in a tub or sink, then flushing the toilet. If the water that is running out of the faucet decreases dramatically, the water pressure is too low. Low water pressure can be caused by an inadequate plumbing system or corrosion within that system. If there is a well, it can also be caused by a problem with the well, a problem with the water pump or pressure tank, or just too low a setting on the pressure control valve.

Next turn on all the faucets and flush all the toilets to make sure they all work. This little exercise also lets you know if all the drain and sewer lines are in working order. Don't be embarrassed to do any of this. I was, until I bought a place that needed a whole new plumbing system—and I mean everything from the pipes right on down to a new water heater (that one cost over $1,000). Needless to say, I am not embarrassed any more. Moral: Always check all the faucets and drains.

Your final check will be to locate the main sewer cleanout. If there is no place to get into the main line before it leaves the house, there may be no easy way to clean out the sewers if they become obstructed. Not having an inside cleanout is no great problem, but its absence could be used as a good bargaining point. Installing an inside cleanout is also no great problem, so don't let its absence worry you.

The material composition of the water and drain lines is important. If they are galvanized, they are at least twenty-five years old and may need replacing in the very near future. If they are copper or plastic, they are newer and less apt to give you problems or need replacing. Copper and plastic are also easier to repair and replace than galvanized plumbing. This is a definite plus when it comes to making changes or repairs.

The water heater is the next thing in the plumbing system you will want to check. Is it in good condition, or does it look as if it's on its last leg? The last thing you will want to check for is the existence of a washer and dryer hook-up. You will also want to check and see if there is a dryer vent.

Electrical system. The first question again is, how old is the system? There may be an inspection tag on the main box (service panel) that will give the date the system was installed, updated, and/or last inspected. If there are no add-on boxes or no new wires running into or out of the main box, the system is probably an original installation. If the box has fuses, it is at least twenty-five years old and probably inadequate for today's use. If it has circuit breakers (switches), it is newer and may be adequate.

A minimum service for today's homes is around 100 amps. An adequate service would be more in the neighborhood of 150–200 amps. If the amp service rating is not stated on the main box, it can be estimated by taking the number of circuits (number of fuses or circuit breakers) and multiplying that number by 15 amps (the number of amps most circuits are wired for). An older home with an electrical system that has not been updated may have only four fuses. This means that it has a 60 amp service (4 fuses × 15 amps), a service that is totally inadequate using today's standards.

Before leaving the main box, you will want to check if there are any fuses (if it is a fused system) over 15 amps or 20 amps. If there are, you can be fairly certain that the system is inadequate, as they were probably put in because the smaller fuses kept blowing out. If there are any 25 amp or 30 amp fuses, you know, without a doubt, that the system is inadequate and, indeed, has been causing problems.

Now you are ready to leave the main box and go through the house checking to see if all rooms have controlled lighting. I'm not talking about pull chains or light fixtures with little knobs or switches; I'm talking about honest-to-goodness wall switches that operate a light fixture or an outlet that a lamp can be plugged into. The absence of controlled lighting or any lighting at all is another problem that you will want to be aware of.

Next, count the number of outlets in each room. As you put down the numbers, you will also want to note if the outlets are two-pronged or the newer three-pronged (grounded) type. If there is a mixture of both types, it is an indication that the house may have had some rewiring or that somebody replaced some of the outlets, incorrectly using the newer type. If you really want to get technical and find out what the story is and if the outlets are indeed wired correctly, you can buy a three-pronged tester at most hardware stores and check them out. This tester is inexpensive and easy to use, and it makes you look as if you know what you're doing.

Getting back to the number of outlets in each room. Why count them? First of all, to find out if all the rooms have at least one outlet. I once bought a great big, older, two-story home without giving this subject any thought. After getting into the house, I discovered that there was only one outlet for the entire upstairs. That one outlet, which was located in the hallway, had somehow to service three bedrooms and a bathroom. Even with extension cords running all over the place, it just didn't work. This house didn't need to be rewired; it needed to be wired. My cost—over $1,000.

Public and/or municipal utilities and services. Are they all hooked up and operational? A meter hanging on the side of the house doesn't guarantee anything. In fact, before I added this item to my housecheck list, I had purchased a home that had passed through every one of the aforementioned check-up items. I had done such a thorough job of examining this house, I was confident that nothing could take me by surprise. Within ten minutes after the closing, I was to have my confidence taken away and a new item added to my growing list.

The house I had purchased was one that was foreclosed upon. It turned out that the former owners didn't like paying their utility bills any more than they liked paying their house payments. When the gas company turned off their gas, the former owners simply broke the seal at the meter and turned it back on. Not to have this happen again, the gas company dug down at the street and disconnected their service. Unaware of this condition, I bought the house. When I called to have the gas turned on, I was told I didn't have service. I was told that I would have to apply for a new service, pay a new service fee, pay for the installation, and wait at least a month for the ground to thaw so that a new line could be installed. The house sat vacant for a month-and-a-half. I could not work on it or in it all this time because of the freezing temperature, and I could not rent it out either. This slight oversight cost me over $1,000, too.

Besides checking to see if everything is hooked up and operational, also check to see that there are no outstanding bills that can become either a lien on the property or your responsibility. If there are, have the seller take care of them before the closing.

Garage or carport. If the house has a garage, you will want to write down its size (one-, one-and-a-half-, two-car, or its actual size measured in feet) and note if it is attached or detached and if it has any electrical service. You will also want to note the condition or age of the roof and note if it has a concrete floor or not, if it is heated or not and if the garage door or doors are in good working order. If there are any other features like an automatic door-opener, work area, hoist, storage shelves, or anything else, you will want to note them also.

Although the existence of a garage can be a definite plus, the absence of one does not constitute a major drawback to the property. Many tenants' major concern is finding a nice home in which to live. If it has a garage, so much the better.

Amenities. These are extras. If there are any (central air conditioning, fireplace, security systems, smoke alarms, etc.), don't forget to check them out.

Financial, governmental, legal questions. If you are assuming any financing, do you have all the necessary information? If you have any questions or doubts about the house and what you can do to it, have you talked to the local building department or building inspectors? Does your locality require an inspection report, and if so, have you seen it? Are there any zoning violations? Are there any easements or rights of way that may be a problem? Are you sure you are getting the mineral rights? Do the survey and the legal description of the property agree with what you think you are getting?

Have you talked to the neighbors? I can't say enough about the neighbors. They are and will always be one of your best sources of information. They can and will tell you things everybody else forgets or at least forgets to tell you about. They know better than anyone else what the neighborhood is like, its good points and its bad, and how it is changing. They also are the ones who, next to the seller himself, know more about the house you are considering buying. Finally, they are also the ones who may know more about the seller and why he is selling than anyone else. Don't forget to check with the neighbors every time you check out a house. In many respects, they are the most important item on this whole list and maybe even in this whole chapter.

HOUSECHECK

_Date ___ Walls ___ Ceilings ___ Floors ___ Floor Plan (draw on back)_

_Owner ___ Kitchen ___ Bath(s) ___ Plumb. Fixtures ___ Elect. Fixtures_

_Property Address ___ Landscaping ___ Exterior Painting ___ Interior Painting ___ Emergency Repairs ___ Drive/Walks/Patios ___ Material ___ Rooms_

LOT ELEVATION
____ Is it the lowest lot in the area   ____ Can it be filled in
____ Does water drain away from house   ____ Can grade be changed
FOUNDATION/CRAWL SPACE/BASEMENT
____ Is it sound (any cracks, washouts, powdering or crumbling mortar)
____ Is it dry and well ventilated (any signs of flooding, water, mildew)
STRUCTURE
____ Are all the floors level and sound
____ Are all the walls square and sound   ____ Exterior   ____ Interior
____ Are there any rotten windows, doors, sills
____ Are there any signs of dry rot (Basement, Sidewalls, Attic)
____ Are there any signs of termites   ____ Inspection ____ Correction
____ Are there any falling porches, awnings, shutters
ROOF
____ How old is the roofing   ____ How many layers   ____ Valley/Cap/Edge
____ Gutters and Downspouts   ____ Chimney   ____ Flashings
INSULATION
____ How much in the attic   What type_____   R Value____
____ How much in the walls   What type_____   R Value____
____ Last year's annual heating bill $_____   Supplier_____
____ Storm doors (____ Type)   ____ Storm windows (____ Type)   ____ Screens
HEATING SYSTEM
____ How old is the unit   _____ Make/Model   ____ Type ____ Fuel
____ Is it properly installed   ____ Last serviced   ____ Condition
PLUMBING SYSTEM
____ City water   ____ City sewers   ____ Hooked up   ____ Assessments Paid
____ Well age   _____ Depth _____ Location   ____ Health Dept.
____ Septic age   _____ Size _____ Location   ____ Health Dept.
____ Check faucets ____ Water Pressure ____ Check drains ____ Sewer Cleanout
____ Water lines/Drain lines (Galvanized, Copper, Plastic)
____ How old is the Water Heater   ____ Fuel   ____ Condition   ____ Safety
____ Washer hookup   ____ Dryer hookup (____ Gas, ____ Electric, ____ Vent)
ELECTRICAL SYSTEM
____ How old is the Main Box   ____ # of Circuits   ____ AMP Service (x 15)
____ Circuit Breakers   ____ Fuses   ____ Oversized Fuses (Over 15/20 AMPS)
____ How many rooms don't have controlled lighting (Wall Switches)
____ How many outlets in each room   ____ 2 Prong   ____ 3 Prong (w ground)
____ Living Room   ____ Family Room   ____ Kitchen   ____ Dining
____ 1st Bedroom   ____ 2nd Bedroom   ____ 3rd Bedroom   ____ Hallway
____ Bathroom   _____   _____   ____ 220 Range
PUBLIC UTILITIES/MUNICIPAL UTILITIES and SERVICES
____ Are they hooked up and operational ____ Gas ____ Elec ____ Water ____ Sewer
____ Any outstanding bills ____ Gas ____ Elec ____ Water ____ Sewer ____ Garbage
GARAGE/CARPORT
____ Size ____ Attached ____ Detached   ____ Electric Service
____ Roof ____ Floor ____ Door(s) ____ Heated ____ Floor drain
AMENITIES
____ Central Air ____ Fireplace ____ Fenced Yard ____ Security System
____ Smoke Alarm   ____
FINANCIAL/GOVERNMENTAL/LEGAL QUESTIONS
____ EXISTING FINANCING Lender_____   Assumable____
____ Balance $_____   Payment $_____   Rate____ % Term____
____ Balloon $_____
____ Building Department ____ Inspection Report ____ Zoning
____ Easement/Right of Way ____ Mineral Rights ____ Survey/Legal Description
HAVE YOU TALKED TO THE NEIGHBORS
____ Location (What is the neighborhood like?)_____
____ House (Is there anything wrong with it?)_____
____ Seller (Why is he selling?)(BESIDES THAT)_____

© 1982 David J. Grzesiek

CHAPTER SIX

PROPERTY APPRAISALS

Half our mistakes in life arise from feeling
where we ought to think, and thinking
where we ought to feel.

J. COLLINS

A good property appraiser can give a fairly accurate estimate of the worth of a property, partly because of his training and experience and partly because he is reasonably objective about the property. An appraiser's estimate of worth is just that, an estimate. It is not a certified, bona fide, or absolute figure. An appraiser's estimate of worth is nothing more than a statement which says, "According to the market conditions that exist today, this is what I figure this particular piece of property will sell for under normal market conditions."

If a seller had to sell his house within twenty-four hours, he would probably end up selling his house far below the appraised value. He would have to do this in order to move it so quickly. If a seller wanted to sell his house at some future date, say five years from now, he would probably be able to sell it for far more than the current appraised value. Time is an important factor, and so is the seller's desire to sell.

The appraiser himself is also an important factor. As impersonal and objective as an appraiser tries to be, his experience and his feelings do enter into his decision. This is why two different appraisers can both look at the same house and come up with appraisals that are thousands of dollars apart. This is an important point to remember when you are seeking financing. Since you want to obtain as large a loan as possible, you want as large an appraisal as possible. You need to know which banks and which appraisers come up with the highest appraisals. It isn't hard to find out this information. All you have to do is ask around. And whom do you ask? Your realtors.

THREE APPROACHES TO APPRAISING

Basically, there are three different ways an appraiser can determine the value of a piece of property. The first and most commonly used is the market approach. This approach represents an educated guess. The second is the cost approach. This approach is generally used to substantiate the figure arrived at using the market approach. More and more lending institutions are now requiring that an appraiser supply them with at least one other form of appraisal besides the market appraisal, and a cost appraisal is usually the one. The third and last approach is the income approach. This approach is generally used when appraising larger income-producing properties.

Market appraisals. Simply stated, a market appraisal represents an educated guess based on known facts. Knowing what similar houses in similar areas or in the same area have recently sold for provides the appraiser with most of the information he needs in order to make a fairly accurate estimate. Notice that the primary factor is the recent selling price of similar homes in similar areas. It doesn't matter how much a home costs to construct, and it doesn't matter how old or new that home may be. What really matters is how much someone is willing to pay for it. When you come right down to it, that is how the value of anything is fixed. Why should homes be any different?

Cost appraisals. A cost appraisal is an estimate of what it would cost to reproduce a particular piece of property. To use this approach on a new house, you would simply take the square footage and multiply it by the current building cost per square foot for that type of structure. Adding the current cost of the land to that figure will give the current appraised value of that house. For an older house the same formula is used, but two more factors are considered in the formula—depreciation (age) and obsolescence (obsolete architectural, functional, and/or economic conditions). To arrive at the current value, you multiply the square footage by the building cost per square foot, add the current cost of the land, and subtract the amounts calculated for depreciation and obsolescence.

Income appraisals. An income appraisal is often referred to as an income approach or a capitalization approach. This kind of appraisal is used only on larger income-producing properties. It is not very accurate when applied to smaller properties, especially single family homes. Basically, this type of appraisal attempts to place a value on a piece of property by taking into account its current or projected earnings. This approach is somewhat complicated and, in most cases, you will never have any need to use or understand it, unless you get into buying apartments or commercial properties. If that time ever comes, your accountant will be more than happy to explain it to you and show you how to figure it out.

There is, however, an easy income approach that you can and should use to estimate roughly the current and projected value of a single family home. That approach is covered in the following section.

YOU CAN BE A PRO

A house is worth only what someone else is willing to pay for it. This includes you. The problem is, how do you determine what a house is worth to you? Since you are going to be looking at that house as an investment, an income-producing investment, your first and major concern is going to be, How much income will it produce? This is a question to which you must know the answer. This is where and why you have to be a pro.

How do you become a pro when it comes to appraising or putting a value on a house? It's easier than you may think. All you have to do is a little foot work. It's not hard, and it's not going to take long. What it is, is important. In fact, it is so important that much of your success as an investor depends upon it.

Before you put on your coat and head out the door to start buying property, you are going to have to know what kind of rental market you want to invest in. This will determine what you buy and how much you pay. Some investors prefer to specialize in low-income areas, and some prefer to cater to high-income individuals. If you are looking for a trouble-free and secure investment, you are advised to stay away from the extremes and devote your time, effort, and money to the largest and most stable group—middle-income wage earners. You need to know what type of housing and what rent level best fit their life-style. Once you know this, you want to find houses that fit into both these two categories.

What type of houses do you look for? First, you look for houses that are in middle class neighborhoods. You don't want to buy a house in the slums, and you don't want to buy one in a high rent district. Second, you look for houses that are suitable for the average size family. You don't want a house that has only one bedroom, and you don't want one with four or more bedrooms. Too few or too many bedrooms limit your market. Small homes may be cozy, but families need room. Large homes may be roomy, but the cost of utilities when added to the rent could be more than a man with a large family can afford.

What rental amount do you look for? You look for one that is at or below the current going rate. Never buy a house that will have to be rented out for more than the average rental amount in your area. How do you find out what the average rental amount is in your area? You got it—ask your realtor. After you get a figure from him, do some market research on your own. Look in the newspaper, and notice which houses and apartments are below that amount and which are above it. Look at back issues of the paper and notice when the ads began. Keep watch in the coming issues to see how long the ads appear. You won't want to do this with every ad, only those that seem to offer the type of housing you are considering buying.

Those ads which run for a long time usually indicate that the house or apartment advertised is priced over the going market rate. Sometimes you will notice that a house or apartment that appears to be at or below the going market rate remains unrented. This usually happens when the property in question is over-priced for either the area or the condition it is in. To conclude your market research, play "prospective tenant"—go out yourself and take a look at the properties that appear for rent in your newspaper. Look at those that rent out right away, and look at those that don't. This procedure will help you determine whether your estimate of the average rental amount for the area is accurate, and it will also confirm your feelings about the type of housing that most appeals to the average middle-income wage earner and his family. You will also find out how other landlords conduct their business.

Now you are ready to become an appraiser. You won't be able to get licensed, but you will be able to come up with some fairly accurate appraisals. In fact, when it comes to the type and price of homes that you are interested in, you should be as good as the men in the field.

A few pages ago I told you there was an income approach you could use to determine the value of a house. Knowing the income a house will produce, you will easily be able to estimate what a house is worth as an investment. To do this, you simply take the monthly income and multiply it by one hundred. If a house is in an area where similar homes are rented out for $150 a month, it is a safe assumption that it will also rent out for that amount. Taking the monthly rental amount and multiplying it by one hundred gives you $15,000 ($150 × 100 = $15,000). Likewise, a house in an area where similar homes are rented out for $100 a month gives you $10,000 ($100 × 100 = $10,000).

No matter what the rental amount, when it is multiplied by one hundred it will give you a figure that represents the highest price you can afford to pay for a particular house. This price not only represents the purchase price, but it also includes the cost of all improvements and repairs you will have to put into the house. For example, if the house that rented for $150 a month needed $1,000 in improvements and repairs in order to bring it up to the level of the surrounding houses, $14,000 is the top price you can afford to pay. Paying over that amount may result in a negative cash flow. Paying under that amount is not only advisable, but it is downright necessary if you want to earn a good return.

This quick and easy income approach to finding the value of a house for investment purposes will save you a lot of time. You will be able to use it as a quick first test to determine whether you want to examine a house further or not. Although it is far from accurate, it will give you a rough, ball park figure. Purchasing a house below that figure should give you an investment that yields a positive cash flow. In other words, the rent should more than cover the mortgage payments and all the expenses (taxes, insurance, maintenance, and repairs). To determine more exactly what your cash flow and your other returns will be, you will need to do some calculations. I have developed a worksheet for that purpose, and we will be covering this form shortly.

Once you have done your homework and you know what type of property and what rental rates you want to specialize in, you are ready to begin preparing to buy. Your first exercise consists of determining what price homes fit into your program and then looking at at least ten of them before you buy your first home. If, for example, you decide to specialize in two- or three-bedroom homes that would rent out for $100 a month, located in stable middle-income neighborhoods, you would set out to see at least ten $10,000 homes which fit that description. Don't forget that a $10,000 home should be one that can be purchased for $10,000 or less, including the cost of all repairs and improvements.

After looking at at least ten homes, you should have enough experience to recognize a $10,000 home when you see one. In fact, you should be able to tell the difference between one that is a good buy and one that is a bad buy. You should also be able, rationally and unemotionally, to look at a house and judge its value as an investment for you. Being able to do this will allow you to move quickly when a good deal comes along and to stand your ground when someone tries to sell you a line.

Nothing I can think of will help you to become a better buyer, and therefore a better investor, than this little exercise. Don't neglect to do it, and don't be tempted to buy your first house until you have looked at at least ten similar homes. Even if the first house you look at is the buy of a lifetime, let it go by. Once you start looking, you will find that the "buy of a lifetime" comes around about every couple of weeks. Don't let your first house be like mine—get your experience first.

One more word on appraisals. Don't take anyone's appraisal as gospel—not your Aunt Martha's, not the realtor's, not the tax assessor's, not even the certified, bona fide, and licensed appraiser's. I'm not saying you should disregard their opinions, but just don't accept them as the final word. Everybody sees things differently. Some people don't see the possibilities in a property, and some people don't see the problems. Only you can look at a house and determine if it is right for you and if you can make it work or not. Consider other people's advice, but make your own decisions.

A final word about appraisals: never let the tax appraisal, the previous selling price, the asking price, or the listing price mislead you. Many times these appraisals bear little or no relation to a property's true value. Most tax appraisers are not well trained, and even if they are, their appraisals often consist of a drive by a house and not a complete inspection. If the owner is friendly with the appraiser or has a friend in the courthouse, the tax appraisal is even more likely to be inaccurate. The previous selling price is also no indication of the true value of a house. It could be low because the home was purchased from a friend or relative or from a person who had to sell quickly. It could even be low because it needed all kinds of repairs and improvements. It could be high because the buyer overpaid, or it could appear high because you don't know what other items the buyer got with the property, which he may since have sold off. The asking price or the list price isn't any indication of the actual value of a house, either. These prices could be high or low because of the seller's ego, ignorance, or greed.

WORKSHEETS

If you are the kind of person who enjoys keeping records and working with figures, this section will appeal to you. If, on the other hand, you are like me, filling out a worksheet is probably the last thing you want to do. Nevertheless, the principles and calculations in this section are important, and it is in your own best interest to understand them.

The worksheet is laid out so that it can be filed right along with the housecheck form you do on every property you seriously consider, and the property address is again the first item you see when thumbing through the files. Although filling out and filing both of these forms may seem like a lot of work, I'm sure you will never regret having done it.

I will be illustrating many of the investment concepts of this book using something called a $10,000 house. I chose this figure for two very important reasons. First, because of the great fluctuations in the price of an average home in various parts of this country, any price I chose would probably be the wrong price in your particular area. Second, $10,000 is a very easy number to work with. I could just as easily have chosen $100,000, but that figure isn't any closer than $10,000 to the average cost of an average rental unit. Besides that, if you were to go out and make a mistake, I would much rather you err towards the $10,000 figure than the $100,000 figure.

WORKSHEET #1

We are now going to analyze two different houses, both of which were purchased for $10,000. Worksheet #1 concerns itself with a house that is in an area of other $10,000 houses where the average rental rate is around $100 a month. Looking along the left side of the worksheet, you will notice the property address (00 Slow Pole Lane) and the top price that the buyer was willing to pay ($10,000). Next is

WORKSHEET 1

$ 10,000	Asking Price
$ 10,000	Appraised Value
$ 10,000	Purchase Price

$$\frac{\text{YOUR GAIN}}{\text{MONEY INVESTED}} = \text{YOUR RETURN}$$

– 0 –	Difference between Appraised Value and Purchase Price				
$ 10,000	Purchase Price	The Down Payment	4,000	2,000	– 0 –
– 0 –	Improvements (2-1)(4-1)	Improvement Cost	– 0 –	– 0 –	– 0 –
10,000	Current Market Value	MONEY INVESTED	$4,000	$2,000	$ – 0 –
1,000	Inflation Rate (10 %)				
$ 11,000	Projected Market Value	*YOUR GAIN	$1,000	$1,000	$1,000
	APPRECIATION	YOUR RETURN	25 %	50 %	∞ %

Annual Rental Income $100 x 12 months			1,200	1,200	1,200
Expenses (30% to 50%) 40% x Annual Rental Income			-480	-480	-480
Interest on Mortgages			-600	-800	-1,000
Depreciation on Structure $9,000 (15yrs. S.L.)			-600	-600	-600
Depreciation on Improvements					
Pretax Gain or (Loss)			(480)	(680)	(880)
Your Tax Rate (30 %) x Above		YOUR GAIN	$ 144	$ 204	$ 264
BENEFICIAL TAX TREATMENT		YOUR RETURN	3.6 %	10.2%	∞ %

Annual Rental Income			1,200	1,200	1,200
Expenses (30% to 50%) (Taxes, Insurance, M & Repair)			-480	-480	-480
Annual Debt Payments $55/$73/$91 (10% of 25yrs.)			-660	-876	-1,092
Cash Flow Amount		YOUR GAIN	$ 60	$ (156)	$ (372)
CASH FLOW		YOUR RETURN	1.5 %	-7.8 %	∞ %

Annual Principal Reduction (1st Mortgage)			60	60	60
Annual Principal Reduction (2nd Mortgage)				16	16
A.P.R. (3rd Mortgage, Notes, Other Loans)					16
Total Equity Build-up		YOUR GAIN	$ 60	$ 76	$ 92
DEBT RETIREMENT		YOUR RETURN	1.5 %	3.8 %	∞ %

Total YOUR GAIN (A+B+C+D)		$1,264	$ 1,124	$984
Total YOUR RETURN (A+B+C+D)		31.6 %	56.2 %	∞ %

Left margin (rotated):

Property Address OO Slow Poke Lane
Owner's Name Mr. Ucuda Donebetta
Realtor Hicem Again
Average Selling Price of Similar Homes in the Area $ 10,000
Average Rental Amount of Similar Homes in the Area $ 100

Top Offer $ 10,000
Phone (111) 555-1212
Date Viewed 6/2

the owner's name, his phone number, the realtor's name, and the date the property was viewed. The last two items are the average selling price of similar homes in the area ($10,000) and the average monthly rental of similar homes in the area ($100).

These last two items are vitally important. Buying a home for which either of these two figures exceeds the average can cause negative cash flows, vacancies, and losses that may never be recovered. These last two items also should confirm the income appraisal discussed earlier (100 × monthly rent = appraised value).

Turning the page upright, notice the figures on the top left-hand corner of the page. The asking price is $10,000; the appraised value (buyer's appraisal) is $10,000, and the purchase price (the price the buyer actually paid for the house) is $10,000.

Dropping down to the box below, you will notice that the first figure is "0," since there is no difference between the appraised value and the purchase price. If the appraised value were higher than the purchase price, the difference between the two would be entered here. If the appraised value were lower, the difference would also be entered here, but it would be entered as a negative number. The next figure is the purchase price ($10,000), followed by the projected increase in value to the house attributed to improvements the buyer is planning to make. Since the house was in fair shape and no improvements were scheduled, there will be no increase in value to the house and "0" is entered here. Totaling these figures, you see that the current market value of the house is $10,000.

To estimate what the house will be worth after holding it for one year, the buyer will have to estimate what the inflation rate is likely to be. The buyer projected a rate of ten percent, and that figure was entered in the parentheses on the next line. Multiplying the inflation rate by the current market value gives a figure of $1,000 (10% × $10,000 = $1,000). Adding this figure to the current market value gives the projected market value of $11,000.

Now the buyer is ready to compute his returns on his investment. Most investments offer three types of return: appreciation, beneficial tax treatment, and cash flow. If you recall, I said investing in real estate offers an additional return: debt retirement. Most homes are not purchased outright for cash. They are usually purchased with a small down payment followed by monthly payments that cover the interest on the loan plus an amount that goes to reduce the principal balance of the loan. Every dollar that goes toward reducing the buyer's loan is a return that decreases his debt and increases his equity. This additional return gives the buyer four different returns to calculate and receive. We are now going to look at these four returns, A, B, C, and D.

Looking at the first column on the right side of the page, you will notice that the down payment is $4,000, or forty percent of the purchase price. Since there were no improvements, "0" is entered on the line for improvement cost. The next line reads $4,000 and represents the total amount of money invested in the house.

The second and third columns have been added to this form in order to show what would happen if the buyer were able to buy the house for $2,000 down (twenty percent down) or for nothing down. We are now going to analyze the four different returns (A,B,C,D) and see how the down payments (forty percent, twenty percent, or nothing) affect the returns in these four areas. (Down payments include buyer's closing costs.)

Appreciation. The buyer projected that in one year his house would be worth $11,000, or $1,000 more than he paid for his investment. This $1,000 gain is put into the space after the words *your gain*. Using the formula in the box at the top right-hand corner of the page, the buyer can take his $1,000 gain and divide it by his $4,000 money invested and find that his return is twenty-five percent on his money invested. Notice how his return jumps to fifty percent with the smaller $2,000 down payment. Notice how his return becomes incalculable when he has nothing down. He is actually earning money on an investment in which he has no vested interest!

Beneficial tax treatment. Since our buyer will be renting out his house for $100 a month, his annual rental income will be $1,200. The expenses (taxes, insurance, maintenance, and repairs) usually run about thirty percent of the annual rental income, if the property is in really good condition. Since the property was in fair condition, the buyer set forty percent as an estimate; therefore, the expenses will equal $480 ($1,200 × 40%). The interest on the mortgage will run approximately $600 the first year on a $6,000 mortgage written at ten percent with a twenty-five year term (it would be $800 on an $8,000 mortgage or $1,000 on a $10,000 mortgage).

Depreciation on the structure amounts to $600. The structure is valued at $9,000 ($10,000 purchase price minus $1,000 for the land).

Dividing the value of the structure by fifteen years (I.R.S. allows you to choose a write-off period of fifteen, thirty-five, or forty-five years) gives you the $600 figure. Writing off the same amount every year is referred to as the straight line method (S.L.). There is also another method that allows more to be written off in the first years and less in the remaining years. That method is called the accelerated cost recovery system (ACRS) and it will be discussed in chapter thirteen. The next line on the worksheet is for the depreciation of the improvements. Since no improvements were made, nothing is entered on that line.

Notice that the before-tax gain or loss in each column is a loss in the amounts of $480, $680, or $880 respectively. (Many accountants signify a negative number, or loss, by putting it in parentheses—as I have done on the worksheets.) If the buyer was in a thirty percent income tax bracket, thirty percent of his loss would result in a tax refund. Thus a $480 loss would enable the buyer to recover $144 in taxes for which he normally would have been liable ($480 × 30% = $144). A $680 loss would allow him to recover $204, and an $880 loss would allow a refund of $264. Dividing these amounts by the various amounts of money invested shows the return on investment to be 3.6%, 10.2%, or incalculable, respectively.

Cash flow. The annual rental income remains the same, $1,200. The expenses also remain the same, $480. The monthly debt payments (mortgage or loan payments) are $55 a month on a $6,000 mortgage written at ten percent with a twenty-five year term, $73 a month on an $8,000 mortgage, or $91 a month on a $10,000 mortgage. Multiplying these amounts by twelve months, the annual debt payments amount to $660, $876, or $1,092, respectively. Notice that with the larger $4,000 down payment, the amount of the cash flow is $60 to the good. Notice that the higher debt incurred with the lower down payments results in negative cash flow amounts of $156 and $372. Putting these amounts into the formula, the resulting returns on investment are as follows: 1.5%, −7.8%, or incalculable, even though there is a loss.

If this analysis of cash flow proves anything, it proves that cash flow is not where the money is in real estate. Many people don't know this, and so they buy real estate thinking that most of the rental income is going to end up in their pocket. At, or even before, the end of their first year they get very disappointed and wonder what went wrong. They should have realized in the first place that they couldn't keep all the rent and that getting rich through rental income is about as impossible as getting rich through earned income.

If you are interested in getting rich, appreciation and beneficial tax treatment are the areas you should be interested in. If a greater cash flow than is indicated above interests you, the house on the second worksheet will show you some of the things that can make it possible.

Debt retirement. It's not always possible to finance the entire purchase using just one loan or mortgage. This section of the worksheet allows all the financing to be broken down and listed separately. The first column shows a $60 annual principal reduction on a $6,000 mortgage ($660 annual debt payments minus $600 interest on the mortgage). The second column shows the same $60 reduction on a $6,000 first mortgage, plus a $16 reduction on a $2,000 second mortgage (at ten percent for twenty-five years) that was needed to finance the $8,000 total. The third column shows the same thing except for the addition of another $16 reduction on another $2,000 in loans (at ten percent for twenty-five years) that made it possible to finance the entire $10,000 purchase price. Putting these total gains ($60, $76, or $92) into the formula results in returns on investment of 1.5%, 3.8%, or, again, incalculable.

Totaling the gains and the returns on investment, you will notice there is not a great deal of difference among the total gains found in the three columns ($1,264, $1,124, or $984). There is, however, a great deal of difference when it comes to the total returns on investment that represent the return on the investment (30.1%, 53.2%, or an incalculable percentage since the buyer had no money invested). These higher returns on investment are a result of the buyer's investing less of his own money, thus making use of something called leverage. Diamonds may be a girl's best friend, but when it comes to getting the highest return on every dollar invested, leverage is the investor's best friend. The chapter on financing will explain what leverage is and how you can use it like the buyer above did to earn that $984 without investing a penny of his own money.

Without even leveraging himself out very far and buying this house with $4,000 down (forty percent down) the buyer still achieved a thirty percent return on his money. As low as this total return may be, it is high enough to make most investors' mouths water. If this is the case, why is the address listed as "00 Slow Poke Lane"? Simply because the buyer could have purchased a house that could have earned him a much higher return in a much shorter period. Such a house is the subject of the next worksheet.

WORKSHEET #2

We are now going to analyze a house that was purchased for $10,000 by Ms. Ing Knomore, an investor who used some of the principles found in this book. The house was bought for slightly less than it was worth, and some improvements were put in to create even more wealth. Looking along the left side of the page, you will notice the property address (1 Easy Street) and the top offer the buyer was willing to pay ($11,000). Notice that although the buyer was willing to offer more than she paid for the house, she was able to negotiate the lower purchase price of $10,000. Notice also that the buyer viewed the house more than one time. The second time she met with the owner privately, and the third time she gave the house and the deal one final inspection before submitting her offer. Notice also that the buyer did the market research necessary to confirm that most of the other similar homes in the area were in the $15,000 price range and that the rents were indeed around $150 a month.

Now turn the page upright, and look at the top left-hand corner. Notice that the seller was asking $12,000. Considering the condition of the house, the neighborhood, and the rental rate in the area, that is not a bad price, but it's not a great one either. Notice that the appraised value of the house is $11,000. The buyer arrived at this figure herself. She didn't take the seller's or his realtor's appraisal of $12,000, and she didn't have any idea of what the bank appraisal might be. She had to rely on herself. She was able to do that and she was able to come up with a good estimate of what it was worth to her because she had looked at at least ten different $10,000 homes before she saw this one. Last but not least, notice that the purchase price was only $10,000. She did some negotiating.

Dropping down to the box below, you will notice that the first figure is $1,000. This is the difference between the appraised value (buyer's appraisal) and the purchase price. This $1,000 discount is very conservative and does not approach the recommended minimum twenty percent reduction in the second of the five steps to success (see chapter two).

WORKSHEET 2

$ 12,000	Asking Price
$ 11,000	Appraised Value
$ 10,000	Purchase Price

$$\frac{\text{YOUR GAIN}}{\text{MONEY INVESTED}} = \text{YOUR RETURN}$$

1,000	Difference between Appraised Value and Purchase Price				
$ 10,000	Purchase Price	The Down Payment	4,000	2,000	-0-
4,000	Improvements (2-1)(4-1)	Improvement Cost	1,000	1,000	1,000
15,000	Current Market Value	MONEY INVESTED	$ 5,000	$ 3,000	$ 1,000
1,500	Inflation Rate (10 %)				
$ 16,500	Projected Market Value	*YOUR GAIN	$ 6,500	$ 6,500	$ 6,500
	APPRECIATION	YOUR RETURN	130 %	216.7 %	650 %

Annual Rental Income $150 x 12 months		1,800	1,800	1,800
Expenses (30% to 50%) 30% x Annual Rental Income		- 540	- 540	- 540
Interest on Mortgages		- 600	- 800	-1,000
Depreciation on Structure $9,000 + $1,000 (S.L.)		- 666	- 666	- 666
Depreciation on Improvements ← (after service)				
Pretax Gain or (Loss)		(6)	(206)	(406)
Your Tax Rate (30 %) x Above	YOUR GAIN	$ 2	$ 62	$ 122
BENEFICIAL TAX TREATMENT	YOUR RETURN	.04 %	2.1 %	12.2 %

Annual Rental Income		1,800	1,800	1,800
Expenses (30% to 50%)		- 540	- 540	- 540
Annual Debt Payments $55/$73/$91 (10% of 25 yrs)		- 660	- 876	-1,092
Cash Flow Amount	YOUR GAIN	$ 600	$ 384	$ 168
CASH FLOW	YOUR RETURN	12 %	12.8 %	16.8 %

Annual Principal Reduction (1st Mortgage)		60	60	60
Annual Principal Reduction (2nd Mortgage)			16	16
A.P.R. (3rd Mortgage, Notes, Other Loans)				16
Total Equity Build-up	YOUR GAIN	$ 60	$ 76	$ 92
DEBT RETIREMENT	YOUR RETURN	1.2 %	2.5 %	9.2 %

Total YOUR GAIN (A+B+C+D)	$7,162	$7,022	$ 6,882
Total YOUR RETURN (A+B+C+D)	143.2 %	234.1 %	688.2 %

© 1982 David J. Grzesiek

Left margin:

Top Offer $ 11,000
Phone (111) 555-0000
Date Viewed "5, "6, "9
$ 15,000
$ 150

Property Address #1 Easy Street
Owner's Name Ms. Ios Knowmore
Realtor Lois Bid
Average Selling Price of Similar Homes in the Area
Average Rental Amount of Similar Homes in the Area

The next figure is $4,000 and represents the increase in value to the house because of the improvements. Although the improvement cost was only $1,000, the buyer got a four to one return on her outlay because she did the work herself. Had the buyer hired out the work, her return would have been reduced to a two to one return. She would have had to increase her improvement cost to $2,000 to get a $4,000 increase in value. Totalling these first three figures shows the current market value to be $15,000. This figure represents what the house will be worth shortly after it is purchased and all the improvements are in. Notice that the current market value is now up to the $15,000 average selling price of the other homes in the area.

Assuming there is a ten percent inflation rate, the buyer's home will appreciate $1,500 over the next year, just like the other homes in the neighborhood. Adding this to the current market value gives the projected market value of $16,500. This represents a $6,500 increase in value over the original purchase price of $10,000. This figure is then put on the line for your gain. Above the $6,500 figure, the buyer has filled in the space with the amount that she invested in order to get that gain. The $4,000, $2,000, and the zero down payments combined with the $1,000 in improvement cost give an amount of money invested of $5,000, $3,000, or $1,000, respectively.

Appreciation. Using the formula, the buyer can take her $6,500 gain and divide it by her $5,000 money invested and find that her return is 130% on her original investment. Notice how her return increases to 216.7% and an amazing 650% when she buys with less or no money down. This is why seasoned investors buy property using little or none of their own money. They don't do it because they don't have the money, and they don't do it for the thrill of getting a house for nothing down, either (although that is exciting). They do it for the returns.

Are you beginning to see how buying with little or nothing down can increase your returns? Are you beginning to see how buying a house for less than it's worth creates wealth? Are you beginning to see how improvements create wealth? I certainly hope so! I also hope you noticed that these two factors, which you can control, in this case created $5,000 in wealth.

I also hope you noticed that inflation, which you can't control or depend on, created only $1,500. Even without inflation, the house on worksheet #2 would have produced an excellent return, whereas without inflation the house on worksheet #1 would have produced almost nothing. Inflation is an added bonus that a smart investor will always want to take advantage of, but he will never want to base his entire return on it.

Beneficial tax treatment. Even though the buyer may end up with one of the most desirable homes in the neighborhood after her improvements are completed, she won't set her rent above the going market rate. Since the going rate is $150, she will set her rents at that amount so as not to encourage vacancies. The first line in this section shows the annual rental income to be $1,800. Since the home has been remodeled and fixed up, it will not require a great deal of money to keep it in good condition, so the expenses should run about thirty percent of the annual rental income, or $540. (Notice that anticipated expenses on worksheet #1 were $480 even though they were based on a higher percentage of the income.)

Interest on the mortgages will be the same as on worksheet #1: $600 on a $6,000 mortgage written at ten percent with a twenty-five year term, $800 on an $8,000 mortgage, or $1,000 on a $10,000 mortgage. Annual depreciation on the structure will be $666 ($10,000 purchase price, minus $1,000 for the land, plus $1,000 for improvement cost, divided by fifteen years). Improvements put in before a house is put into service or in the same year the house is purchased are generally added to the cost of the house, and then they are depreciated together as a whole. Improvements added at a later date are depreciated and entered on the line below for depreciation on improvements.

Notice that the before-tax gain or loss is a loss of $6 in the first column, a loss of $206 in the second column and a loss of $406 in the third column. Assuming, again, that the buyer is in the thirty percent tax bracket, she will realize a tax refund of $2, $62, or $122, respectively. Using the formula, we see her return on investment is .04%, 2.1%, or 12.2%, respectively.

Cash flow. The annual rental income remains the same as above, $1,800. The expenses remain the same also, $540. The annual debt payments are the same as on worksheet #1: $660, $876, or $1,092. The amount of cash flow works out as $600, $384, or $168, respectively.

Using the formula again, we see the return on investment is 12%, 12.8%, or 16.8%, respectively.

Debt retirement. The annual principal reduction on the first mortgage, the second mortgage, and the other loans works out the same as it did on worksheet #1. Even the gain works out to be the same: $60, $76, or $92, respectively. A different return on investment is gotten, though, when the figures are put into the formula because the money invested is more because of the improvement cost ($1,000). The return on investment is 1.2%, 2.5%, or 9.2%, respectively.

Totaling the gains, you will notice that, as on worksheet #1, there is not a great deal of difference in the actual dollar amounts ($7,162, $7,022, or $6,882), but there is a big difference in the total return on investment (143.2%, 234.1%, or 688.2%). Comparing the dollar amounts and the percentages to those found on worksheet #1 makes the figures on worksheet #2 look too good to be true. Well, they aren't! That's why the investor who bought the second house found herself on Easy Street. Figures don't lie. They may seem unbelievable, but they don't lie.

I doubted returns like this myself at one time, that is, until I started buying houses using either method of buying a house discussed earlier, together with the formula for financial freedom. Now, however, I know returns like this are not only possible, but in many cases, very low.

ABOUT THE WORKSHEETS

One of the major points illustrated on both of the worksheets was that the less of your own money you have in an investment, the higher your returns are likely to be. Aside from that, your returns are likely to be their highest in the year you buy a property (because of the profit you receive for buying it for less than it's worth), and in the year or years you put in improvements (because you are creating value). Returns for subsequent years are likely to be lower. They are also likely to change because of changes in the rate of inflation, your personal income, the property's income, and the property's debt. Because of all these variables, the worksheets should be filled out annually if you really want to know how fast and in what direction (A,B,C, or D) your investments are moving.

In chapter four I told you that there were certain things you could do to control or change the four returns you get by investing in real estate. If you have read this far, you are probably aware of, or even familiar with, many of them. If you have already done any investing, you are probably, or should be, familiar with all of them.

Appreciation. Appreciation is, by and large, the quickest and easiest way to create wealth. There are a number of ways to get a property to appreciate, and they are listed here. They are arranged in order from the most desirable to the least desirable method.

1. Buy property for less than it's worth.
2. Buy the worst house in the neighborhood, and then fix it up.
3. Buy property in need of repairs and/or improvements, and then put them in.
4. Buy property that is underproducing and then improve the management.
5. Buy property that will keep pace with the economy.
6. Take advantage of inflation when it exists.
7. Take advantage of the effects of supply and demand.

Beneficial tax treatment. The tax advantages you secure by investing in real estate can be quite pleasing, to say the least. Notice that all the income generated by both houses on the worksheets is completely tax-free. The tax losses (paper or book losses) that occur by virtue of your owning these houses will actually result in a return of tax dollars that would have been paid on your other earned income. This is why investing in single family homes can provide you with enough tax losses to shield legally part or all of your income (both earned income and income from investments) from income taxes. This does work out on paper, and since your taxes are worked out on paper, this tax bonanza is all quite legal and all quite acceptable to the I.R.S. It even has its blessing.

The same tax system that forces you to pay income taxes will enable you to become wealthy, if you let it. The system offers you many different options, so that you can choose the way you want to get there. These options are listed below, with the most desirable methods first.

1. Buy real estate (start creating wealth and lowering taxes).
2. Buy more real estate (create more wealth and eliminate taxes).

3. Improve the property you already own (create more wealth and eliminate taxes).
4. Refinance equity out of your property (get tax-free money and increase interest write off).
5. Increase your write-offs (refinance property, increase the maintenance program, or turn management over to others).
6. Decrease your rental income (don't raise rents when the time comes, or don't raise rents after improvements).

Cash flow. Notice that the cash flow amount on worksheet #1 is only $60 (in the first column), compared to $600 in the first column of worksheet #2. That's quite a difference! Even the negative cash flow found in the second and third columns on worksheet #1 ($156 and $372) is no match for the positive cash flow found on worksheet #2 ($384 and $168). If this isn't enough to convince you that finding the right house at the right price and then fixing it up in the right way is the right way to go, then nothing is.

Before getting into the things that can create a better cash flow, I should mention that the section of the worksheet on cash flow doesn't really take into account the whole picture. In order to arrive at the actual cash flow, the effects of the beneficial tax treatment section (tax refund) must be included. On worksheet #1 the tax refunds of $144, $204, and $264 must be combined with the cash flows of $60, ($156), and ($372). On worksheet #2 the tax refunds of $2, $62, and $122 must be added to the cash flow amounts of $600, $384, and $168.

Below are the two best ways to insure a good cash flow:
1. Buy on your terms (make sure monthly payments don't exceed what you set as a limit).
2. Buy at your price (a lower price should mean lower monthly payments—get them).

The following methods can be used on a property once you own it:
1. Raise the rent (but do not raise it above the going market rate in the area, or you will be plagued with vacancies).
2. Improve the house, and then raise the rent.
3. Lower the expenses (but do not lower the expenses so far that the house begins to deteriorate and lose value).
4. Have the tenant assume some of the expenses, such as utilities (city water and sewer charges or any other utilities you are currently paying) and services (trash removal, yard work, or furnace cleaning).
5. Have the tenant do some of the minor maintenance and repair work

(painting, decorating, faucet repair, electrical switch and outlet replacement).

6. Do the maintenance and repair yourself (buy a book that shows you how to do routine repairs if you don't know how).
7. Buy the maintenance and repair items you will be needing when they are on sale and keep them on hand until you need them (paint, cleaning supplies, switches, outlets, pipes and fittings, light bulbs, etc.).
8. Shop around for people who will do your maintenance and repairs at a better price than your present handyman.

Debt retirement. As mentioned before, the section on debt retirement allows you to break apart the different financing that may have been necessary to put the deal together. The figures used in the section on beneficial tax treatment (interest on mortgages) and the figures used in the section on cash flow (annual debt payments) don't reflect this breakdown. They are the total amounts of all the financing.

I should add that the figures used for the $2,000 second mortgage and the $2,000 third mortgage, notes, or other loans are all low. For simplicity, I treated them as $2,000 mortgages written at a ten percent rate of interest for a term of twenty-five years. In all likelihood, though, these additional loans or mortgages won't be written at the same interest rate and for the same term as the primary financing. The interest rate may be higher or lower, and the term may be considerably shorter or even longer.

When you are making any investment, your primary concern should always be the ABCs. Your debt, or lack of it, will determine to a great extent what your return in these areas will be. Keep these points in mind. When you are buying, refinancing, or financing improvements, you will find first, the higher the debt, the higher your return on the appreciation, the higher the beneficial tax treatment, the lower the cash flow; second, the lower the interest rate, the lower the beneficial tax treatment, the higher the cash flow; and third, the longer the term, the higher the annual beneficial tax treatment, the higher the cash flow.

CHAPTER SEVEN
OFFERS AND NEGOTIATIONS

*A wise fisherman does not bait his
hook with what he likes, but with
what the fish likes.*

ANONYMOUS

Now you know what you want your investments to do for you. You have looked at at least ten similar homes, and you know how to recognize a bargain when you see one. You even know how to figure out what kind and what amount of return you will receive before you invest. All that remains is to find that first home and put in an offer, right? For most investors maybe, but not for you. You want to be better than most investors. You want to be the best in order to increase your chances of getting the best buys and the best returns. But to be the best means you are going to have to take extra time to find out all you can about both the seller of the house you want to buy and yourself.

THE SELLER

Why do you have to know anything at all about the seller? Because if you don't know all about him and his motives for selling, you can't possibly make your best deal. Every person who is selling something is selling it for some reason. It could be to make a profit, or it could be to escape from a problem. There are almost as many reasons for selling something as there are people. Only when you find out why a person is selling can you structure a deal that will give him what he wants. It's almost certain that you will end up getting what *you* want when you can offer the seller something *he* wants.

Some people have the mistaken notion that a good deal occurs only

111

when one of the parties involved clubs the other party into total submission. Once the victim is senseless and defenseless, the victor can strip him of his possessions and his rights. The winner takes all. Needless to say, some people do transact their business in this barbaric way. Eventually, however, they are the losers. Either someone stronger comes along or their reputation precedes them and no one wants anything to do with them. Smart investors don't play the role of Attila the Hun. They presume the attitude of Sherlock Homes (that's Homes, as in single family homes).

How do you become a good detective and find out what the seller wants? It's simple; you ask questions. Your first step is to ask the realtor if he knows why the seller is selling. Your next step is to verify the information by asking the seller himself. Do this after you have viewed the house the first time with the realtor. The purpose of this second visit is to talk to the seller without anyone else present. You don't want anyone (realtor, agents, relatives) to answer for the seller or put his own two cents' worth into the conversation. You want the seller's answers and opinions only.

The best way to open the conversation when you arrive for the second visit is to tell the seller that you were very interested in his house. Ask him if he has a few minutes, and then ask him if you may step in. Once inside, you would be wise to open the conversation with some compliment about the seller's house, his furnishings, or his family. This is a good way to ease tension, start the conversation, and create a feeling of friendship and trust. Never, and I mean never, give false compliments. They are easily seen through, and they do nothing but increase tension, cripple the conversation, and create mistrust and suspicion.

Once the ice is broken, you can carry and direct the conversation any way you want. You can ask the seller about the house, the neighborhood, and himself. Limit your questions to the information you will need in order to make your decision. Do not get too personal or too nosey. Respect people's privacy, and respect their time. Get in and out of the house as quickly as possible. Overstaying your welcome can lose you the deal. Ten minutes is about as long as you want to take.

There may be times when you ask a question and the seller refuses to answer it. If the question is not personal and the answer is important, you need not worry. All you have to do is ask the seller if knowing the answer will keep you from buying his house. If his answer is yes, you should be thankful you found out when you did. If his answer is no, you should politely ask the question again and wait for an answer.

"BESIDES THAT" TECHNIQUE

Many times people answer a question with a standard reply that doesn't tell you too much. These replies are usually the first things that sound good or logical that pop into their heads. You will almost always hear these standard replies or pat answers when you ask a seller why he is selling his home. When you stop to think about it, an answer like "I bought another house" doesn't tell you anything at all. It doesn't tell you if he bought that other house because he couldn't stand his neighbors. It doesn't tell you if the noise and pollution from a nearby highway or factory prompted his decision to move. It doesn't tell you if his taxes, present expenses, or future expenses (like the new sewers that are coming through) forced him out. It doesn't even tell you if he has personal or financial problems he is trying to escape or take care of. If you are going to put together a deal which will benefit both you and the seller, you are going to have to know the seller's real reason for selling.

Remember, there are as many reasons for selling as there are people. Every individual has his own reason for selling and his own set of circumstances. Whatever these reasons and circumstances, most sellers are not going to come right out and tell you and the whole world what they are. It's up to you to find out. The "besides that" technique will allow you to get the information you need. Even old Sherlock Holmes would approve of this one.

Using this technique is simply a matter of asking the seller why he is selling and then waiting for the answer. Once he has answered, follow up with the question, "Well, besides that, is there any other reason you are selling?" (the word "selling" could be replaced by "moving," "leaving the area," "wanting so much money down," or anything else). If you want to check to see if the new answer is the real reason, simply ask the question again. "Well, besides that, Mr. Seller, is there any other reason you are . . . ?"

I have used this technique ever since I have been in this investment game. I have been continually amazed at some of the answers I have received and at some of the deals I have been able to put together because of the information I have received by using it. In all the years I have used this technique, I have never had an unfavorable response or an upset seller. I have found that people will answer almost any question when it is asked in the right way and for the right reasons.

Be a good investor. Be a good detective. Use this technique often; it will help you find the right way to approach any seller. It will even help you find all those motivated sellers (don't wanters) and find out all the reasons that make them so motivated. It's not a bad idea to use this technique on the realtor and the seller's neighbors too.

RED FLAGS

Red flags are those things that a seller may wave in front of your face before the sale to see if you are paying attention. If you don't notice them, you may find yourself waving a white flag after the sale, signaling your financial surrender. Here are four of the most common flags to be on the lookout for.

1. **Beware of a seller who won't give information.** If a seller will not answer any question about the house, its systems, its deed, or its financing, it is almost certain that he is trying to hide something from you. Pleading ignorance and saying, "I don't know," can be another form of refusing to answer a question. Either way, by not telling you what he knows, the seller is telling you that you might not want his house. Listen to him.

2. **Beware of a seller who gives false information.** The seller who intentionally gives false or misleading information should be handled very carefully. Everything he says and does should be taken with a grain of salt. Those things that can't be checked out should be covered using something called a "performance agreement." This is a paper drawn up by your attorney that states both the property and the seller's word is as good as it is said to be. If the seller is unwilling to sign this agreement and have your attorney hold a certain amount of the seller's money in escrow for an agreed-upon time to cover any defects, you should either walk away or use this to negotiate a lower price.

I should mention that many times the information the seller or the realtor gives you may be incorrect. This by no means implies that the seller or the realtor is dishonest. It may only mean that the seller was unaware of the facts, and that the realtor, who got his facts from the seller, didn't check them out. Realtors are supposed to verify all information, but unfortunately they may not do so until right before the closing. At that point it may be a little late to change your plans. Go to the source, and go there yourself. Call the lenders; call the utility companies; call the taxing and assessing authorities.

3. Beware of a seller who is renting to friends or relatives. If the seller is renting his house to friends or relatives, you should proceed cautiously. There may be some special agreements in effect between the owner and his tenants. Maybe the rents are overstated to make the house look like a good investment. After buying the house you may find your tenants moving out and no new tenants interested in moving in at the artificially high rent you thought you could receive. You could also find that the owner was paying all or part of the utilities or providing some other service. Whatever the case, you could find that you made a mistake by judging a house strictly on its stated income. By doing the exercises discussed in chapter six, looking at ten houses and playing prospective tenant, you will know the housing and the rental markets and should never fall into this trap.

4. Beware of a seller who has expenses that are too high or too low. If the seller is renting his house and his expenses (taxes, insurance, maintenance) run over fifty percent or under thirty percent of the gross rental amount, something is probably wrong. If the rent is in line with the market and the expenses are too high, you will definitely want to find out why before you buy. If the expenses are too low, it is probably because of low taxes (which will probably go up after you buy), or a low or non-existent maintenance budget (which will also go up after you buy).

THE BUYER (YOU)

Years ago when milk was delivered by a horse-drawn wagon, a wise old milkman decided it was about time to replace his horse with a stronger and younger one. The old nag that he had been using for so many years just couldn't do the work anymore. Thinking that he could make some money if he could find a sucker to buy his old broken-down horse, he ran the following ad in the paper: "For sale, seasoned horse, excellent stock, first class experience, wonderful disposition, will eat anything, especially fond of children, only $10,000." After he had shown his horse to potential buyers for a few days, a man finally came along who made him an offer. Unfortunately, the offer was for only twenty-five dollars, but the old milkman accepted it on the spot. When asked why he dropped his price so much, he replied, "I knew the old nag was only worth about twenty-five dollars, but I thought I might have been lucky, and found a man who was looking for a ten-thousand-dollar horse."

Horses or houses, it doesn't make any difference. The asking price is no indication of value. Unless you look at at least ten similar homes and have a good feel for the market, you can end up getting emotional and making an investor's greatest error, overpaying. Don't think it can't happen to you. It can, and it will, unless you learn the market you are going to be investing in first. Remember, your heart is closer to your wallet than your head. It's easier to make emotional judgments rather than intelligent judgments. It may be harder to do so, but always rely on your head to make business decisions.

An acquaintance of mine had his house listed for $86,000. It had been listed quite a while, and there had been numerous lookers. He even received an offer of $84,000 but turned it down out of pride (he had built the house himself). After months of not receiving his asking price, he got mad and raised his asking price to over $100,000. Almost immediately the house sold. It sold to a man looking for a $100,000 house. My friend was the winner; the buyer was not.

Knowing the market will protect you from making this mistake and from patronizing the seller who is asking too much. It will also help you to recognize the seller who is asking too little. I have bought a number of homes from sellers who didn't know the market and who therefore asked too little for their homes. Two of these sellers even resisted every attempt their realtor made to get them to ask a higher price. As unbelievable as this sounds, it is nonetheless true. Knowing the market allowed me to recognize these bargains and to take advantage of them. It can do the same for you.

Besides not knowing the market, there are two other ways that you can end up overpaying and missing out on the bargains. The first is to let it be known how much you want a certain house. The second is to let your top price be known. Letting a seller or any realtor (his or yours) know either one of these facts is foolish. Letting both these facts be known is just plain stupid. Your best protection against these two fatal errors is always to have more than one offer out at a time and always convey the impression that the offers you have out are the best you can do under the current conditions. I recommend that you have offers out on at least ten different properties at all times. This will create two great benefits for you. First, you can pick and choose the deals you want, and, therefore, you will be more likely to remain unemotional. You won't get to the point at which you will willingly concede everything to close that one deal you have been working on so hard for so long. Second, you'll benefit from the fact that when the sellers find theirs is not the only property you are considering, they will be more inclined to make concessions.

Even if the realtor is your best friend or a family member, remember, no matter how hard he works for you, he is still legally the seller's agent. That means any information that you give him must be passed on to the seller or used for the seller's benefit. Keep all your thoughts and feelings to yourself because they can and will be used against you.

If you aren't using a realtor and you are doing your own negotiating, remember that no matter what happens you should never be the first one to mention a figure. Every seller has a figure in mind, and you have to make him come up with it. If you are the first one to mention a figure and it is too high, you just may be obligated to buy the house for that amount. Knowing you are willing to pay him more than he was willing to accept may even encourage him to try to force you into the sale. If you are the first one to mention a figure and it is too low (at least in the seller's eyes), the effects can be even worse. Your offer could be taken as a personal insult. Insulting the seller or his house may result in an immediate and irreversible shutdown of all negotiations.

I have lost two excellent deals on account of this very mistake. In the second case the seller actually sold her house to someone else for thousands of dollars less than I had originally offered. I should have known better because of the first deal I lost. I didn't. Unintentionally I insulted her, her family, and her house (the place where she spent the best years of her life). Because of experiences like the one described above, I have found it is to my advantage always to have someone else do my negotiating for me. If your experiences prove to be anything like mine, you will find the same holds true. If the seller is acting on his own and he doesn't have a realtor, have your attorney or a friend represent you. If the seller is working through a realtor, you can use his realtor as your negotiator.

Using a third party as a go-between can be very effective. He will be acting more like a messenger than anything else. Carrying messages back and forth, he keeps you and the seller from ever meeting face to face once the negotiation process has started. Never having to deal directly with each other from this point on will save both of you from the temptation to get emotional and personal. When feelings are left out of the picture, it is easier to come to an agreement. Bringing a third party into the picture often keeps the clouds away.

If you want to play the part of a successful buyer and investor, you will have to know the market, learn to be unemotional or at least hide your emotions, and keep your top price to yourself. Being able to do this will have a positive effect on you and on the sellers you deal with. You will feel more knowledgeable, more decisive, and more confident. You will also appear that way to the sellers. The rest of this chapter will show you other ways to enhance that image.

MAKING THE OFFER

When the time comes for you to make your first offer, and just about every offer after that, you could be making it on something called a standard offer-to-purchase form. Although these forms are used to save time and money (mainly legal fees), they are anything but standard. You will find they vary from state to state, from city to city, and even from realtor to realtor within a given city.

As legal and as formal as these forms may look, they are not unalterable. You can change anything you wish on these forms, without exception. May I add that if you do change or alter the forms, have them approved by your attorney before you sign them or submit them to a seller.

In order to save yourself a lot of time and a lot of legal fees, you may want to come up with your own "standard form." To do this, simply take any standard form and change it to fit your needs. Once you have done that, take it to your attorney for approval and use it from that point on every time you make an offer.

Below are some changes that you should be interested in making to any standard form. These changes will make any form more suited to your specific needs. If ever you run into a realtor who tries to convince you that you cannot make these changes, let him know that you know different. If he persists, don't give in. Find yourself another realtor who is more flexible and better informed.

Escape clause. The first and most important addition you want to put into any offer is an escape clause. Someone once referred to this clause as a "weasel clause," probably because it allows you to weasel your way out of something you got yourself into. In effect, this clause gives you a way to back out of a deal you don't want to go through with and to recover any money you may have put down.

One of the most effective escape clauses you can add to an offer to purchase form is, "This offer is dependent on my obtaining satisfactory financing." Since only you can say what is satisfactory to you, this clause is very ambiguous and, therefore, very effective. If you are ever pushed by a realtor or a seller to be more specific, you can make him sorry he asked. Spell out the lowest down payment, the lowest interest rate, and the longest term you would like. If you do this, make sure your conditions cannot easily or realistically be met. Remember, if all your conditions are met, your escape clause is null and void.

Another escape clause that you can use states, "This offer is dependent upon my receiving a satisfactory inspection report from my contractor." This clause is not as good as the first because you may have to go out and hire a contractor to go through the house. In addition, he would have to give you an unsatisfactory report in order for you to back out of the deal. If you ever do use this clause and you have to have a contractor go through the house, make sure you hire your own contractor. Never hire anyone the seller or his agent recommends, and never allow the selling party to pay for the inspection. The contractor you end up with if you do could have a real ability for downplaying the faults and cost of repair.

Besides using your contractor, you could make your escape clause dependent upon a satisfactory report from your attorney or your accountant. Here again there are inherent problems similar to those you can have using your contractor.

Deposits. Many realtors will try to get you to put a large earnest money deposit with an offer. Don't do it. They may try to convince you that a large deposit will show your good faith and help gain the seller's acceptance. They may try to convince you that a certain amount or a certain percentage of the price is required. No matter what they say, stick to your guns, and stick with a small deposit.

In most cases, you will want to put down as little as twenty-five dollars to one hundred dollars. If a larger deposit is deemed necessary, agree to increase it only after all negotiations have been concluded and the deal is all tied up. The main reason you don't want to put a lot of money down is to avoid having all or most of your money tied up in one deal. You want to be able to take advantage of other good deals if and when they come along.

Acceptance time. Besides keeping your deposits small, limit the acceptance time on your offers. Normally, give the seller three business days to accept or reject your offer. Never go beyond five business days. The main reason for limiting the acceptance time is to prevent the seller and his realtor sitting on your offer until a higher one comes in. Since your offer will be low, you don't want to give them the chance to use it to extract a higher offer out of any other interested buyer. Remember, too, that if the seller does not accept your first offer, a good realtor will try to get him at least to submit a counter-offer to you. You could then counter his offer and from that point on, both of you could keep counter-offers going back and forth for months. This is one more reason for keeping your earnest money deposit small. All the time you are negotiating, your money is tied up.

Title insurance. Many offer-to-purchase forms state that the seller will furnish the buyer with an abstract (title history) or a title insurance policy. You do not want to let the seller decide which he will give you. You should stipulate that he furnish you with a title insurance policy for the amount of the purchase price and that the policy insures you a marketable title. The key word here is *marketable*. Without a marketable title, the property you are buying is virtually worthless. If there are any clouds (defects) in the title, make sure your attorney sees that they are cleared up before you even consider buying or going through with a closing.

A title insurance policy insures you against any loss you may incur, up to the face amount of the policy, for any unrecorded claim or defect in your title owing to forgeries and mistaken identities. The policy will cover you as long as you own the house, and the premium paid by the seller is a one-time payment. No other additional or annual payments will ever occur. In most cases you need never worry about increasing the policy amount as your home increases in value. If there is any reasonable chance that your title is not marketable or has any clouds, the title company will not issue you a title policy in the first place. This is why you should always insist on a policy that insures a marketable title. Besides that, if a title is not marketable, it is very unlikely that your claim to the property will ever be upheld in court, should a problem arise.

A few years back I was sitting around my house when I heard a knock at the door. Answering, I discovered a fellow claiming to be the long-lost owner of one of my houses. Having abandoned the house years ago, he was now moving back into the area, and he wanted his house back. He said he had stopped by the house and couldn't get over the nice job I had done restoring it. He said he was sure grateful for everything I had done, and then he asked for the keys. Needless to say, I was a little shocked and a little unsettled. I told him he had better talk to my attorney and the title company first. As it turned out, I had nothing to fear. The fact that I had used my attorney to check the title commitment before I bought and the fact that I had a title policy protected me. Oh, what a relief it is!

I strongly recommend that you have your attorney review your title commitments. He should do this when you receive them and then again the day of the closing to check for any changes. Have him draw a conclusion about marketability and make sure the restrictions of record and the standard exceptions listed do not adversely affect you. You may also want him to recommend what title company to use in the future, since some companies are more careful in their title searching than others. Finally, you may want to ask him whether you should increase your policy amounts as time goes on. For example, if a house that you paid $10,000 for increases in value to $30,000 and a defect in your title came to light, you could lose the house. In a case like that, the title company would pay you only up to the amount of your policy. If you had only a $10,000 policy, that's all you would get. You would lose your house and all the equity you had in it. If your attorney thinks that increasing your coverage is a good idea, you may want to have an "inflation rider" attached to your original policy or policies. This rider will automatically increase your coverage as time goes on.

Possession. If the seller will be occupying the house after the closing date, make sure that he will be paying a specified rent. This amount can either be set at the current rent for a similar home, or it can be set at a figure that represents the prorated amount of your direct expenses (mortgage payments, taxes, insurance). You may be told by the seller or his realtor that it is customary to give the seller thirty days after closing to vacate the property. This may well be the case, and you should be more than happy to comply, but you should let him know that you are not obligated to let him stay there at your expense. If the seller makes an issue out of it, explain to him that you are an investor and that you are buying his house as an investment that must pay its own way. If he still insists on staying rent-free, tell him you will be more than happy to grant his wish if you can negotiate a further reduction in the purchase price to offset your increased expense.

How you settle the issue of the first thirty days will affect you, but not nearly as much as the period that follows those thirty days. If there is the slightest possibility that the seller will be staying beyond that time, include a clause in your offer that converts the seller to a tenant after his thirty days are up. Have it understood that he will be subject to all the terms and conditions of your rental agreement, and have him sign one before the closing. Don't set the rent so low that it actually encourages the seller to stay, and have your attorney hold at least enough of the seller's proceeds from the sale in escrow to cover his first month's rent and security deposit. (The unused portion of this money is returned to the seller upon his vacating the property.) This is an excellent way to encourage a seller to vacate as soon as possible. Since most sellers won't want to pay rent for their own house and since most sellers want all their money as soon as possible, they will depart posthaste.

If the house is occupied by tenants when you make the offer to purchase, you may want to make the offer subject to the house being vacant before the closing. There are two good reasons for this. One is that you will normally want to get into the house immediately after the closing and start fixing it up. The other is that the seller's reason for selling just may have been his tenants. In that case, you certainly don't want to buy his problems and then spend the next few months trying to evict them. It is a far better thing to let the seller use his time and money to take care of the problem and not yours.

If you do buy a house and plan on keeping the present tenants, make sure you talk to them beforehand, just to make sure no special agreements exist between them and the seller. You should have them sign one of your rental agreements before the closing, just to protect yourself. You may also want to set the closing as close to the rental due date as possible. This way the rent moneys plus the security deposit that will be transferred to you at the closing will cut down on the amount of money you will have to come up with in order to close.

Your name (AND/OR ASSIGNS). If you are going to be wheeling and dealing a lot, you will probably want to include these three words, AND/OR ASSIGNS, after your name in all your offers. If a buyer comes along who is willing to pay more for a property than the price you have negotiated, you can simply assign your interest over to that person for an agreed-upon fee. By doing this you will be able to make a nice profit without going through all the time and expense involved in buying and then reselling the property.

OFFERS, OFFERS, OFFERS

Ridiculous offers. At least ten percent of all sellers are "don't wanters." In times of economic downturns that figure is even higher. Many of these motivated sellers will accept at least twenty percent less than the property is worth and even provide some excellent financing terms to boot. I have purchased many properties for twenty percent or more under the seller's asking price. Nobody was more surprised than I the first time I realized that a seller would even accept such offers. The first ridiculous offer I ever submitted, I submitted because I felt obligated to do something. A very nice real estate agent spent a lot of time showing me a piece of property I didn't want. Since it didn't fit any of my desires, I made sure the offer was so low it had to be rejected. It wasn't low enough, and I ended up getting a $50,000 property for $19,000. I have never regretted this purchase; in fact, I have often wondered what I could have gotten it for. Since that day I have continued to submit ridiculous offers, and the only thing I do differently is include an escape clause in every one of them.

Get into the habit of making ridiculous offers often. The more you make, the better. You won't know how many homes you can buy for a whole lot less and for far better terms if you don't try. You also won't know how many of those sellers out there are "don't wanters." Some sellers and realtors are going to think you are a complete idiot when you make them a ridiculous offer. Don't let that bother you. Other sellers are going to think you are a knight in shining armor riding to their rescue. These are the sellers you want to find.

If you are really serious about getting into this single family home game, making at least ten ridiculous offers a week is one way to prove it. Playing the game by getting that many irons into the fire every week indicates you are not playing around. It also proves to the sellers that they cannot play around with you or your emotions. They will know that their piece of property is not the only one on your Monopoly board. That puts you in a darn good playing position.

Shotgun offers. Shotgun offers can only be made when you find a realtor who is willing and able to work with you. This technique could involve sending out as many as a hundred or more ridiculous offers a month. Each offer contains a weasel clause because you are not necessarily interested in buying each home you put an offer on. What you are interested in is finding out which sellers are "don't wanters" and which aren't. The offers that come back with a positive response are the only ones you will be interested in pursuing. You generally don't put down a deposit on each offer but put a certain amount of money in escrow with the realtor to cover the positive responses.

Armed with a fistful of possible candidates, you head out of your door to look at the homes the "don't wanters" have for sale. Notice you don't waste your time looking at any of the homes you put an offer on until you get back the positive responses. Using this approach to find motivated sellers and bargain properties piles a lot of work on a realtor. Because of this, many of them will be unwilling to work with you. If you decide to try this approach and you find a realtor who is willing to work with you, give that person all your business because he is going to make you rich.

Stacked offers. Sometimes, no matter how fast you act, somebody else beats you to the seller with an offer that he accepts. Even if the house is an exceptional buy at the price and terms accepted, all may not be lost. You can have your realtor submit an identical offer. When doing this, make sure that your offer is dated and that it verifies that you are in the second position. If your realtor tells you that this can't be done, don't waste any time in finding one who knows better.

I have purchased two homes in this way. I know it can be done, and I know that it works. In both cases I was second in line. One of the homes was such a good buy that there were three offers standing in line. I was eventually able to buy these homes because the parties in the first position were unable to obtain the financing needed to close the deals. (Thank heaven those unfortunate would-be buyers didn't know what you are about to learn about financing in chapter eight!) Like the car rental firm that advertises it may not be number one, I have found some consolation in being number two a few times. I encourage you to use this technique if ever you find yourself arriving on the scene a little too late.

NEGOTIATIONS

Rarely does a seller accept your first offer. If he does, it usually means only one thing—you probably offered too much. Usually a good realtor will get the seller to counter your offer rather than just reject it. This is where all the homework you did to find out why the seller is selling pays off. Like a good lawyer, you will be able to anticipate most of the seller's responses. You may even know the seller better than he knows himself.

After both of you have counter-offered back and forth a few times, you will probably end up at what seems to be the lowest price the seller is willing to accept. It is at this point that the negotiating process really begins. At a time when most buyers think they are just about finished, you are just beginning. The following techniques will help you to negotiate an even better price and even better terms.

The "R & R" technique. "R & R" doesn't stand for "rest and relaxation," and it doesn't stand for "railroading." What it does stand for is "repair and replace," and it is an excellent technique for indirectly lowering the price by getting the seller to pay for certain repairs or improvements. For example, you might say, "Okay, I'll buy your place, but first you will have to replace the roof." You could just as easily have asked that the plumbing, heating, or electrical systems be repaired, updated, or replaced. You could even have asked for storm windows, insulation, new carpeting, new plaster or drywall, a new kitchen or bath, a new paint job inside and out, or a new lawn. In fact, you could ask for any or all the items noted on your housecheck.

As you can see, this technique makes the housecheck form you completed a valuable negotiating tool in addition to its already valuable function as an insurance policy against costly surprises. The items on the housecheck are very useful in negotiating, because many of them draw your attention to deficiencies that exist in and about the home. Many times these deficiencies are not that evident to the seller simply because he has lived with them so long. Bringing them to his attention at this point in the negotiation process is one of the best ways to get an indirect, or even a direct, reduction in the price.

The repair and replace technique can also be used to divert the seller's attention from a low bid. This can be very important if you are about to make a ridiculous offer on a house and you want to increase your chances of its being accepted. For example, you might make an offer saying, "I'll buy your house for this ridiculous price if you repair or replace every one of the following items." Many sellers, when presented with this kind of offer, see it as a choice between fixing up their place and selling it at a ridiculous price or just selling it at a ridiculous price (the lesser of two evils). Many times they will tell you they will accept your ridiculous price, but only on the condition that you fix up the darn place yourself. Sometimes a seller may even surprise you and concede to fix an item or two.

The reason this technique works so well is that it offers the seller a choice between something the buyer wants and something else the buyer wants. Many wives use a variation of this technique all the time, with phenomenal success, on their husbands. For example, the old boy comes home from work very tired and very hungry. His wife meets him at the door with a kiss and a smile and says, "Honey, I was so busy today that I didn't have time to fix dinner, and I was wondering if you would like to take me to McDonald's or to that fancy new restaurant right up the street." (Notice that staying home isn't even an option.) The poor guy, thinking he is pretty smart, quickly chooses McDonald's because it's cheaper. Of course, that's where she wanted to go in the first place. If she had wanted to go to that fancy new restaurant, she would have made the other choice a more expensive and more distant place.

All successful negotiators use this principle in one way or another. They always give the other fellow the choice between something they want and something else they want, and then let him decide. All successful negotiators also know that if given a choice between something and nothing, the other fellow will always choose nothing and then proceed to come back with his own terms.

The **"Okay, I'll pay your price, but . . ."** technique. The main concern of this technique isn't the price, but the terms of the sale. For example, the seller has countered with his lowest and final offer. You apparently concede and tell him, "Okay, you win. I'll pay your price, but I want you to include the appliances, all the tools in the garage and the basement, the dining room outfit my wife fell in love with, and the yacht in the back yard that I fell in love with." The list can include anything. In many cases, the seller may surprise you and agree in order to close the deal. The seller may also consider lowering his price even further in order to keep some of his personal possessions to himself.

This technique can also be used to get favorable financing, the most important terms of all. For example, you say, "Okay, I'll pay your price, but I want you to carry a second mortgage for the amount of the down payment, and I want my payments and the interest rate to be . . . ." You can ask for a certain type of payment plan tailored to fit your investment program. You can ask for a rate of interest on the paper the seller carries lower than you could arrange elsewhere. You can ask for and receive just about any kind and amount of seller financing, if you know it will somehow fit into his financial situation.

Another variation of this technique allows you to eliminate all or part of your closing costs. For example, you say, "Okay, I'll pay your price, but I want you to pay my closing costs." Many times a seller will accept this stipulation because your closing costs are usually much less than his, and, therefore, it seems a small concession. In reality, it is really a very big advantage to you. If, for example, your closing costs were going to be $1,000, it means you could actually buy his house with $1,000 less of your cash up front. A concession like this is much more valuable to you than a $1,000 reduction in the purchase price, which would still leave you with almost $1,000 in closing costs. See the benefit?

The "Okay, I'll pay your price, but . . ." technique has still other uses. You can use it to gain immediate possession at closing or to get a reluctant seller to accept a performance agreement he normally wouldn't agree to. You can use it to get just about anything you want, but you have to use it. All I have to say is, "Try it; you'll like it!"

The "Oh no, not again" technique. This technique can be used, if need be, to get final acceptance on an offer. Competition, if you recall the hamburger philosophy, is a wonderful thing. Here it can be put to use for your benefit. Let's say that you have negotiated hard and long, and all you need is a little something extra to get the seller to accept your final offer. Someone else trying to put in a lower offer than your present offer may be all that you need. When faced with the prospect of starting all over again with someone else, a seller is very likely to feel like saying, "Oh no, not again!"

Many times other investors in the marketplace unintentionally provide this service. I know also of cases in which this natural competition didn't exist and the buyer actually went out and created his own. He got someone (a friend or relative without the same last name) to try to submit an offer much lower than the one already in the works.

Besides being used to bring negotiations to a close, this technique can be used to open them up. Estate scavengers use a variation of this technique all the time. They usually work in pairs, but this is never known by or made known to their marks. One of the partners goes to the person disposing of an estate and offers him a certain price for all the furniture. This price is usually lower than the seller is immediately willing to accept. A short time later the other partner approaches the seller and makes a much lower bid. The first partner then contacts the seller again and is usually able to close the deal at the original price.

OTHER IMPORTANT CONSIDERATIONS

REALTORS

Realtors make their living by selling real estate. They earn and receive their commission only when they are able to bring buyer and seller together and close the sale. This fact alone should make it rather obvious that the realtor is at least as interested as the buyer or the seller in seeing a house sold. Because of this, he will work as hard for you as he will for any seller, even though he is the seller's legal agent and the seller is the one who pays him his commission.

As you can see, you don't have to get the realtor on your side; he is already there. All you have to do is make use of his services. One of the most useful services a realtor can render is that of a negotiator.

Realizing that a sale is not likely to occur unless all parties involved receive what they want out of the transaction, he attempts to bring them all to agreement. It becomes evident how important this service is when you take a look at how a realtor submits the most difficult of offers, the ridiculous offer.

Taking a totally unacceptable and possibly insulting offer to a seller may be impossible for you, but it is everyday business for a realtor. All he has to do is approach the seller saying, "Look, Mr. Seller, I have an offer here that, according to the law, I have to submit to you. This offer is so ridiculous that, if it weren't for the fact that I had to take it, I wouldn't even be wasting your time. Now, I will say that the person who made this offer is very interested in your home and that he is a good qualified buyer. I should add that in going through your home he did find a number of deficiencies. If you find his offer totally unacceptable, maybe you could suggest a good counter-offer I could take back to him." See how easy it was for a realtor? You could never have gotten away with submitting an offer like that in person without finding yourself thrown out the front door by the seat of your pants.

Long ago I discovered that I was a lousy negotiator, especially when it came to negotiating for myself. This fact bothered me until I discovered that even professional negotiators very rarely represent themselves in any personal negotiations. They hire someone else to negotiate for them. Like them, I discovered that when I was face to face with the other party I was apt to give away my rights and give up my ground. This is why I like to use the realtor to negotiate for me. All I have to do is tell him my terms and conditions and let him relay them to the seller. If the seller objects or balks, I'm not there to give in or back down. The realtor simply has to tell the seller that that is my offer and that he doesn't think I will change it. If the seller finds it totally or partially objectionable, the realtor can help him construct a counter-offer that he (the realtor) thinks I might accept. Even if I had to pay the realtor's commission, I would gladly do it for this invaluable money-making service that he renders.

LAWYERS

Always use an attorney. If you don't already have a good real estate attorney or if you don't know of one, ask around. The mortgage loan officers at most lending institutions usually know which attorneys in your area are most qualified. Although for business reasons loan officers may not recommend any one in particular, they can give you a list of names. Once they give you these names, ask who their own attorney is. If their attorney's name is on the list, you have got a pretty good idea of whom to use as your attorney. Repeat this little exercise at a number of lending institutions in your area. Notice which names appear most frequently.

Is the size of an attorney's fee important? Yes and no. A high fee doesn't necessarily guarantee the best service. The best attorney for your needs could very well be the one with the most reasonable fees. Cost can be an indication that the individual is highly qualified, but it is not always. Personal recommendations from people in the business (mortgage loan officers and realtors) will always be your best indication. Never assume that because an attorney is good in one area (casualty, trial, divorce, etc.), he is good in real estate also. It just doesn't work that way. Find and use the specialist.

Before you engage any attorney, always check to see if he charges an hourly fee, a standard fee, or a percentage of the purchase price. Most times you will be further ahead by hiring him on an hourly basis. If you have all your work and questions prepared ahead, you will not waste much of his time or much of your money either.

Another way to save time and money is to use the same offer-to-purchase form every time you make an offer. Once you and your attorney have gotten a form to cover and do what you want it to do, use it all the time. Until that time, always have your attorney review all your offer-to-purchase forms before you sign. You should also have him to review any other critical documents, such as purchase agreements, land contracts, deeds, and title insurance commitments.

Is using an attorney important? Yes, yes, yes. There is no doubt about the answer to this question. I will be the first person to admit that nine out of every ten times I have used an attorney, he found everything to be in order. This does not mean that I did not need an attorney, and it does not mean I wasted my money. It does mean that one out of every ten times I really needed him. Those are the times his services really paid off. In fact, I will probably end up never paying as much in legal services over my lifetime as I could have paid out if I had never used an attorney.

Is an attorney's advice important? Yes, especially if you know how to make the best use of his expertise. In order to do this, you have to be prepared when you go to see him. Have in mind what you intend to do and be ready with all your possible questions. It's best to have this all written down on a piece of paper. After you explain what you intend to do, ask him, "What will happen if I do it this way?" Now sit back and listen. When he is finished ask him, "How would you recommend I do it?" Again, sit back and listen, and then come to a mutual agreement.

Never go to an attorney and have as your first question, "How should I do it?" Attorneys are conservative by nature. If they were not, it is doubtful they would be good attorneys. Because of this, they will always advise you to do anything the safest way. Remember the example of the hamburger chain that was able to serve a hamburger 256 different ways? Well, there is usually more than one way to do anything. You don't always have a simple choice between the right way and the wrong way but a choice among many different ways. You make the best possible use of your attorney by asking "What if?" and not "How?" Also remember that since your attorney earns his fee no matter what you do, you can count on his advice being objective and unbiased.

ACCOUNTANTS

If you are just starting out, chances are you probably don't have an accountant. You may even think that you won't need one for quite a few years. Let me tell you that once you realize that you need one, it is usually a little late to go out and start looking. Your best bet is to start looking right now. Find a good C.P.A. firm in your community which has a younger member new to the staff. This accountant will be eager for new accounts and will have the time to answer your questions and give you the advice you need. All you may have for him to do at first is your income taxes, but as you grow in your profession, he will be growing in his. When you need a good C.P.A., you will have one, and you will be one of his regular accounts.

Just like a good attorney, a good accountant costs no more than a poor one. In fact, you probably won't pay any more to have your taxes done by a professional than you already pay some poorly trained tax preparer to do them for you. The money a good C.P.A. saves you in taxes and tax planning more than pays his fees. A good C.P.A. also cuts down your chances of being audited because the I.R.S. is not as likely to pull your return when it has been prepared by a reputable firm. Add to this the benefit of having a year-round tax consultant as close as your phone, and you just can't lose.

Finding an accountant or C.P.A. who is well versed in real estate isn't any harder than finding an attorney who is well versed in real estate. Ask the lenders, realtors, and other investors in your area for recommendations. Once you find out who their accountants are, you want to ask one more question. This question is, "How many times have you been audited lately?" If they have been audited much at all, stay away from that accountant, C.P.A., or firm. Frequent audits may mean that that person or firm is on the I.R.S.'s hit list because of certain practices. Don't set yourself up for annual audits by using these people, no matter how highly recommended they are.

INSURANCE AND INSURANCE AGENTS

Hazard insurance. Whenever you buy, finance, or refinance a house, the lenders who hold any paper on that house will require you to protect their interest by insuring the house and property against loss. They also require that they be listed on that insurance policy as a mortgagor or trustee. This provision protects them against a policy holder's pocketing any insurance money he may receive because of a loss, rather than using those moneys to repair or restore the property. This insurance is usually referred to as hazard insurance and is usually available in three different forms, the basic form, the broad form, and the special form.

Basic form. This form insures against loss caused by fire and lightning and covers the removal of all debris associated with the loss. It usually includes these extended coverages:
1. Windstorm and hail
2. Explosion
3. Riot and civil commotion
4. Aircraft
5. Vehicles
6. Smoke
7. Vandalism and malicious mischief

Broad form. This form may also be called optional perils or additional perils. It covers all the perils listed under the basic form above, plus the following:
1. Falling objects
2. Weight of ice and snow
3. Collapse of building
4. Sudden and accidental tearing asunder of heating systems and appliances

5. Breakage of glass
6. Accidental discharge of water or steam
7. Freezing of plumbing, heating, or appliances
8. Burglars
9. Sudden and accidental injury from electrical currents

Special form. This form may also be called all risk. It usually covers all loss or damage from all causes except those specifically listed in the policy.

It has been my experience that it is well worth the additional cost of taking out a special form policy. In all the years that I have been carrying this extra coverage, I have had three losses that were covered by the provisions of this special policy. On those three occasions, the losses totaled over $1,000 each. Considering that this policy costs only about $10–15 more than a basic policy, it's a bargain.

Co-insurance. Most insurance policies (basic form, broad form, and special form) carry a co-insurance clause. This clause stipulates that in return for a reduced rate, you must insure your house for at least eighty percent of its value or its replacement cost. If you fail to do so, you must bear a proportion of any loss, thus making yourself a co-insurer of your house along with the insurance company. For example, let's take the $10,000 house on worksheet #2. Let's see what would happen if the buyer had gotten a $10,000 basic form insurance policy and she incurred a $3,000 loss after the house was fixed up and worth $15,000.

If the loss is covered by the policy, since the house is still insured for $10,000 (the buyer did not increase the policy as she increased the value of the house), it is only insured for two-thirds or sixty-six percent of its value. Since this amount is under the required eighty percent, the insurance company is responsible for only two-thirds of the $3,000 loss, that is, $2,000. The other $1,000 of the loss must be borne by the buyer, since she is the co-insurer. In some cases, the loss may not be covered by the policy. Notice that the buyer got a basic form policy. If the loss were caused by any of the perils listed under the broad form or anything covered by the special form, it wouldn't matter how much or how little she had the house insured for ($10,000 or $15,000). Her loss would not be covered and would therefore be all her responsibility. She would have to bear the whole $3,000 loss.

As you can see, it pays to carry the right amount of coverage (at least eighty percent of the value of the house) and the right policy (special form). The added cost is small compared to the cost you will incur if you have a major loss.

Liability insurance. In addition to hazard insurance, you should also have liability insurance. There are two different types of liability insurance you should be familiar with, bodily injury and property damage, and personal injury.

Bodily injury and property damage. This coverage insures (up to the policy limits) you against a loss you may incur because of a loss, damage, or injury done to others, and a loss, damage, or injury to the property or assets of others. Most policies have a standard $25,000 limit on the liability coverage. You can and should increase this limit to its maximum (usually $300,000). This additional coverage costs surprisingly little, only a couple of dollars more a year for each house. Considering your increased exposure as a landlord, it is well worth the investment.

Personal injury. This coverage insures you against the following:
1. Bodily injury, sickness, disease, disability, shock, mental anguish and mental injury
2. False arrest, false imprisonment, wrongful eviction, wrongful detention, malicious prosecution or humiliation
3. Libel, slander, defamation of character, or invasion of rights of privacy
4. Assault and battery committed for the protection of persons or property.

If you presently own your own home, bodily injury and property damage and personal injury protection can be obtained at a very low cost by adding your rental units to the personal liability of your homeowner's policy (the policy you have on your own home). Most homeowner's policies will allow you to add up to six units. Once you have over six homes, you will probably have to talk to your insurance agent about an O.L.T. policy (owner/landlord/tenant policy). This is a policy that is specifically written to provide liability coverage for landlords with a number of rental units. The cost per house will be higher if you insure your houses on an O.L.T. policy than if you add them to your homeowner's policy, and that is in part because you may have better coverage.

Many O.L.T. policies have a minimum premium. Whether you have one house or six houses, the premium is the same. Once you have over a certain number of houses (or units), each house over the minimum carries an additional charge. Have your agent explain this policy, its provisions, and its cost to you.

Umbrella policy. One other liability policy you should be interested in is an umbrella policy. This policy provides an additional $1,000,000 or $2,000,000 coverage (whichever you elect) above the $300,000 limit on all your other policies. This policy basically increases and expands all the coverages provided on your other liability policies to an all risk category, and at a cost that can be as little as $150 a year. See your insurance agent about getting one of these policies, especially if you have a lot to lose. Remember, too, that the biggest benefit of any liability policy is the fact that your legal defense is provided free, and the cost is not deducted from the amount of coverage your policy provides.

Insurance rates. Shop for insurance just as you shop for anything else—compare coverage and compare rates. Once you do, I'm sure you will find that the cost for similar coverage can and will vary by as much as twenty-five percent or more. This cost difference doesn't have anything to do with the profit the local insurance agent is making. It has to do with the type (stock, mutual, or mixed) and payout record of the companies he represents. What does have something to do with your local insurance agent is his ability and willingness to go to bat for his clients (you) when they have a loss or claim. Before you buy any insurance, you will want to know about your agent. You also want to find an agent who will take the time to sit down to talk with you and answer your questions. The service he offers is going to be just as important as the cost of the insurance, so both of these items should be at the top of your shopping list.

Binders. You should always ask for and receive a binder whenever you take out any kind of insurance. A binder is a temporary contract of protection issued pending the preparation and execution of the permanent policy. There is no additional charge for a binder, and even if the insurance company refuses to issue a policy, it is bound to provide coverage for the term of the binder (usually thirty days) or until noon of the first business day following its refusal. Because of the possibility of a loss, and the possibility that it may not be covered, you should always make sure you have a written binder (not a verbal one) and that it stipulates the exact type and amount of coverage you want.

A final word about insurance. All insurance policies contain exclusions, even all risk policies. Make sure you know what these exclusions are before you buy.

POINTS TO REMEMBER

1. Use the "besides that" technique to find out all you can about the seller. Use it on the realtor, the seller's neighbors, and the seller himself.
2. Watch out for red flags.
   A. Beware of a seller who won't give you any information or one who gives you false information.
   B. Beware of a house whose expenses are too high (over fifty percent) or too low (under thirty percent).
   C. Beware of a house that is rented out to friends or relatives of the seller.
3. Watch yourself.
   A. Don't let your ego, your pride, your emotions, or your lack of knowledge get you into overpaying.
   B. Never let anyone know how much you want a certain house because the knowledge can and will be used against you.
   C. Never let your top price be known because it can and will be used against you.
   D. Remember, the first person to mention a figure almost always loses.
   E. If you are a poor negotiator, always get someone else to negotiate for you, even if that someone else is the seller's realtor.
   F. When negotiating, try to outwit your opponent by remaining silent. Don't give away your position or your feelings; keep him guessing.
   G. When negotiating, remember that every time you open your mouth, money falls out.
4. Watch out for people who tell you you can't change a standard form.
   A. Always use an escape clause.
   B. Always get title insurance that guarantees marketable title.
   C. Always limit acceptance time to three to five days.
   D. Always ask for possession on closing.
   E. Always keep your deposits small.
   F. Always consider using the words "and/or his assigns."
5. Learn how to make successful offers.
   A. Make ridiculous offers.
   B. Make shotgun offers.
   C. Make stacked offers.

6. Learn how to negotiate the best price and the best terms, and how to close the deal.
   A. Use the "R & R" technique.
   B. Use the "Okay, I'll pay your price but . . ." technique.
   C. Use the "Oh no, not again!" technique.
7. Learn how to work effectively with and use the expertise of your realtor, lawyer, accountant, and insurance agent.

To help us get to know you better, pick the *one answer* that most closely describes you, and then put the corresponding number in the box.

NUMBER OF DEPENDENTS *(include yourself)*	one .... 1 two or three .... 2 four or five .... 3 six or seven .... 4 over seven 5	NOD
TIME WITH PRESENT EMPLOYER	under one year .... 1 one to four years ...... 2 five to ten years ...... 3 eleven to fifteen years ... 4 over fifteen years 5	TWPE
WEEKLY TAKE HOME INCOME *(applicant only)*	under $100 .... 1 $101 - $150 .... 2 $151 - $200 .... 3 $201 - $250 .... 4 over $250 5	WTHI
LIVING FACILITIES	living with parents ...... 1 renting .... 2 buying on land contract . 3 buying on mortgage .... 4 own free and clear 5	LF
TIME AT PRESENT ADDRESS	under 1 year .... 1 1 - 3 years .... 2 4 - 7 years .... 3 8 - 10 years .... 4 over 10 years 5	TAPA
TOTAL MONTHLY INSTALLMENT PAYMENTS *(excluding rent or mortgage)*	over $200 .... 1 $151 - $200 .... 2 $101 - $150 .... 3 $51 - $100 .... 4 under $50 5	TMIP
MONTHLY RENT OR MORTGAGE PAYMENT	under $100 .... 1 $101 - $150 .... 2 $151 - $200 .... 3 $201 - $250 .... 4 over $250 5	MR/MP
OTHER SOURCES OF INCOME*	none .... 1 pension .... 2 part-time job .... 3 co-applicant employed 4 other 5	SOI
MONTHLY AMOUNT OF OTHER INCOME	$ 0 - $100 .... 1 $101 - $175 .... 2 $176 - $250 .... 3 $251 - $325 .... 4 over $325 5	AOI
YOUR AGE	18 - 24 .... 1 25 - 34 .... 2 35 - 54 .... 3 55 - 65 .... 4 over 65 5	AGE

Secret Credit Test (see page 146)

CHAPTER EIGHT
FINANCING

An empty pocket or an empty head never stopped anyone, only an empty heart.

HENRY FORD

"EXTRA! EXTRA! READ ALL ABOUT IT. Little old lady lifts 3,000 lb. car using only one hand!" Have you ever seen a headline like that in your local paper? Probably not, because it is something that happens every day. Just about anyone can accomplish the same feat. Even a small child can do it. All a person needs is leverage. Of course, leverage is easy to apply when you use a tire jack.

LEVERAGE

Leverage is a wonderful thing. You can use it to accomplish many things that otherwise might be impossible. Teeter-totters, pulleys, and even tire jacks are just a few of the devices that use the principle of leverage. Financially, it is also possible to use the principle of leverage to accomplish seemingly impossible feats.

Every time you purchase something on credit, you are using leverage. Buying a house should be no different from buying a stereo at K-Mart. Both items can be leveraged out all the way, that is, both items can be purchased for nothing down, with all the moneys needed to cover the purchase being borrowed or charged. The only problem is that the same person who buys a stereo and finances the entire purchase thinks nothing of being asked to put thirty percent or forty percent of the purchase price down when buying a home. Needless to say, this same person would scream and holler up a storm if he were

139

asked to put down thirty percent or forty percent of the purchase price of his stereo before he could put it on his credit card.

It doesn't matter whether you are buying a stereo or a house, both of these items can be leveraged out all the way if you so choose. Of course, it may be a little more difficult to buy a house with no money down than it is to buy a stereo with no money down, but it certainly isn't impossible. As we saw on the worksheets, the benefits of leveraging out all or most of the purchase price make it well worth the time and effort involved. The easiest way to illustrate the benefits of this leveraging would be to take our good old friend, the $10,000 house, and demonstrate them.

We are going to look at three different ways to buy that house. We are going to assume that the house is going to increase in value ten percent, or $1,000 in the coming year ($10,000 × 10% = $1,000). We are also going to assume the increase is due to one or all of the following: inflation, supply and demand, improvements, and buying it right.

Example #1. House purchased for $10,000 cash:

$$\frac{\$1,000 \text{ (YOUR GAIN)}}{\$10,000 \text{ (MONEY INVESTED)}} = 10\% \text{ (RETURN)}$$

Example #2. House purchased with $4,000 down payment:

$$\frac{\$1,000 \text{ (YOUR GAIN)}}{\$4,000 \text{ (MONEY INVESTED)}} = 25\% \text{ (RETURN)}$$

Example #3. House purchased with only $1,000 down:

$$\frac{\$1,000 \text{ (YOUR GAIN)}}{\$1,000 \text{ (MONEY INVESTED)}} = 100\% \text{ (RETURN)}$$

(If the formula above looks familiar, it should. It is the same one found at the top of the worksheets.)

Notice how the return jumps from a mere ten percent to a respectable twenty-five percent when leverage is used. Notice how it jumps to a fantastic one hundred percent when more leverage is used. Just think what the buyer in example #1 could have earned if he had used his $10,000 to purchase ten homes with $1,000 down on each home. He would have earned $10,000 instead of $1,000. Just for fun, figure out what his return could have been if he had used his money to purchase twenty homes at $500 down or one hundred homes at $100 down. What would his return have been if he had purchased his homes for no money down?

As you can see, he who benefits most is he who has the least amount of his own money in an investment. This is why most of the big boys won't buy a piece of property unless they can get it without investing a lot or any of their own money. They know where the good returns are, and they know their investments have to be leveraged out as far as possible to get these returns. Of course, they realize that their financing costs may, but will not always, be higher as they finance more and more of the investment. They also realize that once they have no money of their own in the investment, any return they receive is all gravy.

When I started investing in single family homes, I was like a babe in the woods. I knew nothing about leverage. All I knew was that I didn't want to give anybody my hard-earned dollars for the privilege of borrowing his money. Once I figured out what it would cost me, I was even more sure that I didn't want to do it. I figured out that when buying a $10,000 house with $4,000 down, I would have to pay a lender over $18,957 for the $6,000 loan I needed (if I had a thirty-year mortgage at ten percent interest, I would be making monthly payments of $61.44). I found that financing the entire purchase would raise the payback to over $31,593. The thought of doing that made me ill. I thought that I would be much further ahead by scrimping and saving until I had enough money to buy the house outright. I thought that by doing so, I would be able to use the money I would have paid in interest to buy myself some more homes or maybe some of the extras in life like a couple of new cars or a yacht or a trip around the world for my family and me.

Although I felt that way, it didn't take me long to realize that it would take me forever to save up the money I needed. I also realized that even if I was able to save up the money, it would take so long that by the time I had it, it wouldn't be enough to buy the same house at its newly inflated price. Besides that, somebody else would have bought the house long before I ever would have been able to. Then and there, I decided that if I wanted to get anywhere at all, I was going to have to borrow the money and pay for the privilege. It boiled down to a simple choice between doing that and getting somewhere or not doing it and getting nowhere. And I wanted to get somewhere.

Although I unknowingly started using leverage, it wasn't until many years later that I discovered what it was and how really to put it to use. By the time you are finished with this chapter, you are going to have a pretty good idea of what leverage is and how to use it. By now you already know that buying a house with thirty or forty percent of the purchase price down is a form of leverage. You also know that practically anybody who has the money can buy a house using that kind of leverage. What you may not know is that there are many ways you can buy a house with little or no money down. When you can do this, you are really using leverage. Later in this chapter I am going to show you thirty-eight different ways you can buy a house and leverage the purchase out all or most of the way. Once you are able to do that, you will have elevated leverage from a function to an art.

OTHER PEOPLE'S MONEY

It's no secret that it costs money to borrow other people's money. What is a secret is that when it is used for investments, borrowing can *make* you an awful lot of money. I mentioned one page back that the payback on a thirty-year mortgage for $10,000 was $31,593 (at a ten percent interest rate). What I didn't mention then was that a house that was worth $10,000 could be worth $80,000 in thirty years (with a seven percent inflation rate).

If inflation were to average just seven percent a year, the cost of a home would double every ten years. A $10,000 house would be worth $20,000 in ten years, $40,000 in twenty years, and $80,000 in thirty years. If after thirty years the cost of financing the entire purchase ($31,593) was deducted from the new value ($80,000), there would be a gain of $48,407. As you can see, it doesn't cost to use OPM; it pays!

If the $10,000 home in question was like the home on worksheet #2 (worth $15,000 after improvements), here is what would happen. It would be worth $30,000 in ten years, $60,000 in twenty years, and $120,000 in thirty years. This time the gain would be not $48,407, but $88,407!

Notice that even though the interest rate on the mortgage is three percent higher than the rate of inflation, the two examples above illustrate a rule rather than an exception. Interest rates usually run about two to four percent above the actual rate of inflation, and although it doesn't seem possible, the person who uses OPM always benefits rather than suffers. The reason for this is simple. As the mortgage (and the interest paid on it) decreases, the value of the house (and the equity in it) increases. It doesn't take long before the build up of equity surpasses the cost of the loan. From that point on, the person who uses OPM is the net winner.

BANKS (LENDING INSTITUTIONS)

Contrary to popular belief, banks really do want to lend money. In fact, if banks didn't lend their money, they would go bankrupt. It's the interest that they receive from their loans that keeps them in business and pays their expenses (rent, taxes, utilities, and even the interest they pay their depositors). Every time a dollar comes in from a deposit or a loan repayment, banks must turn around and put it to work or it will end up costing them money.

Banks are constantly trying to balance their flow of incoming and outgoing funds. When you are shopping for mortgage money, this becomes apparent. At a time when one bank may have a lot of money to lend, the bank across the street may be completely out of mortgage funds. Both banks will make a mortgage loan to one of their customers. The only difference is that the bank with the funds available may require a smaller down payment and offer much better terms. A month later the tables may be turned and the other bank may be in a position to offer the better loan.

Money is to a bank as bread is to a bakery: when there is a lot of it on hand, the price is cheap, and when there isn't, the price goes up. Money is a commodity just like bread or anything else. Its price fluctuates with its supply and its demand. When one bank finds its supply running low, it marks its price up, even though the bank across the street may have so much on hand that it is putting its money on sale. Shopping for money as you shop for anything else you buy is a skill you should develop. What is really surprising is that only ten percent of all home buyers shop for their loans. Developing this all-important skill is easier than you may think. All it entails is being able to answer a simple question and ask one in return.

The question you will have to answer is, "Are you a customer at our bank?" It's not a difficult question, and answering "yes" is not difficult either. Before you approach any bank (or any lender) for any kind of loan, always make sure you are a customer of the institution first. Becoming a customer is as simple as opening a savings and a checking account. If the bank offers a credit card program, applying for and receiving one of its cards will gain you extra points. It doesn't take a lot of money to do these things as the amount of money you have in these accounts isn't important at this point in the game. If your experience is anything like mine, you will never be asked how much you have in your accounts, only if you have them. Make sure you can answer, "yes."

Once you have answered that simple question, follow up with one of your own. Ask the loan officer, "How is your bank set at the present time for mortgage funds?" If he says that the funds are low or depleted, ask him when he expects them to be available again. After you know whether or not he has funds available, get his bank's present interest rate and terms on the kind of financing you have in mind.

BANKERS (LOAN OFFICERS)

Many mortgage loan officers are not well versed in the investment field. Most of their time is taken up dealing with people who are buying homes for themselves. Investors in larger properties usually deal with the bank's commercial loan officer. The commercial loan officer is well versed, but he generally doesn't make loans on single family homes. Since you and the mortgage loan officer are going to be stuck with each other, it is imperative that you know how to work with him.

Any good mortgage loan officer is conservative by nature and unwilling to take any risk whatsoever with his depositors' money. This being so, you had better be prepared to prove your case. Doing that won't be a hard job at all if you have a worksheet and a housecheck form completely filled out on the house you want to buy. On these sheets you will have all the information you will need to present an intelligent and persuasive case in favor of his lending you the money you require. The facts and figures on those sheets will show him how you are going to take that house and turn it into an even more valuable piece of property. He likes that kind of security. He will be able to see with his own eyes both how much the house is going to be worth when you are finished with it and how much income it is going to generate.

How much income your house is going to generate and how much money your house will be worth will be his main concerns. Why? Because in lending you the money, he will want to know if there will be enough income to meet the payments and enough collateral to secure the loan. He is going to be as knowledgeable of rental rates and housing prices as you are, and he will know if your figures are realistic or not. Since your projected income will be based on rents that are at or below market, he should feel secure that your house will easily produce its projected income. Since the projected value of the house will be comparable to that of the surrounding houses, he should also feel that your house will be a safe place for the bank to put its money.

Net worth statement. Before leaving our discussion of bankers, we have to cover one other subject, the net worth statement, or personal financial statement as it is sometimes called. This statement or form can be obtained free from just about any loan officer. If you have any questions on how to fill it out, the loan officer will be more than willing to show you and to answer any other questions you may have.

Basically, you use this form to list all your assets (everything you own) and all your liabilities (everything you owe). After all your assets and liabilities are totaled separately, the figure that represents your liabilities is subtracted from the figure that represents your assets. You hope the answer you get will be a big one, or at least a positive one.

There will be times when you apply for financing when you are asked to submit a net worth statement. The loan officer is not doing this because he is nosey; he is doing it because it is necessary to establish your credit-worthiness and financial strength. When you fill out a net worth statement, there are a few points you should keep in mind. First, keep the value you place on your cars and personal items very conservative. Most bankers are familiar with the value of these items, and if the value you place on them is out of line, they will conclude that the other assets you have listed are also overstated. Second, make sure the value of your personal property does not exceed one-half the value of your personal residence. If you live in a house or apartment that is worth $50,000, it is very unlikely that you will have over $25,000 worth of furniture, clothing, tools, appliances, or anything else. The only way you could have a total over one-half is if you own a private art collection or a fortune in jewelry. If you do own anything that valuable, you had better be prepared to prove it.

Besides the fact that a banker will usually lend you up to ten percent of your net worth unsecured, keeping track of your net worth also provides you with some important information. It lets you know how well you are doing at this game of life. It is your scorecard. Checking your net worth every six or twelve months allows you to examine and chart your growth. It gives you the chance to see how much of the money you made you actually kept. It lets you know if you are a financial master or an indebted slave.

HOW TO GET A LOAN

Have you ever noticed how easy it is to borrow money when you don't need it? The reason is that bankers just love to lend money to people who don't need it. They know that if you don't need it, you won't have any trouble paying it back. Of course, when you do need it or they think you really need it, it's a different story. If you don't want to be treated as if you have the plague every time you want to borrow some money, you are going to have to create the impression that you don't really need it.

It always used to amaze me how a loan officer could determine in just a few minutes whether a person was a good credit risk or not. What was even more amazing was that the interview he held with the prospective borrower seemed more like a friendly chat than an information-gathering interrogation. It took me a number of years and a seat on the board of directors of a lending institution to find out how he was able to make his decision so quickly.

The method is extremely simple. While the prospect is telling the loan officer about his wife and family, his job at the plant, the new recreation room he just put on his house, and the store where he got the best price and terms on the material he used, the loan officer is taking mental notes. He then uses these notes to compute a score on a secret test. This score tells the loan officer whether or not the prospect is a good candidate for a loan.

When I finally saw this secret test, I was shocked. It really wasn't that secret. In fact, it is the same test that had appeared on the application form for a major credit card for many years. The only difference between the two tests was that one was filled out by the loan officer whereas the other was filled out by the applicant himself. I have reproduced the test here. Does it look familiar to you? Why not take a minute to compute your score. (See page 138.)

Did you get any low scores? If so, you don't have to worry too much unless you got one on the sixth item (total monthly installment payments). The other scores are not unimportant and you can work on bringing them up, though it may take you quite a while. Fortunately, the really important one, the one that can kill all your hopes of qualifying and getting a loan, is the only one you can usually do something about in a relatively short time. Your total monthly installment payments include all those payments that you have from bank charge cards, credit cards, charge accounts, medical bills, short-term loans, and any other short-term debts on which you are required to make monthly payments. The only thing not included is your monthly rent or mortgage payment.

Debt ratio. The figure that represents your total monthly installment payments is important in obtaining your debt ratio. Your debt ratio is important because it indicates what kind of credit risk you are. Your debt ratio is computed by taking your total monthly installment payments and dividing that figure by your total monthly net income (take-home income). The example below shows how this is done.

$$\frac{\$180 \text{ (total monthly installment payments)}}{\$900 \text{ (total monthly net income)}} = 20\% \text{ (debt ratio)}$$

If your debt ratio is twenty percent or less, you are considered a safe risk. If your debt ratio approaches thirty percent, the loan officer will be reluctant to lend you any money. If your debt ratio is close to forty percent, he will know you are having problems, and he won't want you to become a problem for him. If your debt ratio is around fifty percent, you are a candidate for bankruptcy, and nobody will want to have anything to do with you. A low debt ratio is a goal to work towards because it represents your ability to repay the loan.

Once you start acquiring some property or other investments, a lender will also want to take a look at your investment portfolio. He will analyze it much as he analyzed your personal finances to arrive at your debt ratio. If his analysis shows that your portfolio is in trouble, you will have trouble getting him or anyone else to lend you any money. Your portfolio and your debt ratio are both different sides of the same coin. If either side is in trouble, you're in trouble, and it doesn't matter how good the other side of the coin may be. Getting your debt ratio down by watching your spending should not take long. Getting your portfolio up by spending your time buying houses the right way should not be too difficult either. Getting both sides of this coin looking good will go a long way toward getting a lender on your side.

Before leaving the subject of the loan officer's secret test, I should mention that not all lending institutions use this test or any other form of credit scoring. Those that don't still have to screen a loan applicant. Regardless of what method they use, they still make their decision using basically the same facts as those covered in the test you just took. If you can pass this test, you should be able to pass any test any loan officer uses. Remember, anybody can pass any test if he knows what is going to be asked and has the time adequately to prepare. You now have both. Give yourself an "A."

BUILDING A GOOD CREDIT RATING

Having a low debt ratio is a must for anyone applying for a loan. Of course, if you pay cash for everything and you owe no one anything, your debt ratio will be zero. Although this is as good a rating as is possible, you will still have a tough time obtaining a loan if you haven't established credit anywhere. Establishing credit and demonstrating that you are a good risk is a rather easy and enjoyable process.

When I started earning a living and paying my own bills, I thought that the best course to follow was to pay cash for everything and owe nothing. I felt that if I couldn't afford to pay immediately for whatever I wanted, I simply couldn't afford it. I also felt that it was stupid for me to pay interest or carrying charges on my purchases, since those fees only added to the cost of the item. I also felt that it was a financial sin to go into debt for any personal purchases. I felt that way then, and I still feel that way today.

On the other hand, I do not think that it is a financial sin to go into debt for investment purposes. In fact, I consider it a sin not to. Using other people's money to leverage out your investment increases your return and, therefore, your profit. Successful investing in real estate depends heavily on the wise use of credit. Unless you have an abundance of cash, you will need to use your credit not only to get started, but to keep going and growing.

If you are wondering where to start building your credit rating, your local lending institutions are probably your best bet. Since you are trying to impress your local loan officers in the first place, you should start with them. Once you have opened a savings and checking account, apply for a credit card if that institution handles them. Just about anybody can apply for and receive a credit card with a couple of hundred dollars charge limit. After you receive your card, use it every time you make a decent-sized purchase. Remember, the purpose of having the card is not to buy things when you don't have the money, but to buy those things when you do have the money and to use the card to pay for your purchase. When your credit card statement comes in the mail, you then use the money saved for the purchase to pay your balance. There may be no interest or carrying charge if your account is paid in full shortly after you receive your first statement. Even if you do incur a charge, it is likely to be very small because of the short period over which it is imposed. The charge, if any, is a very inexpensive way to build your credit. It is also a small price to pay for so great an asset.

You may want to apply for and carry a card from a number of different financial institutions. As you use your cards, your credit limit on each card should be increased at various intervals. If the institution that issued the card doesn't automatically do it, you should request an increase. The institution's officers will be more than happy to increase the credit limit on any paying account, especially if they think that because of the new limit you will be apt to charge larger amounts and therefore take a longer time to pay them off. Why would they be interested in having you take a longer time to pay off your balance? Because then they would make more money off your card. Are you going to let them do that? Of course not.

Besides getting credit cards, open a few charge accounts at some stores. The stores where you do most of your shopping are the best ones, and it doesn't matter if they are small, local merchants or large, national chain stores. You may even want to open an account at your local lumber company and hardware store, especially if you will be using them when you start working on your houses. You should use these charge accounts just as you do your credit cards, never charging a purchase unless you have the money to pay for it in the first place.

$10,000 IN TEN MINUTES OR LESS

Credit cards and charge accounts are necessary in order to establish a credit rating. Although you could stop right there, you want to raise your sights even further and establish a line of credit at various lending institutions. A line of credit is simply an open line that allows you to borrow up to a certain amount of money on your signature alone. The money you borrow will all be unsecured and therefore require no collateral. If the loan is for a short term (thirty, sixty, or ninety days), it usually takes the form of a note. Notes don't have any monthly payments but are due (principal and interest) at the end of the term. If the loan is to be for a term longer than ninety days, the loan will more likely than not be amortized, or payable in equal monthly installments much like a car loan or a mortgage.

You go about building a line of credit much the same way as you go about building your credit rating, using credit cards and charge accounts. Borrow money to purchase something for which you already have the money set aside. For example, you have saved the $300 needed to purchase the new carpet you want for your bedroom. Before you go out to buy that carpet, go to the bank and borrow the $300 to buy your carpet. You will sign a three-month note at the bank, saying that in ninety days you will repay that $300 plus interest. A couple of weeks before the note is due, you should call the loan officer and tell him that you will be coming in the next day to pay off the note early. Ask him please to figure out the amount due so that you can bring in a check for the exact amount.

The interest on most notes is straight, or simple, interest. Since it is not compound interest it is easy to compute and much less expensive than a compounded rate. If you borrowed $300 at a twelve percent annual rate, your interest charge would be one percent a month. One percent of $300 is just three dollars a month or approximately ten cents a day. If you paid off the note at the end of two months (sixty days), your interest would amount to only six dollars. If the original $300 that you kept in your savings account earned interest at the rate of six percent annually, it would have earned three dollars interest during those two months. Six dollars of interest expense minus three dollars of interest income would give you a total cost of three dollars on that $300 note for two months. That's an awfully cheap way to borrow money and to start building your line of credit at the same time.

Usually when you go in to pay off a note, the transaction will be handled by a teller at one of the windows. The person who made you the loan will be unaware that you have paid off the note, or that you have paid it off early. You don't ever want it to appear obvious, but you do want the loan officer to know that you not only pay your debts, but do so ahead of time. Besides reinforcing your good repayment record, this practice gives you the chance to talk to him more often and reinforce your name in his memory. When it comes to borrowing money, nothing can beat the good reputation and the name recognition this exercise can provide. Use it, and use it often.

Many people who already have money in savings will borrow money before they ever think of taking money out of their savings. Many people who have thousands and thousands of dollars in savings would rather borrow a few hundred dollars and be committed to paying it back than take that money out of their savings. People who borrow when they have more than enough money in their savings are people who remember how hard it was to get that money there in the first place. When the lender makes a loan to these kinds of people, everybody ends up happy. The lender is happy because he made a loan to somebody who really didn't need it, and will, therefore, have no trouble in repaying it. And the borrower is happy too because he didn't have to touch his savings. Very rarely, if ever, will a lender ask a borrower why he just doesn't take the money out of his savings. The lender knows darn well why. Besides that, the lender is more than happy to lend a borrower his own money and at the same time retain the borrower's savings account at his financial institution.

At this point, you are probably wondering what all this has to do with getting $10,000 in ten minutes or less. It has everything to do with it. Most financial institutions that offer unsecured loans (lines of credit) have a $5,000 to $10,000 limit. Your ultimate goal is to have a line of credit up to the limit open to you at each institution. Depending on your current financial situation and credit rating, it could take you only one visit or it could take you one year or more to achieve this goal.

Once you have your lines of credit open, you will be able to walk into any of the financial institutions you deal with and borrow up to your credit limit on your signature alone. If you call before you arrive, the papers will all be prepared and awaiting your signature. Your check will also be waiting for you. If you don't call, you will probably end up waiting five or ten minutes for the paperwork to be completed.

Assuming that you call ahead and that the lending institutions are close together, it is possible to get in and out of two of them within ten minutes. Even if they have a $5,000 limit each, you will end up with your $10,000 in ten minutes or less.

Now the question is, why would you want to borrow $10,000 in less than ten minutes anyway? Well, what if you came across an excellent buy on a house, but you didn't have the money to swing the deal? With open lines of credit at a number of lending institutions, you could borrow enough money immediately not only to make the down payments, but to buy the house outright and still have money to spare. The deals that you can now arrange are limitless. You are now ready to move full steam ahead with your investments, and you will be doing it using the magic of OPM.

MORTGAGES (DEEDS OF TRUST)

Basically, a mortgage is a lien upon real estate given by you to the lender as security for the money borrowed. Generally, a mortgage will run from ten to thirty years and will be paid off during that time with monthly installments that cover both interest and principal payments. Mortgages that aren't amortized over the life of the loan may have a final balloon payment. Some mortgages, especially government-insured or loan-guaranteed, will require you to make an escrow payment along with or included in your monthly payment. This escrow payment is held in a trust fund by the lender and used to pay your taxes, hazard insurance, and special assessments. The amount of the escrow payment is computed by taking your anticipated annual expenses and dividing them by twelve to arrive at a monthly figure.

When applying for a mortgage, always ask if an escrow account is required. If you have the option of using or not using an escrow account, you should probably elect not to use one. You should be able to use that money much more effectively and earn a much better rate of return than the lender can pay. In fact, some lenders do not pay any dividends at all on the money you have in escrow. If you are not confident enough yet that you can set aside the funds to pay the expenses yourself, you may want to use an escrow account the first time or two. Do whatever you feel comfortable with, but remember that a good investor likes to control his money as much as possible himself.

Many mortgages have a due-on-sale clause written into them. This clause states that if you ever sell or transfer the property to anyone else, the entire unpaid balance of the loan becomes due and payable immediately. The due-on-sale clause is not the only acceleration clause that can cause the entire unpaid balance of the loan to become due and payable. If you fall behind in your payments, fail to pay your property taxes, fail to pay your insurance, or take out another loan on your property, you could find your loan being called in. Keep these clauses in mind every time you apply for or assume a mortgage or do anything that might activate these clauses in your mortgage.

There was a time not so long ago when most lenders held their mortgages. Nowadays, many lenders sell their mortgages in the secondary mortgage market to big investors (insurance companies, pension funds, and government corporations set up to buy mortgages). Because of this secondary market and because of new consumer protection laws, mortgages have become more and more standardized. Before this mass standardization took place, it was possible to negotiate various terms in and out of most mortgages. Now about the only time you can negotiate any changes is when you run across a lending institution which does not use the secondary market for all its mortgages.

Why would you be interested in negotiating any changes, and what changes would you make? If you were not going to be keeping your house very long, you may be interested in a mortgage that makes it easy for you to sell your house when the time comes. Clauses that would not allow an assumption of your mortgage or a release of your liability are not in your best interest. Of course, if you are going to follow the investment strategy recommended in this book, you are not going to be selling (at least in the near future). If, however, for some reason, you are going to be selling, you would be interested in what changes you should try to negotiate into or out of your mortgages. These changes center on the two items mentioned above, the assumption and the release.

Assumptions. Some mortgages allow assumptions and others do not. Some states have their own banking rules and regulations that address themselves to this issue and dictate what lenders can and cannot do regardless of what is or is not stated in the mortgage. Even the federal government is in on the act. Whatever the current situation at the individual institutions in your area, whether you are planning to get a new mortgage or assume an existing one, be sure you understand what you can and cannot do. If you are planning to sell a property shortly after purchase, you may want to look for a mortgage without a due-on-sale clause that will keep you from financing the buyer if you do sell.

Releases. Any time you sell a house and the buyer assumes your mortgage, you should be interested in a release. If there is a simple assumption, the buyer assumes your mortgage at the same rate and terms that you had. With a simple assumption you are not necessarily released from the obligation of seeing that the mortgage is paid in full. Most lenders will not be too thrilled at the idea of granting you a release, but they might do so if you offer to pay a slightly higher rate of interest on your loan (at the time you originally get your loan) or if you agree to pay a fee at the time you want the release. If there is a formal assumption, you will automatically be released, but the buyer may find the interest rate adjusted up and a whole new set of documents to sign.

How important it is to get a release is a purely individual matter. It will depend upon your financial situation, the amount of equity the new buyer has in the house, and your view of the future. Only you can decide, and only you know if you want to go for an assumable mortgage or not. You have to know your plans for the future, and then you have to take the necessary steps to insure that your plans work out. Keep in mind that the laws and regulations which govern the ways mortgages are written and what lenders can and cannot do are subject to change. Keeping current and keeping informed will not be difficult if you keep in touch with your friendly neighborhood loan officers. Keep in mind also that even with all the standardization, some mortgages can be changed (especially those not designed for the secondary market). Last, but not least, keep your attorney close by to approve all mortgages, both those you change and those you don't, before you sign them.

With that out of the way, let's look at some of the places you can get a mortgage. Banks are a good place, but they are only one of your alternatives. Savings and loan institutions are another good source because they are set up primarily to make home mortgages. Mortgage companies are also primarily in the home mortgage market and, therefore, another good alternative. Many larger credit unions also make home mortgages, but in order to get one, you have to be a member of the union. Once you get out and shop these different places, you will find that there may not be a great deal of difference in the interest rate you will be paying. In fact, many of the other charges will also be similar. What will be different is some of the types of mortgages they offer and their terms. What will really be different and what will account for the greatest difference in closing costs between one institution and another is the points they charge for processing your loan. I will discuss points in just a minute, but first I should mention something about first and second mortgages.

First and second mortgages. Many times you hear a mortgage referred to as a first mortgage or a second mortgage. This may all sound rather confusing, but it really isn't. A mortgage is a mortgage. Two identical mortgages could be drawn up at the same time, for the same amount, and on the same piece of property, and neither of them would be anything more than a mortgage until they were recorded. Usually, the mortgage recorded first becomes the first mortgage, and the next one recorded becomes the second mortgage. The date a mortgage is recorded and the number of recorded mortgages that stand before it usually (but not always) determine whether it is a first, second, third, or fourth mortgage.

Whoever holds the first mortgage is the first lienholder of record, and, therefore, entitled to be in the first position to recover his moneys if the buyer defaults. If there is a second mortgage and the buyer defaults, the lienholder in the second position can foreclose simultaneously with the first mortgage holder or buy out the first holder's position and then foreclose. Either way, the lienholder in the second position hopes there is enough equity to satisfy his debt. As you can see, lenders who hold second mortgages are not in a good position. Lenders who hold third mortgages are in an even less enjoyable position.

Mortgage positions can change or be changed. Let's look at our $10,000 house again and see how. On worksheet #2 the buyer purchased the house using a $6,000 first mortgage, a $2,000 second mortgage, and $2,000 in cash received from some personal loans. Let's say that after the improvements were in and the house was worth $15,000, the buyer decided to refinance. Applying for a loan at a different lending institution from the one at which he had the original first mortgage, he discovered he qualified for a $9,000 loan (sixty percent of the new $15,000 appraisal). The new lender agreed to the new first mortgage only if the original first mortgage ($6,000) was paid off and if the holder of the second mortgage agreed to maintain his second position. This is why. When the original first mortgage was paid off, the second mortgage would become the first mortgage of record (automatic change of position). The new lender, not wanting to be in the second position, got the smaller lienholder to subordinate his mortgage to the new one and maintain his second position (controlled change of position).

Insured mortgages. A number of lending institutions offer government or privately insured mortgages. An insured loan isn't a loan that insures you; it insures the lender. What it insures him against is the possibility of losing the funds he advances above his normal lending limit. For example, if a lender normally makes sixty percent real estate loans, the most a borrower can get on a mortgage for a $10,000 house is $6,000. If the lender offers insured loans, he might be able to offer the borrower as much as a ninety-five percent loan, or $9,500. The additional $3,500 the lender can advance is insured against loss if the loan goes bad. In effect, the lender is still only risking the $6,000 he normally would on any real estate loan.

Who pays for this insurance? The borrower does. He pays for it by paying a slightly higher rate of interest (one-fourth to one-half percent) on his loan. This higher rate of interest remains in effect (to pay the insurance premium) until the loan is paid down to sixty percent of the appraised value of the house. The interest rate could drop before that time if the borrower negotiates for it to do so. All he has to do is negotiate that the rate will drop once the value of the property increases to the point at which the loan balance is less than sixty percent of the new value.

Points. One point is equal to one percent of the amount of the mortgage. On a $6,000 mortgage, one point is equal to $60. On a $9,500 mortgage, one point is equal to $95. You can end up paying as much as ten points or more on a government or privately insured loan. In addition to that, many lenders charge you points just for the privilege of making you a loan. These points go by many names, such as origination fees or loan preparation fees. No matter what they are called, you can be sure of one thing—they are going to cost you money, and a lot of it. More than anything else, points account for the greatest difference in closing costs between one lender and another.

LAND CONTRACTS

Known by various names (contracts of sale, conditional sales contracts, conditional contracts of sale, agreements of sales, contracts for deeds, and real property sales contracts), the land contract is widely used. Basically, it is a contract between a buyer and a seller which states that the seller will convey title of the property to the buyer after certain conditions and payments have been met. Even though the buyer does not yet hold title, he is considered the equitable owner of the property and has all rights of possession and the right to treat the property as his own for all tax purposes.

Buying a house on land contract is similar to buying a house with a mortgage. The main differences can be seen when you look at the advantages of a land contract and its possible disadvantages. The advantages are that a house can be purchased with little or no money down, the interest rate is usually much lower than for a mortgage (there may be a legal limit), and the terms are much more flexible. But there may be disadvantages too, with respect to title, encumbrances, and defaults.

Title. Because you do not hold title to the property, you need to protect your interest. The best way to do that is to have your contract recorded immediately and have a title insurance policy issued in your favor. (You can do this yourself or have your attorney handle it.) If you do not record your contract immediately and the seller resells the house to somebody else, goes bankrupt, becomes incompetent, or dies, you would have to go to court to protect your interest and, you hope, get title.

Encumbrances. The seller could pledge his contract with you as security for a loan, thus adding an encumbrance to the title. To protect yourself against this, have an encumbrance clause added to your contract. This clause will, in effect, tell the seller that he cannot further encumber the property without your written permission.

Defaults. If the seller does not own the house free and clear at the time you purchase it from him, you should notify all lienholders of your interest in the property (lienholders include anyone else who has an interest in the property, like any bank or banks that hold a mortgage or any other person or persons who hold a land contract or other lien on the property). You will want them to know that you have added a default clause to your contract with the seller.

This clause puts them on notice that they are obligated to notify you any time the seller, or any other party who is responsible for making payments on any lien against the property, defaults. Upon notification, you can make payments directly to the affected lienholder and protect your property from a possible foreclosure. Without this clause you may wake one day to find your property in foreclosure even though you personally have never been late or remiss in any of your payments.

SELLING YOUR HOUSES ON LAND CONTRACT

If the day ever comes when you decide to sell any of your homes and you do so using a land contract, you should take certain precautions with respect to the down payment, the insurance, taxes, and encumbrances, in order to protect your interest.

Down payments. As a seller you should demand and receive a sizable down payment or pledge of some of the buyer's assets as collateral. This is the opposite of what you yourself look for as a buyer. Why the switch? Because you want to find a buyer who will have enough vested interest in your house to want to take care of it and not walk away from it if the going gets tough.

Insurance. You should have the buyer list you on the hazard insurance policy as an "additional name insured" (land contract holder), and you should have him furnish you with a copy of the policy. Furthermore, you should have the insurance company notify you immediately any time the buyer changes the policy, is late in his payments, or cancels the policy. These precautions will protect you in case of a loss and also in case the buyer tries to pocket the insurance moneys if there is a loss and leave you with a damaged or worthless home.

Taxes. You should also have the buyer furnish you with a copy of his paid property tax bills. If there are special assessments or other obligations, ask for proof that they have been paid also. This will keep you from seeing your house listed in the annual tax sale because the buyer forgot or refused to pay his taxes.

Encumbrances. You should always add to the contract the provision that the buyer cannot further encumber the property or physically change it in any way without your written permission. This will keep him from pledging the property as security for any loans or for any other reasons. It will also put him on notice that he cannot change or alter or even cause a change or alteration in the property without your knowledge and written permission.

I know of a couple who sold their house on land contract. They sold it for a very small amount down to a buyer who immediately embarked on an extensive remodeling project. Before the work was completed, the buyer stopped making all payments, not only to the sellers, but also to everyone else involved. The contractors slapped a mechanic's lien against the property, and the sellers had to start foreclosure proceedings. By the time they regained possession of their home, completed the abandoned work, paid off the contractors, paid the legal fees and all the mortgage payments, taxes, and insurance that had piled up between the time the buyers stopped paying and the time they were removed, the poor sellers had learned an expensive lesson. Don't ever let this happen to you. Use the precautions mentioned above when selling, and use a good attorney.

PRIVATE SOURCES OF MONEY

Besides commercial lenders and sellers, there are many private individuals and groups that will lend money for the purchase of real estate. Some of these people run ads in the newspaper. Those who do are usually looking for buyers who can't get financing anywhere else. Borrowing from them can be very expensive. A better source of private financing can be found by asking your realtor. He will be able to tell you who currently has money to lend and at what rate and terms the loan will be made.

If you are a professional, if you are self-employed, if you own your own business or corporation, or if you have your own retirement or pension fund, you may be able to borrow the money you need from yourself. There are certain regulations that you have to abide by when borrowing money from yourself and you should be aware of them before you begin proceedings.

Your accountant and your attorney can best advise you on what you can and cannot do and on what will be the best route to take. Don't overlook this source of money if it is available to you. In most cases, the interest on the loan is tax deductible when you pay it and tax free when you receive it, especially if it is borrowed from a pension fund or retirement account. You win both ways.

Whenever borrowing money, from yourself or anyone else, always have your attorney look after and protect your interest. Never enter into any kind of private or commercial financing agreement without an attorney. Don't be tempted to operate without one just because the lender had his attorney check over all the papers and approve them. The lender's attorney is looking out for the lender's interest, not yours. If you are foolish enough to sign away your rights and protections, he will let you. Don't be foolish. Forewarned is forearmed.

FORECLOSURE

Foreclosure does not mean the bank or other lender is going to take your house away from you. Foreclosure simply means that the full amount of your loan is immediately due and payable and that the lender has the legal right to apply your house to the payment of that debt if you cannot pay it. As mentioned earlier, a number of things can trigger an acceleration clause in a mortgage or note to make the full amount due at once. Most of the time, though, this happens because you have defaulted or missed your payments.

Between the time the foreclosure proceedings are initiated and the time your house is actually sold to satisfy your debt, you have several options. You can pay off the loan balance in full if you have the cash, or you can refinance the house and get the cash to satisfy the debt. If you don't do either of these things and your house makes it all the way to the sheriff's sale on the courthouse steps, you can still get your house back. All you have to do is bid one dollar over the bank's bid. The bank's bid will always be the total of the balance of your loan, its accrued interest, and the bank's legal fees and other expenses. Of course, if you had the money to bid one dollar over the bank's bid, your house probably wouldn't have been sold on the courthouse steps.

If your house is sold on the courthouse steps (to the bank or anyone else), you may still have anywhere from six months to a year to redeem it. The redemption time depends on how much equity you had in the house and/or the type of foreclosure and whether you signed the house over to the lender for a release of liability. This redemption time allows you one final chance to protect your equity and get it out. If ever you find yourself facing the possibility of a foreclosure, contact your attorney immediately and have him advise you what steps to take to protect your equity. Waiting too long or not doing the right thing at the right time could cause you to lose everything.

When you buy a house that has been foreclosed upon, the redemption period can also affect you. It doesn't matter whether you bought it at the courthouse steps yourself or from a bank or from anyone else. The party who lost the house can redeem it at any time before the redemption period ends. It goes without saying that this can cause quite a few problems for you as a buyer. In order to avoid these problems, make sure either that the redemption period has lapsed or that there is a release before you buy any foreclosed or repossessed property.

The bottom line of any foreclosure is that the bank doesn't want the house; it wants its money. If the bank has to buy the house to protect its investment, the first thing it is going to do is try to sell that house. Using our $10,000 house as an example again, let's see what would happen once the bank sold it. If there was a $6,000 balance due on the mortgage and the bank was owed an additional $1,000 in accumulated interest, legal fees, and expenses, the bank would have to get at least $7,000 to clear its books. If it were able to sell the house for $10,000, it would net an extra $3,000. This money would be its to keep unless the conditions mentioned above (redemption, release of liability) altered the situation. If, on the other hand, the bank was only able to sell the house for $6,000, it would end up $1,000 short. In most cases this would not bother the bank officers a great deal. They would know that it was only a temporary condition that could be corrected with a deficiency judgment.

Deficiency judgments. A deficiency judgment may be handed down by the courts when a lender does not receive enough funds from the sale of a property to cover his investment. For example, if you had owned the house in the example given above, the court would order you to pay the bank the $1,000 it had lost. If you did not pay, the court would allow the bank to secure some of your other assets to cover the debt. There are two ways you could avoid this problem. One involves an action you take before getting your financing (exculpatory clause), and the other involves an action you take after you find yourself in trouble (release of liability).

Exculpatory clause. You can protect yourself against a deficiency judgment with an exculpatory clause. When this clause is inserted into a mortgage or any other agreement, it states that your liability is limited to the property alone. If you are foreclosed upon and a deficiency does exist, you and your assets will not be threatened. Before you try to insert this clause into every mortgage you get, let me tell you that most lenders will not be inclined to let you do it. About the only people they allow to use this clause are purchasers of very big and expensive pieces of property. Even then, a lender usually makes them pay for the privilege (usually by charging a higher interest rate), unless they happen to be taking a big problem off the lender's hands (for example, a repossessed property).

Aside from this, there will be a number of times you can and will want to use an exculpatory clause. Any time you buy a house on land contract or use any other kind of seller- or private financing, you should include this clause in your agreement. If a seller shows any signs of resisting, it could be a sign that he knows his house is not worth what he is asking. If that is the case, reopen the negotiations and go for a lower price.

Release of liability. Another way to protect yourself against a deficiency judgment is to use a release of liability. The best time to get a release is before a foreclosure has been started. Once a foreclosure is under way, you may still be able to obtain a release, but you will not be able to get it as easily. This release of liability releases you from any possible deficiency judgments that could arise if the lender was not able to sell your house for the amount he had invested in it. In order to obtain this release, you have to sign over your house to the lender. Now the question is, why would the lender be willing to do this? Because he knows that if he has to go through all the time and expense to foreclose, he may come out a net loser, especially if you have no attachable assets. By giving you a release and securing immediate possession of your house, he figures that he will probably come out ahead. Of course, if you have all kinds of money or other assets he could attach, he may not give you a release. He will push for a foreclosure, knowing that if there is a deficiency, he will be able to collect his money.

If for some reason you do find yourself drifting towards a possible foreclosure, there is something you should do. Go and talk to your lenders. Don't wait until you are late with any of your payments. Do it right away, and explain the situation to them. See if you can work out a possible solution. If not, consider signing your house over to them for a release. And, as always, talk to your attorney, and let him guide you.

LAND CONTRACT FORECLOSURES

Everything I have previously discussed about foreclosures on mortgages and notes applies also to land contracts, that is, everything except the part dealing with the person who holds the contract on the house you just lost through foreclosure. In a land contract foreclosure, the person who holds the contract (it could be the seller, a person he sold it to, or one of the seller's debtors) can resell the house for more than you owed on it and legally keep the difference. Using our $10,000 house again, let's say the balance due on the contract was $6,000 and the contract holder was owed an additional $1,000 in accumulated interest, legal fees, and expenses. If he resold the house for $10,000, he would be able to keep the $3,000 he received above his $7,000 investment. If you have a lot of equity in a house that you lose through a land contract foreclosure, you might feel really bad, but the other guy will certainly feel really good. Remember this point when buying or selling on land contract. Also remember that land contracts frequently allow faster repossessions than mortgages.

UNIQUE FINANCING TECHNIQUES

The standard mortgage with its monthly payments that stay the same until you have the loan paid off is not the only type of conventional financing around. Although the standard mortgage has served as the basis for many different variations of financing in the past, we are seeing the birth, today, of many new techniques, and no doubt we will see more new financing techniques as time goes on. Here is a summary of some of the most popular older and newer variations currently in use.

Balloon loan. Perhaps this loan got its name because the last payment has the same effect on the borrower as a pin has on contact with a balloon. Whatever the origin of the term, this type of loan is very common. On the worksheets we analyzed the financing of a $10,000 house purchased using a $6,000 mortgage at ten percent interest. This mortgage was to run for a term of twenty-five years with payments of $55 a month. The bank or person granting the loan could make the loan balance due and payable at any predetermined date before the twenty-five years and therefore create a balloon loan. If, for example, the loan was to run for five years, there would be fifty-nine payments of $55 each and a final payment of approximately $5,600. That makes a total of sixty payments.

The short-term advantage of a balloon loan is that the buyer has payments of only $55 a month rather than payments of $128 a month (the amount needed to amortize the loan over five years). This short-term advantage would help produce a positive cash flow, whereas the higher monthly payments of a fully amortized loan would help produce a negative cash flow. The disadvantage of a balloon loan is that the buyer must either come up with the balance of the loan in five years or renegotiate a new loan. The properties we analyzed could not support payments of $128, and a balloon loan is one way of solving the problem. The only problem is that using a balloon loan may create another difficulty further down the road.

In all likelihood, any house purchased on a balloon loan will be worth more in five years than it is today. The house may also have had some improvements, thus guaranteeing an increase in its value. But there is no guarantee that satisfactory financing will be readily available at the end of five years. As unlikely as it is that you will be unable to get that financing, it is still advisable to put a renegotiation clause into all balloon loans. This clause simply states that the lender will, upon request, refinance the amount outstanding at the end of the loan period for another specified length of time. Try, at the same time, to get a ceiling on the interest rate included in all renegotiation clauses. In other words, work into the agreement the provision that the new interest rate will not exceed a certain amount.

A final word of advice on balloon loans. If you ever have any of these loans, do not wait until the loan comes due before you start looking for new financing. You could find yourself over a barrel and be forced to accept some bad terms in order to gain new financing. Start early. Better yet, follow the market, and refinance whenever you think you can get the best terms. Do this even if it is years before your balloon comes due. If you do refinance and rates drop even further, refinance again. You are never tied in—the lender is. Keep it that way.

Wraparound mortgage. A wraparound mortgage exists whenever a lender assumes an older mortgage at a lower rate of interest and then issues a new mortgage for a larger amount at a higher rate. Let's use our $10,000 house again with a $6,000 existing mortgage at ten percent interest. If you wanted to buy the house with only $2,000 down, you could find a lender willing to make you a new $8,000 mortgage, or you could find a lender willing to make a wraparound.

Let's say you found that new mortgages were being written at twelve percent, or two percent above the rate on the existing mortgage. Let's say that you also found a lender who was very interested in making wraparounds. By assuming the old mortgage and advancing you the extra $2,000, the wraparound lender is able to offer you a new $8,000 mortgage at eleven percent. Your payments on this loan would be only $78 instead of the $84 you would owe on the twelve percent loan.

In effect, the wraparound lender uses the first $55 of your payment to meet the obligation on the $6,000 assumed loan and the remaining $23 of your payment to cover the $2,000 loan you have with him. By offering you this lower blended rate, the lender is able to earn about fourteen percent interest on the new funds he lent you. With this kind of deal, you both come out ahead. If the original loan is held by the lender you are dealing with, he may be even more interested in offering you this blended rate, or wraparound mortgage.

Blanket mortgage. A blanket mortgage is one that encumbers two or more properties. It is used when the primary property borrowed against does not provide enough security for the size of the loan. If you will be borrowing more than the lending institution normally advances, the loan officers will require that you pledge some other property or asset to cover the extra funds. Many times the other property or asset you are pledging could be of such value that it would allow the lender to advance you enough funds to buy the new property outright. This creates the possibility of your buying a house without using any of your own funds. If you ever do make use of a blanket mortgage, just make sure that you include a release clause in the mortgage. This release clause states that once the loan is paid down to a certain point or the property in question increases in value to a certain point, the lender will release the extra property or asset you pledged. This will free you to use it again to buy another house.

Open-end mortgage. An open-end mortgage allows you to go back to the lender and borrow again, up to the amount of the original mortgage. If you originally had a $6,000 mortgage and had it paid down to $4,500, you could reborrow the $1,500 you had already paid off. Depending on the original agreement, you could just continue with your present payments unchanged, but the payment schedule would be extended to cover the added amount. Or the payments could be increased, so that you end up paying off the loan in the agreed-upon time. Or the entire loan could be renegotiated at a new rate and a new term. If you arrange an open-end mortgage, make sure you understand what will happen if you exercise your option to reborrow money.

Shared appreciation mortgage (S.A.M.). Often referred to by its initials, the S.A.M. offers you a below-market interest rate on your loan. The loan has a fixed monthly payment calculated on a thirty- or forty-year maturity schedule, but the loan is really a balloon loan with the balance due and payable in ten years (in many cases). In exchange for the low interest rate, you agree to give the lender a portion of the increased value of your home when the loan is payable. If you sell your home before the ten-year period, the lender's share is due then. If you don't sell your home, an appraiser will show up at your door before the ten years are up, in order to determine the new market value of the house. You will then be called upon by the lender to come up with his share of your home's appreciation plus the balance of the mortgage.

You will be allowed to deduct the cost of any improvements you made to the house, but you will not be allowed to deduct anything for your own labor. If you don't have the money to pay off the mortgage plus the lender's share of the appreciation, you will have to get a new mortgage to cover the amount. If your house only doubled in value during those ten years, you could find that you owe the lender almost twice the amount of your original mortgage. This is not a way to finance a house if you plan to keep it. The higher debt and the higher house payments you end up assuming may eat up all of your profit. They may even eat you up too.

Appreciation participation mortgage (A.P.M.). A.P.M.'s are basically the same as S.A.M.'s.

Variable rate mortgages. Variable rate mortgages are much like conventional thirty- or forty-year mortgages, the only difference being that the interest rate on the loan can be adjusted up or down by one percent every six months. If the lending institution elects to adjust the rate annually, it may adjust it by two percent. When the index the lending institution uses goes up, its officers may raise the interest rate if they wish. If the index goes down, they must usually lower the interest rate.

Other mortgages and loans. Today there are virtually hundreds of different types of conventional financing arrangements available. Because of this great variety and the constant changes, trying to list them all is both impossible and impractical. For the most part the newer programs are not in the borrower's best interest, and definitely not in your interest as an investor because you can't control your financing or its cost.

If you want to keep abreast of what is available in your area, I encourage you to visit your lenders and your realtors. Both of these sources have some excellent booklets that will explain what's new and what's presently available.

REAL ESTATE AND FINANCING

The real estate market is no different from any other market. It fluctuates constantly and is either a seller's or a buyer's market. When conditions make it a seller's market, you have to hunt and negotiate hard and long to find and close a good deal. On the other hand, when conditions make it a buyer's market, you can afford to be very selective and very demanding. Add to this the advantage of reaping the huge profits that can be yours when the market favors the seller again, and you have the makings of a great investment. Actually, every downturn in the economy and every upturn in interest rates is a blessing in disguise to the investor who is astute enough to recognize the opportunities these conditions can create.

Of course, if you don't want to miss these opportunities, you have to stick your neck out. If your head is firmly attached and if you are using it, you won't end up losing it. In fact, you won't end up losing anything. You have everything to gain. All successful investors know that the best time to sell is when everybody is buying. Although this is contrary to what everybody else in the market is doing, these investors have learned that they can sell back at a profit what they bought at a discount. They have learned how to use the forces of the marketplace. You can use these forces too if you have enough faith in yourself and in the system.

Do high interest rates stop you from investing? They shouldn't if the investments you make can produce enough income to pay all your finance charges and still maintain a good and acceptable profit. It's far better to borrow money at practically any cost and show a profit than not to borrow and show no profit. The profit that you make will always be the difference (spread) between what you have to pay out and what you get to keep. Remember this every time you make or consider making an investment. Cost is an important factor, but your ability to show a profit is even more important.

If you can show a profit by making an investment, by all means borrow the money. Never be concerned that the rate you are paying is high by comparison to yesterday's rate. Never be concerned that the rate may be lower tomorrow. If the rates are lower tomorrow, you can always refinance at the lower rate. If the rates go up, you can sit back unconcerned, if you were smart enough to lock in the rate you do have. By using a little forethought, you can virtually have in your possession a no-lose hand. It's up to you how you play your cards.

Are you worried because you can't find any lenders jumping at the chance to make you a mortgage equal to the full value of your property? Even when I started out, there weren't any lenders like that around. I am here to tell you that I have never gotten a mortgage for over seventy percent of the appraisal value on any of my homes. In fact, most of my mortgages have been written for only sixty percent of the appraised value. Sure, there were ninety-five percent mortgages available, but they were only available to individuals buying their personal residences. These types of mortgages never were, and probably never will be, available to the investor who is buying a home he will never live in himself.

How then was I able to do so well working under these limitations? Simply by buying my houses right (way below value) and fixing them up right (making those improvements that have the highest returns). Many times all it took for me to recover my cost (down payment and improvement funds) and to get my profit (money left over from new mortgage once my cost and original financing were paid off) was a mortgage equal to sixty or seventy percent of the new value of the improved house.

I used this buy-fix up-refinance technique many times when I was starting out. In the beginning, though, I bought my homes with a conventional first mortgage. Within a month after purchase I would apply for a new mortgage and use those funds to pay off the existing mortgage, pay off my improvement costs, and pay myself a profit. The major drawback to this plan was that I was giving up a lot of my profit by paying two sets of closing costs (one on the original mortgage, and one on the refinancing). I solved this problem by eliminating the first set of closing costs by buying the property for cash. I got the cash by borrowing it short-term (ninety-day notes), using my lines of credit (to be covered again shortly).

Below is an example of how this whole process works, using a property I bought. The purchase price was $11,000, and the improvement costs were $3,000 (figures rounded off to the nearest thousand).

$21,000 mortgage ($30,000 appraisal, 70% mortgage)
−11,000 purchase price (90-day notes)
 −3,000 improvements (90-day notes)
$ 7,000 profit (tax free)

You are probably a little confused now about why I spent so much time earlier in this chapter on mortgages, especially now that I seem to be saying you may not want to use them initially to buy your homes. There are many ways to buy a home without getting a new first mortgage from a conventional lender. Most of these other ways offer you not only better terms but also a much lower interest rate on the money you borrow. If this is the case, why do you need to know anything about mortgages? Simply because mortgages will be the primary tool by which you will extract your money and your profit from your homes once you own them. Other than that, the only other time you will want to make any extensive use of new first mortgages is when mortgage money is abundant and cheap and when the terms are in your favor.

CREATIVE FINANCING

In the early 1970s when I started investing, very few people knew anything about creative financing and fewer yet knew how to use it. Today it's a whole different story. Many people have found that by using creative financing, they can put together deals that make the conventional financing of the good old days look anything but good.

The thirty-eight nothing-down strategies we are about to cover will show you some of the places you should first look for financing. Whenever money is tight, you will find more and more buyers and sellers turning to some of these alternative ways of financing. As an astute investor, you should use these alternative methods of financing at every opportunity. Don't use them only when conventional financing isn't available. Using these strategies will allow you to get bargain financing in any market, regardless of the conditions. They will show you that the days of making it big in real estate are always around for the investor who can find a bargain and a way to finance it creatively.

Creative financing means more than buying a house without using conventional financing. Creative financing is the art of buying a house with little or nothing down. When a buyer uses creative financing, it does not mean that the seller receives little or no money when he sells his home. What it does mean is that you will be using little or no money of your *own* to purchase his home. In effect, you will be using all borrowed funds to close the deal.

As you recall from the worksheets and our discussion of leverage, it may cost more to use all borrowed funds. Although it may cost more, you should also recall that the less of your own money you have in an investment, the higher your return on that money can be. Creative financing allows you to get those higher returns. In order to use creative financing though, you are probably going to need two or more sources of money. The following strategies will give you some idea of where to look.

The list we are about to go over is by no means complete. You may come across some new items to add to this list or even come up with some creative adaptation or combination of your own. You will be limited only by your imagination and your ability to sell your proposal to the person who is trying to sell his house to you.

As you go through these techniques, pick one or two that especially appeal to you and start to use them. Don't try to master and use all of these techniques. The most successful investors I know became successful by mastering just one or two. They then made their fortunes by putting together deals that allowed them to practice these techniques.

TECHNIQUES USING YOUR ASSETS

1. **Sell or borrow against personal items.** Do you have a car, a boat, a lot, or anything else you don't need anymore? Sell it to raise the cash you need. If you don't want to sell any of these items, you could use them as collateral for a loan.

2. **Barter your personal items.** Do you have anything the seller may want? Many times he will accept something you already own in lieu of the down payment. What you have is often worth more as an item of trade than you could sell it for. Even if what you have doesn't interest the seller personally, he may still accept it. Many "don't wanters" agree to take something other than cash as the down payment in order to sell their property quickly. I even know of one elderly seller who accepted a motorcycle as a down payment, and he didn't even like motorcycles or the people who own them!

3. **Barter the use of personal items.** Do you have a motor home, a cottage, a condominium, a boat, a truck, any special tools, or an exclusive club membership? Anything you have that the seller might be interested in using can take the place of a down payment. All you have to do is work out an agreement whereby he can use it so many times a year for so many years.

4. **Barter your professional services.** Are you a doctor, lawyer, dentist, contractor, landscape architect, painter, accountant, bookkeeper, teacher, mechanic, or anyone else who possesses certain skills? You can offer a specified number of hours of your time in lieu of any money. No matter who or what you are, if you really look hard, I'll bet you can come up with a number of marketable skills you never knew you could capitalize on.

5. **Refinance your home.** You can get a new mortgage on your home to release the equity that you have in it. You can even get a second mortgage and not disturb the low interest rate you may have on your existing first mortgage.

6. **Refinance other properties you own.** Do you own any other houses, lots, or buildings you could refinance either on a new first mortgage or through a second mortgage?

7. **Create your own paper.** You can give the seller a note secured by any of your assets. The note could be secured by the equity that you have in your home or any other piece of property, or it could be secured by any personal item. The note can be set up so that you pay it off on any schedule and at any interest rate that you can sell the person who is trying to sell you his property. If that isn't enough, consider the fact that creating your own paper is very inexpensive (hundreds or even thousands of dollars less than getting a conven-

tional mortgage), it's quick (it can be done in a matter of minutes), and there's usually no procedure to qualify you for the loan (no credit check, no red tape). Your only investment in time and money will be the small amount (as little as twenty-five dollars) it takes for your attorney to write it up and record it. Last but not least, when you create your own paper, you can borrow and use all your equity. Your loans are not limited to sixty percent or seventy percent of your property's appraised value. You can use one hundred percent of your equity.

8. **Borrow against paper that you hold.** Do you have any notes from anyone else? Are you holding any land contracts or second mortgages on property that you have sold? You can put these pieces of paper up as collateral for a loan.

9. **Borrow against stocks or bonds.** You can usually borrow up to fifty percent of the value of any stocks or bonds that you may own. Sometimes the lender will hold these certificates in his possession as collateral.

10. **Borrow against savings accounts, certificates of deposit, or money market certificates.** Do you currently have savings accounts, certificates of deposit, or money market certificates that you do not want to disturb? Would you like to be able to use them and have them continue to earn interest? Most savings institutions are more than happy to lend you your own money for a percent or two above what they are paying you in interest. All you have to do is pledge these accounts as collateral for the loan.

11. **Borrow against a trust.** Do you receive any income from a trust? Most lenders will be more than happy to lend you any amount you have in mind as long as the income from your trust will cover the payments.

12. **Borrow against an inheritance.** Do you receive an income from an inheritance? Are you scheduled to receive any benefits in the future? This, again, is excellent collateral for a loan.

13. **Borrow the "cash value" from a life insurance policy.** Many life insurance policies build up a cash value after so many years. This money can be borrowed at some very low rates. If the policy is an older one, these rates can be as low as six percent or less.

14. **Trade property you have for property you want.** Although the seller may not want a piece of property you have, you can still get him to take it on trade if you have a buyer for it. If he takes it and immediately sells the property for exactly the amount he credited you with, he ends up with neither a tax gain nor a tax loss. You, on the other hand, are able to postpone (possibly indefinitely) any tax

due on your gain (if there was one). This whole process is called a tax-free exchange, and everyone involved ends up happy. There will be more about this in the chapter on taxes.

STRATEGIES USING FEW OR NONE OF YOUR OWN ASSETS

15. **Use the seller's equity.** Rather than tie up any of your assets, use the property you are buying as collateral. If you buy on land contract with no money down, or if you assume and have the seller take back a second mortgage for the difference between the selling price and the assumed amount, the property you are buying should be adequate collateral. If the seller doesn't think it is, he must not think the property is worth what you are paying. If this is the case, tell him you want to renegotiate the price down to an amount that he thinks is adequate to secure the financing.

16. **Use "soft paper."** More than a new strategy, this is a refinement of #7 (create your own paper) and #15 (use the seller's equity). Soft paper refers to loans that have low payments in the beginning and higher payments at the end. You may pay interest only, or less, at first and then pay more until larger and larger amounts go towards the principal. Many times you can offer to give the seller his asking price or more if he will give you soft paper. Often soft paper will make your total payments and/or interest cost less than you would have paid on a smaller loan. Many lenders will also give you soft paper if you help them out by taking a repossessed house off their hands.

17. **Use one or more unsecured notes.** Even if you don't have a rich Uncle Harry, you at least have a bunch of friends and relatives. All these people are sources of venture capital. Getting a lot of people to lend you a little bit of money is usually a lot easier than getting one person to lend you a lot of money. If you don't know how to set up a note, consult your attorney the first time. From that point on you can do it yourself, and don't forget to try for soft paper.

18. **Use lines of credit.** Many lending institutions allow you to borrow up to $5,000 or $10,000 on your signature alone once you have established a line of credit with them. Depending on your credit and your financial condition, you may be able to borrow up to the limit immediately. Once you are established with these institutions, you may even be able to borrow beyond these limits. Having this kind of money available to you at a number of different institutions means there is virtually no limit to the number of deals you can take advantage of when they come your way.

19. **Use your statement of net worth.** Many lenders will allow you to borrow up to ten percent of your net worth unsecured. These financial statements are available free from most lenders, and they will even show you how to fill them out if you are unsure. Your net worth is the difference between your assets and your liabilities.

20. **Use an "appreciation participation kicker."** Offer the seller or whoever will be holding your paper a certain percentage of the property's increase in value at the end of a certain number of years. This is a good way to encourage someone to carry all or part of the financing and to give you a better rate of interest and better terms. For your own protection, it is advisable to set a dollar limit (or cap) on the actual amount of the appreciation the holder will end up getting. For example, to make the offer really interesting to him, you could agree to give him fifty percent of the increase in value, but protect yourself by limiting his proceeds to no more than $1,000.

21. **Use the seller's debt.** If the seller is going to use his equity in the property to pay off some of his debts, you could offer to assume his debts in lieu of a down payment. If this is agreeable to him (and it should be), all you have to do is contact his creditors to work out the arrangements. If you are in better financial shape than the seller, you will be helping his creditors out considerably. Because of this, you should be able to arrange for a considerable discount (fifty percent or more) on the debts you are assuming. You should also be able to arrange a repayment schedule that fits comfortably into your program (try for soft paper here, too).

22. **Use the land.** Let the seller keep the land as collateral. This should make him feel secure, and it really doesn't affect your investment. The house produces all the income and the tax benefits, not the land. If you are going to do this, lease the land from him for a small annual fee. Also get an option to buy the land on or before some future date. Have the option state the price and the terms.

23. **Use the mineral rights.** If you are in an area where there may be some advantage in owning the mineral rights, let the seller hold them as collateral. As with the land in the example above, always get an option to buy them back on or before some specified date, and have the price and terms worked into that option. If you don't and oil is discovered on the land, you will never see even one dollar in royalties.

24. **Use closing credits.** When the house you are buying is rented, setting the closing on or close to the rental due date will net you that month's income. If there is a security deposit, that will also be transferred to you. If the real estate property taxes are not prepaid

in your area, you will receive a prorated amount from the seller to pay the taxes when they come due. Many times the figures from these closing credits can add up to an amount large enough to cover the small amount of money you need to get into the deal.

25. **Use the real estate commission.** Many times the broker or the salesman will lend you their commissions on the sale in order to help the sale go through. Try to arrange to pay back the commissions in a way that won't jeopardize your cash flow (for example, by using soft paper).

26. **Use the realtor.** Many of the best brokers and salesmen have extra income they are looking to invest. If the house they are selling you is a real bargain, they will know that their money is well secured and, therefore, safe. If they know you and are aware of your abilities, so much the better. Remember, you hold the cards that could win them a sale. Let them help you play your hand. It's up to you to make them an offer they can't refuse.

27. **Use an offer to pay more.** Many times offering a seller more money in order to get him to accept your offer or a lower interest rate works wonders. When the interest rate is lowered, the monthly payments needed to amortize the loan drop. It is very possible that the monthly payments on a larger loan at a lower interest rate will be less than the monthly payments on a smaller loan at a higher interest rate.

   Here is an example of how offering more can actually lower your monthly payments *and* the total amount you will end up paying for the loan. Let's say a seller isn't interested in selling and holding any paper for $10,000 at a ten percent interest rate for twenty-five years. (Monthly payments on this loan would amount to $90.88, for a total repayment of $27,264.00.) He may be interested, though, and he may agree to a lower rate if you offer to pay him more. If you offer $11,000 at an interest rate of seven percent, your monthly payments will be only $77.75, and your total repayment will be $23,325.00. You could even offer him $12,000 if he would agree to a seven percent interest rate, and your payments would be only $84.82 (which is still less than the payments on $10,000 at ten percent), while your total repayment would be $25,446.00.

   Mortgage amortization tables are available free from many real estate agents and title companies. They can also be purchased at any bookstore. These books are one of the most useful tools an investor can own. Look into getting one today.

28. **Use "sweat equity."** The F.H.A. has a provision that allows you to receive credit for the labor you put into fixing up a house. About the only stipulation is that you receive credit only for the things that

bring the house up to F.H.A. standards. You can also use "sweat equity" in a repair partnership like the one mentioned below. Since "sweat equity" covers all or most of the down payment, it can help produce a positive cash flow.

29. **Use a repair partnership.** If the house you are buying is in need of extensive repairs, you may consider getting together with a general contractor, a plumber, an electrician, or anyone else whose services or skills you will require. Each of you will receive an agreed-upon percentage of ownership, and yours should be the largest because you are the one who found the deal and put it together. When the seller sees how you are going to upgrade his property, he should feel very secure in granting you a second mortgage or other instrument to cover the entire purchase price. With the house all fixed up and worth more, the seller will have little doubt about the security of his position. He may even go to bed each night praying that you default so that he gets his house back all fixed up.

30. **Use a "lone arranger" approach.** Finding people with money to lend and having them assume all or part of the financing is not hard to do (especially if you already have a good deal lined up). Many newspapers and magazines carry ads placed by people who have money and are looking for a place to invest it. If there aren't any such ads running at the time, consider placing one of your own. Your ad might read, "Investor with excellent property looking for investor with money who wants excellent return."

Answering or placing ads is a good way to arrange your own financing, but one of the best ways is to let your fingers do the walking. This involves turning to the Yellow Pages of your phone book and calling doctors, lawyers, and other high-income professionals. Many of these people not only have money to invest, but they also want and need to invest in real estate. Their main problem is that they don't have the time or the expertise to do so and manage the investment successfully. If you have these necessary ingredients but you don't have any money, this could be a perfect marriage. Many of today's most successful investors owe their success to a few phone calls—you can too.

31. **Use a real estate future contract.** By using a real estate future contract, you can offer an investor who is looking for a good return a chance to get it. In return for making the down payment he will receive a real estate future contract. The future states that at maturity (one to five years) he will get back his initial investment plus an agreed-upon percentage of the increase in value that occurs.

Make his percentage high enough to be interesting, but put a dollar limit on it. When it is time to pay off the future, you can

refinance, sell, or issue a new contract with the original investor or
someone else.

32. **Use a partnership mortgage plan.** When you use a partnership
mortgage plan, you can offer an investor who is looking for a good
return or some tax relief a chance to help both of you out at the
same time. He makes the down payment and receives an agreed-
upon percentage of ownership. He then receives that percentage of
all income and pays that percentage of all expenses. He also gets
that percentage of the tax benefits and that percentage of all the
equity.

33. **Use an assignment of rents agreement.** As security for a loan, you
can offer a lender or seller an assignment of rents agreement. This
agreement gives the lender the right to impound the rents to pay
the loan in case you default.

34. **Use a co-signer.** Many times when you can't get a loan on your
own, all you need is someone to co-sign for you. A co-signer could
be a parent, a well-to-do relative, a friend, or an acquaintance, or it
could even be your employer. Remember, whoever signs for you is
putting his own good name and credit on the line for you—don't
let him down.

35. **Use your employer.** Are you scheduled to receive a raise or a
bonus? Your employer might be more interested in buying a house
and leasing it to you instead. The tax advantages to both of you
could be very impressive. In addition, you can arrange to buy it in
the future at book cost and at some excellent terms to boot. As an
employee benefit program this could be better than profit-sharing,
pension, and medical coverage all rolled into one! One of my
friends did this with his employer—and everybody won. Use your
profit-sharing or pension funds. If you are in business for yourself
and have no employees, in many cases you are allowed to self-
direct the funds in your profit-sharing or pension plans. If you
have any employees, however, you will need to check exactly what
you can and cannot do with those funds.

36. **Use a lease back to the seller arrangement.** If the seller doesn't
have any place to go after the sale, you could offer to lease the house
to him rent-free for a set period in exchange for the down payment. If you are planning any renovation inside or outside the
house during that time, you should make sure the lease lists what
you will be doing and that your plans have the seller's approval.
Otherwise, he might object to your working on the house while he
is there and make you wait until he is out.

37. **Use a lease with an option to buy.** Many "don't wanters" will
accept a lease with an option to buy. Once you come to an agreement on the price, tell the seller you will lease his house from him

for two years (or whatever term you set) at whatever his current payments are. To sweeten this offer, you may even offer to pay him more than your agreed-upon price. Since the house should appreciate all by itself during the lease, you aren't taking much of a chance even if you agree to pay more than the house is presently worth. Since you have an option, you really aren't taking any chance at all.

To make the seller feel even better, tell him that while you are leasing his house, you will agree to make all the repairs and take care of renting it out. Tell him he won't have any problems at all; they will all be yours.

You could even go on and tell the seller that you will put in certain improvements (list them on the offer) at your expense so that if you choose not to exercise your option to buy his house at the end of two years, he will get it back with all the improvements paid for.

Finding the money for the improvements shouldn't be a problem. If, for example, you could rent the home out for $100 above your lease payments, you would gain $2,400 over the two years of the lease. That kind of money should more than pay for the improvements you plan to put in. If at the end of the lease you decide not to exercise your option to buy, you can turn around and walk away, and all you will have lost is your time.

You should include in your agreement the stipulation that if and when you do exercise your option to buy the house, the seller will finance all or part of the purchase. Don't wait until the option is about to expire before you try to find or arrange financing. It may well be too late then. Get it all set up while you're holding the cards.

38. **Use a "let the seller pay you" arrangement.** As unbelievable as this sounds, some sellers will actually pay you to buy their house. If the house is overmortgaged, condemned, or financially and emotionally draining the seller, he can be negotiated into paying you in order to get himself out. Situations like this exist more often than you would believe. If the seller believes that you will assume his burden and that you have the ability to handle it, he will advance you the funds and give you the terms you require.

TEN FINANCING POINTS TO REMEMBER

1. **Don't worry about going into debt.** Going into debt to buy a good house is just about the best investment you can make. If it wasn't

such a good investment, the people who finance the lion's share wouldn't risk hundreds or thousands of dollars for every dollar you invest. In fact, when you buy with nothing down, other people are assuming almost all the risk. If they aren't worried, you shouldn't be either.

2. **Always know how you are going to pay off the debt.** When you know and understand how your investment will generate the money to service your debt, both you and the lender will feel very secure. Use the worksheet if you are not sure.

3. **Always try to borrow more than you need.** If you are afraid of being caught short because of delays or unexpected expenses or anything else when remodeling, you should borrow more than you expect to need. If you can't borrow more than you need from one source, at least have another source available in case you need extra funds. These extra funds can be used in emergencies to meet the payments on your other loans, thus protecting your credit rating and giving you the time to straighten things out.

4. **Never borrow more than the property will support.** This statement does not conflict with the third point above, but rather qualifies it. For you to be interested in buying a house, it will have to have an income that will more than cover any indebtedness you will have to place upon it. Unless you are in a very high tax bracket and looking for a way to shelter some of your income, you never want to buy a house that will create a negative cash flow. Never.

5. **Don't worry about the high cost of financing.** If you're like most people, you don't like the idea of paying for the privilege of borrowing money. When interest rates are high, you probably like this idea even less. Although you always want to keep your cost as low as possible, don't let high interest rates stop you from getting into an investment that can pay these costs and still make a lot of money for you.

Another factor to consider in financing costs is your net interest rate. The interest that you pay on borrowed funds is a tax-deductible expense. Because of this deduction, you will get back income taxes that you would normally be liable for, and therefore your net interest rate is much lower than the stated rate. The effect of the refund depends upon the tax bracket you find yourself in. The table below shows approximately what your net interest rate is when taking your current taxable income into account.

NET INTEREST RATES

TAXABLE INCOME	APPROX TAX RATE	STATED INTEREST RATE vs NET INTEREST RATES											
		7%	8%	9%	10%	11%	12%	13%	14%	15%	16%	17%	18%
$20,000	22%	5.5	6.2	7.0	7.8	8.6	9.4	10.1	10.9	11.7	12.5	13.3	14.0
$25,000	29%	5.0	5.7	6.4	7.1	7.8	8.5	9.2	9.9	10.7	11.4	12.1	12.8
$30,000	33%	4.7	5.4	6.0	6.7	7.4	8.0	8.7	9.4	10.1	10.7	11.4	12.1
$40,000	39%	4.3	4.9	5.5	6.1	6.7	7.3	7.9	8.5	9.2	9.8	10.4	11.0
$50,000	44%	3.9	4.5	5.0	5.6	6.2	6.7	7.3	7.8	8.4	9.0	9.5	10.1
$70,000	49%	3.6	4.1	4.6	5.1	5.6	6.1	6.6	7.1	7.7	8.2	8.7	9.2

6. **Shop around for the best deal.** Compare the interest rate, the terms, and the closing costs at various lenders. If you don't plan to keep the house until the mortgage is paid off, you might want to negotiate out the prepayment penalty clause and negotiate in an assumption and a release clause.

7. **The seller may be the best source of financing.** Don't forget that the seller can be motivated to offer you more flexible financing at a better interest rate and better terms than any commercial lender. Find out what he wants and needs financially and then work out a mutually beneficial agreement.

8. **Banks want to lend you money.** Never try to walk into a bank on your knees because it's a poor and uncomfortable position to bargain from. Walk in on your feet, confident that you are going to get what you are after. If you have established yourself as a customer, established your credit, and can establish the worthiness of your investment, you have nothing to fear.

    Never let a lender know how much you want or need his money. If he thinks you are desperate, he will extract the most painful terms and conditions. If he thinks you don't need him or his money, he can be most cooperative. Remember, banks love to lend money to people who don't need it. Banks are in business to lend money. Banks need customers to lend that money to. Become a valued customer.

9. **Owner-occupied houses qualify for better terms.** If you are going to use conventional financing and you are not going to be living in the house you are buying, you will find yourself having to come up with a larger down payment and having to live with less favorable financing than if you were buying the house to live in. The solution to this problem is to buy the house and move into it yourself. You may have to live in the house for a while to qualify for the better rate and terms, but it may be well worth it. Check to see what the current conditions are in your area.

10. **If you are turned down for a loan, let it be known.** Possibly one of the worst things you can do if you are turned down for a loan is to try to cover up the fact. Since it will probably come out anyway when you are applying somewhere else, it is far better that you bring it up right at the start. By doing so, you disarm the new lender and cast some doubt on the judgment of the person who turned you down. If you do this, just make darn sure that person didn't have a good reason for turning you down.

CHAPTER NINE
CLOSING

*I'm not afraid of tomorrow, for I have
seen yesterday, and I love today.*

WILLIAM ALLEN WHITE

Closing is the transaction during which the purchase of the house is completed. The closing can take place anywhere, but it usually takes place at a bank, a title company, a realtor's office, or an attorney's office. Prior to the closing you should have your attorney check over all the papers that you will be signing, along with any other documents you will be receiving. If your attorney thinks that his presence is needed at the closing itself, by all means take his advice.

The Real Estate Settlement Procedures Act (R.E.S.P.A.) went into effect in June 1975 and protects you against being caught unaware by high and unexpected closing costs when dealing with most commercial lenders. The act also puts a ceiling on what your monthly escrow payments can be. Under the act, the lender must supply you with a settlement costs booklet that explains in non-technical language the various closing cost terms. The lender is also required to give you a written "good faith estimate" of what your settlement costs will be.

This act provides you with the right to cancel the whole transaction at least twelve days before the closing if you don't like any of the charges. The only danger of cancelling the closing at one lending institution at this late date is that your sales agreement may call for a closing by a certain date. If this is the case, you will not have enough time to look for a better deal from a different lender. An escape clause to the effect that the sales agreement is contingent on your approval of the closing statement could protect you from this danger.

183

Of course, the best solution would be to work out an agreement with the seller whereby he pays all of your closing costs. If you recall, this was one of the techniques suggested in chapter seven when offers and negotiations were discussed. Closing costs average about four percent of the selling price in a normal market under normal conditions. That may work out to only $400 in closing cost on our $10,000 house, but it adds up to $2,000 on a $50,000 house. If the economy is tight, the cost could be much higher. Different areas have different customs and guidelines, but the following list presents the usual division of cost between buyer and seller.

THE BUYER'S COST

Depending on how you take title to the house and what you require, you may be responsible for all or some of the following costs. The source of your financing, your legal work, your insurance, your inspections, and any other services you use will affect the price you pay.

1. **Discount points.** A point is equal to one percent of the mortgage amount. Lenders charge points to increase the yield on their loans. Some lenders don't charge any points, and some lenders charge many. Points may go under different names, such as origination fees, loan preparation fees, and mortgage discount points.
2. **Legal fees.** These legal fees cover the cost of having your attorney look over the papers and/or attend the closing.
3. **Credit report.** The lender must be reimbursed for his cost in getting your credit history.
4. **Lender's title policy.** A lender's title insurance policy protects the lender against loss of his interest in property owing to unforeseen flaws or clouds in the title.
5. **Hazard insurance.** Hazard insurance protects you against loss to the property caused by fire, windstorm, and other common hazards. Any lender will want to be listed on the policy as a mortgage holder or an "additional named insured."
6. **Recording fees.** Recording fees are the fees charged by the courthouse to record your deed and mortgage.
7. **Assumption fees.** Assumption fees are the fees you may have to pay the lender in order to assume the seller's mortgage.
8. **Survey.** A survey is often required by a lender to assure him that the house is sitting on the land your deed describes. This survey, which is usually called a mortgage survey, is not as involved or as expensive as other types of survey.

9. **Prorated taxes.** If the property taxes in your area are prepaid, you might find yourself having to reimburse the seller for part of the taxes he paid in advance.
10. **Termite inspection.** If it is not required and paid for by the seller in your area, have your purchase agreement state that you will pay for termite inspection but that the seller is to pay for any service and repairs that are required.
11. **Structural, plumbing, and electrical inspections.** Again, if structural, plumbing, and electrical inspections are not required and paid for by the seller, you may want to hire your own contractor to inspect the house and its systems. You or the seller may also be required by certain municipalities to have the property inspected by the building department for building code compliance.
12. **Appraisal fee.** The appraisal fee covers the cost of having the lender's appraiser appraise the house and property you are going to buy.

THE SELLER'S COST

1. **Commission.** If the seller had a realtor handle the sale of his house, the seller will owe him the agreed-upon fee.
2. **Points.** Buyers are prohibited from paying points on H.U.D. or V.A. guaranteed loans. Sellers, however, can and do pay these points.
3. **Title insurance or abstract.** In many cases, the seller is required to furnish the buyer with title insurance or an abstract. If the seller has an existing title policy on the property in question and it is less than ten years old, he may be able to turn it in and receive up to sixty percent of its cost as a credit when buying a new policy. The same goes for the lender's title policy. Remember this if you ever sell or refinance one of your houses.
4. **Legal fees.** The seller pays his attorney for his services.
5. **Preparation of the deed.** The seller pays the cost of having a new deed prepared.
6. **Documentary stamps.** Documentary stamps are also called state or local transfer taxes. They are required on deeds and mortgages when title passes from one owner to another.

TAKING TITLE

When it comes time to draw up the deed, you had better know in whose name and in what way you want the deed drawn. In most cases, your attorney is the only person who can legally and intelligently advise you. Once the deed is drawn and you have received and recorded it, it will be very hard to change. That is why you ought to talk to your attorney and discuss what effects the way you take ownership will have on your taxes, your estate, your family, and your control over the property in question.

Joint tenancy. Joint tenancy is by far the most widely used form of ownership. Most husbands and wives take title this way because it gives equal ownership to both parties. If one or the other dies, the right of survivorship allows the interest in the property to pass immediately to the surviving spouse. Since the property does not have to go through probate, it won't be tied up until the estate is settled. Because of this provision, a joint tenant cannot will his or her interest in the property to anyone else, since it passes automatically to the survivor.

Tenancy by the entirety. Tenancy by the entirety is a special form of joint tenancy between spouses. However, it is not recognized in many states.

Tenancy in common. Tenancy in common allows two or more parties to have equal, or unequal, undivided interest in a property without the right of survivorship. In other words, you can take title to a piece of property with another person, and you can have a fifty percent interest each, or you can have a seventy-five percent interest and the other party can have a twenty-five percent interest. You can divide up the interest in the property any way you like among as many people as you like. You can sell your interest, assign your interest, and even will your interest to anyone you choose. Of course, anyone else who has an interest in the property can do the same. For this reason, you may want your attorney to draw up a partnership agreement to protect your interest.

Regardless of how you take title, make sure that your deed is recorded as soon as possible. If for some reason someone else recorded a deed on your property before you, he may be adjudged the legal owner. Also, when it comes time to record your deed, you may want to leave off all mention of your purchase price (some states require this information to be stated on the deed). If the purchase price is not on the deed, it makes it harder for the tax assessor or anyone else to determine what you paid. If this or anything else we have covered so far overwhelms you, relax, because all the legal and complicated stuff we have covered is usually handled by an attorney.

In fact, he and your realtor will be able to answer most of your questions and handle all the paper work.

Before leaving the subject of the deed, I should mention that any time you receive a deed, make sure it is a warranty deed. A warranty deed is one in which the seller guarantees the deed to be free of others' claims and free of all liens and encumbrances except those specified on the deed. In contrast to the warranty deed, there is a deed called a quitclaim deed. This deed does not profess that there is any valid title. All it does is pass on to you any title, interest, or claim the grantor may have on the property.

COMMITMENTS AND BINDERS

Never show up at any closing without three particular forms in your possession. They are absolutely vital. These three forms are a title insurance commitment, a loan commitment (if you are obtaining financing), and a hazard insurance binder stating the kind and amount of coverage you have.

Besides having these forms in your possession, you should take one other precaution. Either you or your attorney should call the title company just prior to closing to see if any last minute liens, claims, or encumbrances have been filed. This happens quite often when people who have any claims hear that the property is going to be sold. The only way you can protect yourself any more than this is to have the closing take place in escrow. Normally only larger properties are closed this way, and there usually isn't any need for it when you are buying a home. Still, if conditions exist that would make this a better way to close, your attorney can advise you.

CLOSING CHECKLIST

This is a final checklist you should go over before you show up at the closing. I take this list with me to the closing, and you may want to do the same. It's much better than trying to rely on your memory.

CLOSING CHECKLIST

BEFORE GOING TO THE CLOSING

   ___DEED (Warranty) (Is it all in order)

   ___TITLE INSURANCE (Marketable Title) (Current Commitment/Phone)

   ___LOAN (Have you seen the Papers) (Do you have a Commitment)

   ___HAZARD INSURANCE ($_____) (Do you have a Binder)

   ___PROPERTY TAXES (Current and Paid)

   ___PRIVATE ASSESSMENTS, DUES, CHARGES, LIENS (Current and Paid)

   ___PUBLIC ASSESSMENTS (Current and Paid)

   ___MUNICIPAL UTILITIES (Hooked Up) (Current and Paid)

   ___PUBLIC UTILITIES (Hooked Up) (Current and Paid)

   ___RENTAL AGREEMENT (Signed by staying seller or current tenant)

   ___CLOSING COST AMOUNT ($_____)

   ___CLOSING LOCATION (_____), Date (_____), Time (_____)

   ___ATTORNEY (Has yours verified all the above)

GOING TO THE CLOSING

   ___IMPORTANT PAPERS (Are you responsible for taking any to the Closing)

   ___MONEY (Do you have your Checkbook and or the Necessary Funds)

   ___ATTORNEY (Is yours to meet you Before, After, or At the Closing)

BEFORE LEAVING THE CLOSING

   ___IMPORTANT PAPERS (Are they all Signed, Sealed, and Delivered)

   ___MONEY OWED BY SELLER (Collected or Deducted from his proceeds)

   ___RENTS and SECURITY DEPOSITS (Collected or Transferred to you)

   ___CLOSING STATEMENT (Received) (Personal Property shown separate)

   ___KEYS (Received all of them) (For every Door and every Lock)

   ___ATTORNEY (Will yours Receive, Recheck, and Record all documents)

NOTES and ADDITIONAL ITEMS TO CHECK

CHAPTER TEN
IMPROVEMENTS

Whatever your lot in life, get busy
and build something on it.

ANONYMOUS

Next to buying a house for less than it's worth, making the right improvements can make your investment appreciate more than anything else you can do. Making the wrong improvements can end up costing you time, money, energy, and potential profits. Over-spending and overdoing it are the main dangers you will face when starting out. There is a strong temptation to make the house you are improving a monument to your good taste and abilities. Make a solemn oath here and now not to let your emotions overrule your head. Leave the building of monuments to public officials. Your only interest in making any improvements should be in building profits.

One of the easiest ways and, in fact, the only way that I know of to keep yourself in check is to set a spending limit right at the start and then stick to it. You can estimate what you can afford to spend on improvements by using the worksheet. One of the most important things the worksheet shows you is that the more money you have invested in a house, the lower your returns. If you want to raise your returns on your improvement dollars, you will have to look for ways to get the most results for the least amount of money. As a rule, you should not spend over ten percent of the purchase price of the home on improvements.

I once advised a young couple starting out investing in their first home how important it was to set a limit on their home improvement budget. I told them I knew how easy it was to get carried away, because it had happened to me on one of my first houses. I emphasized this point so much and so often that I was sure it was indelibly burned into their minds. Unfortunately, their hearts were closer to their wallets than their heads were. Once they got started, nothing was too good or too expensive. They even went so far as to have custom cabinets built for the kitchen and bathroom at a cost that was way over what their whole improvement budget should have been. When they were finished remodeling the house, they found they had so much money in it that the rent they could charge would not cover their expenses. They decided to sell. The good news is that they were able to sell the house for over $30,000 and did not lose any money. The bad news is that they bought the house for $16,000 and did not make any money.

You are probably all familiar with the three Rs you were taught in school. But are you familiar with the three Rs of home improvement? They are repair, replace, and restore. Just about every time you buy a house, you will be faced with repairing, replacing, or restoring part of it. Knowing what you will have to do (emergency repairs) and what you would like to do (improvements) is important. Knowing what your cost will be is even more important.

IMPROVEMENTS vs. REPAIRS

There's a big difference between improvements and repairs, especially when it comes to counting your profit. As a rule, repairs usually don't increase the value of a house beyond their cost, so that no return is earned on the extra investment. Don't take this as a case for not making repairs; it isn't. Many homes can be purchased far below their present value simply because they need so many repairs. The fact that you may not make any money by taking care of the repairs shouldn't discourage you. The fact that so many things are wrong should excite you about the possibility of making money by buying the house at a substantial discount.

Repairs, especially emergency repairs, have to be done, and so the only decision you must make is how to do them the best and most economical way. Improvements, on the other hand, require you to make a number of decisions. Before you start any project, you must realize that for economic reasons you will probably never be able to do everything you want to do. You may not even be able to make the improvements you do make in the way you would like. In any case, you need to use the money you set aside for improvements wisely. If you had budgeted $1,000 for improvements and decided to use that money to put on a new roof or replace the heating system (both of which were still serviceable), you could find that the house might not be valued at a dollar over the appraisal that was done right before you bought the house. Why? Because the appraiser would walk through the house and still notice the same old kitchen, the same old bathroom, the same old worn carpets, and the same old chipping and peeling paint that produced the original appraisal. In a case like this, the $1,000 you put into improvements didn't raise the value of the house, and in effect you ended up losing money by making the wrong improvements. It would have been better to spend a few dollars to patch the roof and get the furnace serviced. The rest of the money could then have been used on the right improvements.

The right improvements are those you and the appraiser can really see. These are the improvements that use paint, paneling, wallpaper, and carpet and all kinds of good ideas. Improvements like these give the highest returns, and they don't take a lot of money, a lot of time, or a lot of expensive licensed help that requires you have a building permit. If you want to make a lot of money making improvements, buy houses that need this kind of work. And don't forget that making repairs won't make you a lot of money; when a house needs repairs, buying it right does that.

SETTING YOUR PRIORITIES AND YOUR BUDGET

From the worksheet you should know your budget. As I mentioned before, you should be able to keep it under ten percent of the purchase price of the home.

Selecting what you are going to do and then trying to figure out how you can get the best results can be habit-forming. If you are anything like me, you will enjoy this as much as or more than any other part of this single family home game. I can guarantee you that once you have the habit, you won't want to give it up. In fact, you will probably wonder how any smart investor can live without it. The truth is, he can't—at least not very well or very long.

Okay, you know what your budget is. Now you have to determine your priorities. This is done by going over all the items on the housecheck form that need work and listing them as either an emergency repair or an improvement. Let's take a look at these two categories and see some of the items that might be listed under each and how they might be taken care of.

EMERGENCY REPAIRS CHECKLIST

Emergency repairs can be anything that needs to be repaired or replaced immediately, such as broken windows, broken doors, missing and malfunctioning locks or security devices, broken or malfunctioning electrical and plumbing parts and fixtures, damaged ceilings and walls, damaged floors, leaky roofs, and plugged-up chimneys. These kinds of repairs must all be done immediately, and your only thought should be how to do them for the least amount of money. Any dollar you save here is one more dollar to invest in improvements.

After you have taken all the emergency items off your housecheck form and placed them on your emergency repair list, go back over your housecheck and list all the items that may need replacing or repairing in the future, such as an old roof, an old furnace or water heater, an inadequate electrical system, an outdated plumbing system, or an old fence. If your budget will allow the immediate replacement of any of these items, fine. If it doesn't, you may want to take steps to help them last as long as they can. Regardless of what action you take or don't take on these items, they should still be listed at the bottom of your emergency repairs checklist under the heading of future repairs and replacements.

IMPROVEMENTS CHECKLIST

This is the list that you are going to work from to create some wealth for yourself (see the section on return ratios in chapter five). The items on this list will be the remaining items on the housecheck form and all those other improvements you would like to make. This is the enjoyable part, when you come up with ways to get the most done on the budget you have to work with. In setting your priorities, you will want to break your list down into two categories, outside improvements and inside improvements.

Outside improvements. People who look good are said to have sex appeal. Houses that look good are said to have curb appeal. When I started out buying and fixing up houses, I spent most of my time and money improving the inside of the house. I figured that since people spent most of the time inside, the inside should be my top priority. I labored under this misconception for quite some time. I was slow to realize that it didn't matter how nice a house looked inside; if it didn't look good from the outside, nobody would take the time to mosey on in.

You want your houses to have curb appeal even if it means foregoing some—or even all—of the improvements on the inside. The reason is that if it looks good from the street, many more prospective tenants will take their time to look at your house. Believe it or not, when given a choice between a house with curb appeal and a crummy interior and a house with a crummy exterior and a nice interior, most tenants will take the first choice. Why? Simply because most of their friends and acquaintances never see the inside of their house, but they all see the outside. John and Mary Tenant would rather have all these people think they live in a really nice place and not a dump. Once they move in, John and Mary Tenant are also more likely to fix up the inside for you, since that is where they spend most of their time.

Since first impressions are so important, you will want to start outside. In fact, you may even want to start with the yard. Ask yourself, what the yard is like. Does the grass need reseeding? Do the shrubs need trimming? Are there any shrubs at all? If you are going to have to put any money into the yard, what should you do? Remember, landscape architects will tell you that $100 of well-placed landscaping can add as much as $1,000 or more to the value of a home. Need this landscaping be expensive? No—in fact, your best buys and your sturdiest plants will be the less expensive varieties. Besides that, they tend to grow faster, and that means that they will fill in faster. These are important points because you don't want anything that requires a lot of care and takes years before it looks right.

The next thing to put on your list may be the outside condition of the house. Would a new coat of paint help? Any siding (brick, aluminum, asbestos, wood, or anything else you might have) can be painted to look good. Before you buy your first gallon of paint, find an established paint store in your area with a knowledgeable manager. He will be able to tell you what kind of paint to use and how to apply it. He will also be able to help with any special problems. This advice is worth more than the money you will ever save by buying bargain paints. Besides that, better paints also have a tendency to last longer, so that you have to paint less often. Since it costs far more to pay someone to apply a gallon of paint than it does to buy a gallon of paint, over the long run you actually end up spending less money for the better paint.

After you have found a store and a person you have confidence in, tell him what you are doing and tell him you want to buy all your paint and supplies from him. Tell him that you want to set up an account at his store, and ask him what kind of discount he will give you. You can expect a minimum discount of at least ten percent and a maximum that is many times greater. Of course, the discount will depend on what items you are buying and how much business you actually plan on doing at that store. You may also want to check whether he gives an additional discount if you pay cash.

Unless you know for sure what color you want and you know what it will look like once it is on the house, don't rush out and buy a couple of cases of a specially mixed paint. Many people have chosen a color from a color chip in the store and then found after they had it up that it looked horrendous. Paint stores are not in the habit of taking paint back once it has been mixed, so you had better be certain that the color you choose is the color you use. The only sure way of getting a color you can live with is to look around for another house that is painted with a color or color combination you like. When you find one, ask the owner where he bought his paint and if he knows the color name and number. Most people will consider your interest the highest form of compliment and will help you all they can. Go into the store the paint came from and get a color chip. Stop by the house again to check that the color matches before giving it to your man to mix up the paint.

Before you move inside the house, one last thing to check is the entrance. Is the sidewalk decent? Are the steps and the porch in good shape? Is the door attractive? If you are going to be doing any other work to the outside, this is the area on which to spend the most effort. This is probably the only area where the people going into the house will be close enough to it to notice any chipping, cracking, and peeling. Everything in this immediate area should be carefully painted, even if it means stripping off the old paint before you apply the new. The extra care you give this area will enhance the overall character of the house.

Inside improvements. Now that your house has curb appeal, you are ready to start work on the inside. Are there any particular rooms you should start with first? You bet. You should look first at the kitchen and then the bathroom(s). These rooms will date a house more than any other room or feature in the entire house. Of the two, the kitchen is usually more important. Families tend to spend a lot of time in the kitchen, especially the member of the family who does most of the cooking. The cook has a lot to say when it comes to making a decision about renting a house. If the cook doesn't like the kitchen, he or she will probably vote against getting the house.

Unfortunately the kitchen can be the most expensive room in the whole house to remodel. Mind you, I said can be. Sure, you can spend all kinds of money if you want to. You can put in new everything if you want to, but you don't have to. You can put in a few good ideas instead. A good idea has always been worth more than a lot of money, and when it comes to remodeling, this rule couldn't be truer. If you don't have good ideas or a good imagination, find someone who does. People are always willing to tell you what they think. Give them a chance. If you don't know any people who can think, you're still in luck because I will soon tell you where you can get all the ideas and professional help you need at little or no cost. When I say professional help, I'm talking about some of the best decorators in this country. And when I say no cost, I'm talking about free.

When you are making improvements, the bathroom can be the next most expensive room. Just like the kitchen, however, it need not cost a fortune to improve it. Before you think of tearing out those old fixtures, stop and consider what people are paying for replicas of those fixtures today. Many of the top-of-the-line manufacturers are reproducing old fixtures for people who want to spend a lot of money to capture the look of yesterday. Maybe all you need is a good idea or two to highlight what you already have. A new tub, sink, and stool won't give a bathroom class and make it unique. Only you can do that. Look for good ideas, and then use them.

The rest of the house can easily and inexpensively be updated and improved. Replacing an ugly old light fixture, for example, or putting one where there was just a bare light bulb before will help a lot. As a rule, you should use standard and inexpensive fixtures that you can buy at any department, discount, or hardware store. The only exception to this rule is that you should put a nice fixture in the entrance hall, dining room or any other room that is used often. Pick the one room that will highlight the rest of the house, and put in a nice (not expensive) fixture. You will give the whole house a touch of class and quality you couldn't get by putting the same amount of money into any other improvement.

Sometimes a ceiling can be a problem. If it is in bad shape and a coat of paint won't be enough to make it look good, try to do more than just fix it. Here again, a good idea can save you a lot of work and money and end up giving you something unique. You could put up a suspended ceiling, but they usually look as if you are trying to cover something up, which you are. What about paneling the ceiling? What about patching the ceiling and then going over it with textured paint or a textured wall covering? What about putting up new drywall and then putting beams at the joints instead of taping them? These are only a few of the ways you could cover up a bad ceiling using less time and money than you would repairing it. Besides, you will end up with something unique, and people living in sterile, mass-produced housing (such as most apartments) can't resist the urge to have something unique.

Walls also sometimes need more help than a coat of paint can give them. If you want to add some character to the room or just find an easy and inexpensive way to hide a bad wall, here are some possibilities. You could carpet or panel one wall. This will give you an accent wall that will set off the whole room. Very rarely will you want to do all four walls, because it will look as if you are trying to cover something up. If all four walls need attention, you might consider wainscoting part way up using carpet, wallpaper, or paneling. You could also use molding to put boxes on the walls. You can then texture or paint around the boxes and wallpaper the inside area. Techniques like this will allow you to use fewer materials and get more effect for your money. Of course, these techniques will also make your house unique.

Although you should not go to the expense of hanging curtains or drapery, you should make sure the rods are provided. If you don't provide them, you will find your woodwork destroyed by each set of new tenants who put up their own rods when they move in and take them down when they move out. You should also provide shades. Besides giving immediate privacy for your new tenants, they tend to make the house not look so empty if it happens to be vacant when you are showing it. The least expensive shades will do, and if you glue or sew a piece of fringe along the bottom, you will add a lot of class. The fringe is an inexpensive extra—use a color that complements your color scheme.

The floors are the last thing you will be working on, because you wait until all the dirty work is out of the way before you put down any new flooring or have the existing carpets cleaned. Carpeting is the easiest and the fastest way to cover a floor. Carpet will cover a multitude of sins and you won't have to spend a lot of time and money in surface preparation. Carpet also has a dramatic effect, giving life to a sterile room. The lower the pile and the tighter the weave, the longer the carpet will wear and the easier it will clean. Carpets with these two characteristics are also less expensive than the plusher varieties.

CONTRACTORS vs. DOING IT YOURSELF

CONTRACTORS

When you pay a contractor to do improvements, you should end up with a better job. In addition, the job should be completed in less time than it would take you. Although these two things should happen, they don't always happen. This is why you should check out thoroughly any contractor you will be hiring. As always, the easiest way to do this is to ask around. Check with your local building department and talk to the inspectors. Check with your realtor. Check with your local loan officers who make construction and home improvement loans. Check with the lumber yards and supply houses. Finally, check with anybody he has done work for in the past. (He will be able to give you some references if he is good.) Just be careful that the people you talk to are not his friends or relatives. Why? Because they might be a wee bit biased.

Once you have the names of a few good contractors, you are ready to start shopping. Shopping in this case consists of getting bids. If there is one thing you have to know about bids, it is this: always get a firm bid, and get it in writing. Never go for a time and materials arrangement, no matter how much a contractor says you will save. I once had a firm bid of $650 from a contractor for a small roofing job. I then made the mistake of letting him talk me into having him do it on a time and materials arrangement. Although he assured me that he could get the job done for less that way, I ended up having to pay him

$1,100. Even though he apologized for taking so long and explained that he was delayed by unexpected problems, I didn't feel any better when I made out the check. You won't want to repeat this or any of the other mistakes that I have made. Never let a contractor convince you that he can do the job cheaper on a time and materials arrangement than he can on a firm bid. Don't let him scare you into it either, by telling you that he has to figure all his bids on the high side in order to protect himself against unexpected problems. Tell him that if he wants your business, he will have to submit a good competitive bid, and tell him he will have to do it in writing.

Get at least three bids if possible. Sometimes it's not possible, simply because you can't find three licensed contractors willing to bid on a small job. Once you have your bids, compare them to see if they all specify the same quality of workmanship and materials. You should also compare starting and completion dates. Then compare the cost. All other things being equal, you should probably choose the middle bidder. The lowest bidder may end up cutting corners and giving you a shoddy job. The highest bidder may be trying to add enough profit to the job to discourage you from hiring him or to get you to pay for his annual vacation to Hawaii.

Before you sign any contract or hire any contractor, it is wise to have your attorney look over the contract to make sure you are protected. Since laws and regulations vary from state to state, I can't tell you everything you will need to know, everything you will need to do, and everything you will have to include in your contract with the contractor. That is why you should consult your attorney and have him look out for your interest. Below are some of the items you may want to include in your contract or at least have your attorney inform you about.

Mechanic's lien. A mechanic's lien is a lien that can be placed against your property if a contractor, his subcontractors, or his suppliers are not paid. Even if you pay the contractor in full, these other people can get a lien against your property to guarantee their payment. Without taking the proper precautions, you could end up paying twice for the materials or labor used on your job.

Bonding. By requiring your contractor to be bonded, you can protect yourself from the possibility of a mechanic's lien and guarantee that the job will be completed. However, if you do certain things, you can nullify the bond and therefore still be vulnerable. Basically these things include making changes in the agreed-upon work or in the contract after the contract has been signed.

Lien waiver. Have the contractor give you a notarized statement containing the names and addresses of all the laborers, subcontractors, and material suppliers he will be using. As the job nears completion, have him deliver to you a lien waiver signed by all the above parties. If the contractor cannot or will not do this, you should proceed to contact all these people and verify the amounts they are owed. Then when you pay the contractor upon completion, make the check payable jointly to all the parties concerned.

Contractor's affidavit of completion. Before making your final payment, have the contractor deliver to you a notarized statement in which he states that all parties have been paid except for those he has listed. If there are any parties listed, check with them to verify the amounts he says he owes them. As above, issue your check payable jointly to all the parties concerned. Most statutes often require you to hold back ten percent to twenty percent of the final payment until you receive this affidavit.

No-lien clause. This clause is a statement to the effect that no liens will be filed. Some states don't recognize a no-lien clause as a protection, but if your state does, you may want to include it in your contract.

Any time you hire a contractor to do any work that costs over a few thousand dollars, you should definitely protect yourself by using at least one of the precautions listed above. Although taking these steps may not eliminate your chances of having a mechanic's lien placed against your property, it will cut them drastically. If ever you do find that someone has placed a lien against your property, don't get shook up and don't run out and pay off the filing party (at least without notifying the contractor first). By not giving the contractor written notice or getting his signed consent, you may still find yourself liable to the contractor for the full contract amount. Chances are that you will never have to worry about any of this, but if a lien is ever placed against your property, consult your attorney before you take any action.

Keeping your cost down and your profits up. If you are interested in keeping your cost down, you might consider finding a contractor who will do part of the job and then allow you to finish it or a contractor who will allow you to work along with him. I have found both, but let me tell you that most contractors will be reluctant to go along with either of these propositions unless you know what you are doing. Why? Because if he lets you finish a job and you don't do it right, he is the one who gets into trouble with your local building department. If he lets you work along with him and you don't know what you are doing, you will actually slow him down and cost him money. I once had a contractor tell me that he figured his time at a straight ten dollars an hour on all his bids. He added that if I wanted to watch, he would have to charge twenty dollars an hour, and that if I wanted to help, he would have to charge fifty dollars an hour. I think he was only joking, but his point was well taken.

Whether or not you decide to work along with a contractor, if you are interested in keeping your profits up, you may decide to multiply yourself and your efforts by working on many houses at the same time. There are only so many hours in a day, and you are only one person. It doesn't matter if you are working by yourself or with a contractor, you can only work on one house at a time. But suppose you had a dozen different houses and a dozen different contractors working on them all at the same time. Probably in less time than it would take you to finish the work on one house, you could have twelve houses ready and rented out. That's multiplying yourself and your efforts, to say nothing about multiplying your profits.

Another way to keep your cost down and your profits up is to hire cheap help. High school students, college students, moonlighters, retired folks, ambitious or out-of-work tradesmen, and even your tenants can be sources of cheap help. All you have to do is find people who are looking for a few extra bucks. Where do you find these people? You find them all over. They might be the kid next door or the retired gentleman across the street. They could be anybody, any age, male or female. You can use ads in the newspaper, notices on bulletin boards, phone calls to the counselors at your local high school or college, or personal contacts you made at the lumber yards and supply houses in your area. Finding such people is easy if you know where to look.

Hiring cheap help is easy too. Have them make a bid, just as you would a contractor. You don't want to hire them by the hour because they could end up taking so long that their final bill is more than a professional's would have been. It's also a good idea to know about what a professional would charge for a job before you start getting your bids. Once you get your bids, select the person who is most skilled for the job who charges the most reasonable price.

Before you go out and hire all kinds of cheap help there are two don'ts you should obey. First, don't always take the lowest bid. Suppose you have a $500 job, and somebody says he will do it for $100. If you hire him, you will probably be sorry. Either he will do a poor job which may have to be redone, or he will walk off the job when he finds it is more work than he thought. Getting cheap help is one thing; taking advantage of people is another. You will never win doing the latter. Second, don't ever hire anybody without checking with your insurance agent first. If someone were injured while working for you, you could find yourself hit with a big workman's compensation suit. Know the risks, and cover them the best you can.

DEALING WITH CONTRACTORS

The following is a list of things you should check before you hire any contractor:

1. **Is he reputable?** Have you checked him out? Is he an established contractor? Is he local? Be careful when dealing with new contractors, and be doubly careful when dealing with new construction firms—they may go out of business and leave you hanging. Avoid dealing with out-of-state contractors or firms. If there are any problems, they will all be yours, and there may be no legal recourse. Finally, watch out for contractors and firms which spend a lot on advertising or offer you some special deals. If they were really good, they wouldn't have to advertise or promote as they do.
2. **Never sign an incomplete contract.** Make sure that the contract is completely filled out and that you receive a copy. Better yet, don't sign it until your attorney has seen it.
3. **Don't ever prepay.** Never pay for a job before it is completed to your satisfaction or before all possible laborers, subcontractors, and material suppliers are paid in full. Prepaying leaves you with no

guarantees and no protection. It only encourages a dishonest contractor to skip town with your money and leave you with an unstarted or uncompleted job.

4. **Limit your payments**. If a contractor requires some money down, limit it to twenty-five percent of the total amount, and don't give him that until he has started the job. Future payments of twenty-five percent can be made upon completion of agreed-upon steps. Do not make the final payment until all clearances have been obtained and the job has been done to your satisfaction.

5. **Get your own financing**. Some contractors and firms offer their own financing and payment programs. These are usually very expensive. You will get a much better rate and much better terms if you arrange your own financing through the established lenders in your area (most lenders have their own home improvement loans or offer F.H.A. Title I home improvement loans). Don't be misled by any easy payment plans or low interest gimmicks. Shop and compare the bottom lines, that is, the amount you actually end up paying over the life of the loans.

6. **Check the contractor's workman's compensation policy**. Make sure that the contractor has a workman's compensation policy and that it is broad enough to cover you. Check with his insurance company, or have him furnish you with a copy of his policy. Without this coverage, you could find yourself liable for the compensation due to a person injured or killed while on your job.

7. **Consider getting a bond**. If the job is going to cost over a few thousand dollars, you may want to have a contractor get a bond, especially if you don't know how financially responsible he is. If the job is going to be over $5,000, you should always require the contractor to carry a bond. A good contractor will have no difficulty in securing a bond and will be able to do so at a reasonable price (usually about one percent of the job estimate). Without a bond, you are wide open to liens, the contractor's unpaid bills, and the cost of completing the job if the contractor fails to do so. With a bond you are protected from these things in case a contractor declares bankruptcy, becomes disabled, dies, or has any of a number of other problems.

8. **Read the contract thoroughly**. Make sure you understand all the terms and conditions of the contract. Make sure that the contractor pays for all the required documents and permits. Make sure that there will be no additional charges for anything whatsoever unless you first authorize them in writing. Make sure that if certain materials are going to be used, they are listed. Further note that no

substitutions can be made without your written approval. You may even want to note that all workmanship and materials shall be of good quality and that all materials shall be new.

9. **Set a completion date.** Many contractors have a habit of starting a job and then disappearing for a couple of weeks or more. But you want to get your houses rented out as soon as possible. By adding a damage clause to the contract, you will encourage the contractor to keep on schedule so that you can keep to your investment program schedule. Most contractors will not be happy with this clause, but if they truly think that they can complete your job by the date stated, they shouldn't put up a big fuss. Depending on the size and the importance of the job, you could choose almost any figure, but about twenty-five dollars a day is a good amount. This amount is deducted from your bill every day the contractor goes over schedule. You could even include a ten-dollar-per-day bonus for jobs completed ahead of schedule.

10. **Be reasonable.** Although you should take as many steps as necessary to protect your interest, you do not want to impose so many terms and conditions that no contractor will bid on your jobs. You should also be reasonable when it comes to minor disagreements. Long ago I realized that nobody could do a job to my complete satisfaction, even myself. That being the case, I learned not to be a perfectionist. You should too. This doesn't mean that you should accept a shoddy job, only that you should be reasonable. Throwing dirt is a good way to lose ground; throwing dirt at a contractor can lose you more than that.

DOING IT YOURSELF

When you decide to do the work on your houses yourself, you have to realize there will be a few disadvantages. One of the biggest disadvantages is that there is a limit to how much you can accomplish each day when you are working by yourself. Not being a skilled tradesman, you will not be able to turn out as much work each hour as the man who does it for a living. Granted, this may not deter you, but you should know what you're up against.

The advantages of doing it yourself may make the disadvantages seem inconsequential. Whenever you do anything yourself, it should cost you far less than it would to have a professional do it. Even if you mess up and have to do the whole job over, you can still come out ahead. Many times the money you save by doing it yourself will more than pay for all the tools you will need to do the job.

Many products on the market today are put there with the do-it-yourselfer in mind. If a product doesn't have the directions attached, there is a pamphlet or book available somewhere that will show you how to use it. Never in the history of the world has it been so easy for a person to repair, replace, or restore whatever he wants. The knowledge that you pick up by doing all of these things will pay you dividends for the rest of your life. You will be not only more self-sufficient, but also more apt to avoid being taken by unscrupulous contractors and repairmen.

After you have finished working on a house yourself, you will know that house and its faults better than anyone else. In many cases you will be able to catch potential problems before they become problems. When problems do arise, you will be able to spot and fix them quickly and easily. You will also be able to live better with your investment because you won't be worrying about what could possibily go wrong next with the place. You will know that it is in good shape because you saw to it yourself.

Last, but not least, you may be the kind of person who gets a deep satisfaction out of being able to do a job yourself. Being able to stand back and admire your work and say "I did that" is a feeling you just don't get out of every investment. The psychological return makes what you earn on your investment that much more rewarding. And as long as we are talking about return, don't forget that by working on the house yourself, you should increase the value of the property by at least four dollars for every dollar you put into improvements, while if you have the work done by a contractor, you should increase the value of the property by at least two dollars for every dollar you put in.

BUILDING PERMITS

If you recall, most of the improvements listed in chapter five didn't require a building permit. The outside improvements which give your house curb appeal, like landscaping and painting, do not require permits. The inside improvements like painting, texturing, wallpapering, putting up moldings, and putting down carpeting can all be done without a permit. So can hanging up shades, putting up curtain rods, and changing the light fixtures. About the only time you will need a permit is if you make any major changes to the structure or its mechanical systems. The more ideas you can come up with that utilize the existing features of the house without changing the structure or its mechanical systems, the better off you will be.

Sometimes, though, you will have to face the fact that you are going to have to do some major remodeling and get a permit or two. If the house is a rental property, you may not be able to get a permit to do the work yourself. You will be told by the local building department that you will have to have a licensed contractor do the work. If you had your heart and your pocketbook set on doing the work yourself, you might be able to find a contractor who will get the permit for you. Because this puts the contractor in an awkward position, it may be difficult for you to find one who is willing to take the risk. You will probably be much more successful if you can find a contractor who, for a fee, will get the necessary permits and then oversee your work. In effect, you would be one of his subcontractors and the fee you would be paying him would be part of the profit he would normally make by subbing out the work.

If this all sounds like too much trouble, you will be glad to know that there is an easier way around this whole problem. The solution is to move into the house yourself, and then obtain all the permits yourself as the homeowner. In fact, in order to do this, you don't even have to move into the house. Having your mailing address changed to your new purchase is one way of proving intent. When they buy a new house, many people get all the remodeling and mess out of the way before they move in. Getting the necessary permits is not difficult for them, and it won't be difficult for you either. Once the job is done and has passed inspection, you can then decide to move in yourself or rent it out. Be warned, though, that if you don't move in and the people at the local building department notice your change of heart, they may be very reluctant to issue you any more homeowner permits in the future.

DECORATING TIPS

Do you remember a few pages back that I told you there was a way to have some of the best decorators in the country guide and advise you at little or no cost? I wasn't lying. Pictures and articles that represent the best in decorating appear in many national magazines each month. Many of them show you how to use color, how to use different materials, how to decorate on a budget, and how to solve any number of decorating problems. Besides showing the best, these magazines present a collection of the latest and the newest. And the beautiful, full-color pictures do something that the best words and wisest advice in the world can't do—show you what the finished product will look like.

Many years ago I started tearing these pictures and articles out of magazines. Since I couldn't see buying these magazines for the few pictures I would choose from each copy, I picked them up free after others were through with them. As my collection grew, I set up a file system. I labeled a folder for each room—living room, dining room, family room, kitchen, bath, bedroom, playroom, laundry room, and workshop. I also labeled folders for other special categories—ceilings, walls, windows, doors, cabinets, stairways, lighting, fireplaces, exteriors, and landscaping. Every time I got a picture, I put it in my file. I found another excellent source of pictures, information, and ideas in the many brochures available free at most furniture stores, flooring stores, paint stores, and lumber companies. All this valuable free material helped my files to grow and grow. And as my files grew, so did my storehouse of ideas.

When it came time to do some remodeling, decorating, or problem-solving, I simply pulled out the appropriate files and thumbed through them. It didn't take long to take one idea from here and one from there and combine them into the perfect solution for my problem. Most of my attempts turned out well enough to be in a magazine themselves. Whenever I receive a compliment on my work, I secretly wish that I could take credit for all those brilliant ideas, but I can't. Being a modest and honest individual, I always admit that the great results are due in part to the beautiful pictures I found in *Better Homes and Gardens*.

Setting up and using some files of your own will be one of the best things you can do for your investment. They will make your improvements not only much easier, but also much more profitable. First, you will profit by saving time that would have been spent in indecision. Second, you will profit by learning to use a good idea to solve a problem, instead of throwing a lot of money at it. Third, you will profit by having a house people will want to rent. Fourth, you will profit by having a house that is worth more. And fifth, you will profit psychologically because you were so darn smart to do what you did in the first place.

A word of caution. Before you hang out your shingle and become your area's most talked-about decorator, keep in mind that you are working on a house that you will, eventually, be renting out. Since there is no way to know the color and print of your future tenant's furnishings, you will want to do most of your decorating in neutral colors and subdued prints. If your decorating is too vivid, it may clash with his belongings and his taste. Remember, one man's wild and wonderful is another man's gaudy. Don't turn off your prospective tenants by trying to impose your taste and style on them.

In addition, you should always stay in the character of the house. If you are redoing an older, two-story house, for example, don't try to go too modern. Wall graphics, shag carpet on all the walls, mirrors on the ceilings, and shiny chrome light fixtures just won't fit. If you want to try your hand at that sort of thing, find a house that will accommodate that style. Older houses lend themselves very well to traditional and early American designs and most people will find these decorating themes to their liking. Finally, always keep your cost and design in line with your potential market, and you won't have any problems.

POINTS TO REMEMBER

1. **Don't overimprove.** The temptation to go overboard is easy to give in to. Keep your emotions and your ego in check. Remember that you are not going to be living in the house but renting it out. Remember that the house is an investment and that your objective is to get as high a return as possible.

2. **Problems are opportunities to make more money.** Many houses I have purchased had one or more problems that turned other buyers away (for example, exposed heating ducts, exposed water and drain lines, too many doors and windows in one room, no closets, no privacy, unused areas, poor layout, poor traffic patterns, abandoned chimneys in rooms, or botched attempts of the owner at remodeling and decorating. These problems allowed me to negotiate and buy the houses for less than I normally could have. Solving them helped me to make more money than I ever could have if those problems hadn't been there in the first place.

3. **A good idea is worth more than a lot of money.** You are probably tired of hearing this, but I keep mentioning it because it is so

important. Maybe you're not creative. Maybe you don't know the first thing about decorating. But you know what you like. When you see a picture of what you like, you can tear it out and put it in your file. Decorating involves nothing more than knowing what you like. People who need decorators are people who don't know what they want. You already know what you want. You want the best results for the least money. Start your file today.

4. **Have a timetable.** Every day your house is not rented out is a day of lost income that you will never be able to retrieve. If you are anything like me, you will want to start working on your house as soon as you leave the closing. It is best to get a house in shape before the first tenant moves in. If you shoot for a completion date of less than a month, the first house payment can be made with the rent money you receive from your new tenant. The idea that the tenant, and not I, will be making the first payment has always motivated me to finish on schedule.

The added benefit of remodeling before you rent out the house is that your investment is then in prime condition and ready to be refinanced if need be. It is also easier to get homeowner permits to do the work if the house has not been rented. And after spending a month working on the house, you will have found and corrected most of its current and potential problems, so that the chances of your getting calls in the middle of the night to fix this or that are practically nil. Being able to sit there with a more valuable and virtually trouble-free investment is not a bad position to be in at all.

5. **Don't try to live in it.** One of the hardest ways to remodel a house is to do it while you are living in it. The next hardest way is to remodel a house while a tenant is living in it. Either way, you will find that you spend most of your time getting everything ready to start working and getting everything cleaned up and put away. Those activities leave very little time for getting anything done. When the house is vacant, you can spend all of your time getting it whipped into shape. Of course, not having your telephone, television, easy chair, and refrigerator close by helps.

6. **Do your own repairs.** So maybe you're not a handyman. Maybe you don't know one end of a screwdriver from the other. Maybe it's about time you learned. Most of the repairs you will be faced with will be minor. Many tenants plead ignorance if a faucet washer, a light switch, or a fuse needs replacing. Calling in a plumber or an electrician to do these small tasks will result in a big bill. You could end up paying at least thirty dollars to have a fifty-cent part replaced by a licensed tradesman. You could find a handyman to do it for five

or ten dollars, or you could do it yourself for the price of the part alone.

Today there are many well-written and well-illustrated books that cost less than the price of one service call. You can find them in your local bookstore or in the book and magazine section of many larger department stores. Some of the books are so well illustrated that you don't even have to be able to read—you just follow the pictures. Don't forget, too, that these books are tax-deductible business expenses. If you can't find any information on how to repair something, you may have to call in a professional to do it the first time. When he is there, watch what he is doing so that you can do it yourself the next time. If you have any questions, ask. You may as well get your money's worth out of a service call. After all, you are paying for it.

CHAPTER ELEVEN

REFINANCING

*There is no trick in taking the rabbit from
the hat; the real trick is ever getting him
in there in the first place.*

HOUDINI

Refinancing is the method by which you can mine the gold out of your housing investments. Many people who own property fail to realize that locked inside every house is a private gold mine just waiting to be worked. Others fail to realize that these gold mines produce riches day in and day out, year after year after year. Out of either ignorance or the desire to make a quick buck, they sell their gold mine to the highest bidder. I'm sure that if they ever found out what they had really sold, they would kick themselves.

Worksheet #2 illustrates what can happen when you not only buy a house the right way but also improve it the right way. A house that was purchased for $10,000 increased in value in a short time to $15,000. Many people would be delighted by this appreciation and want to rush right out and sell the house to reap their profit. But let's see how much you would really end up with by selling. If you sold the house for $15,000, this is how the sale would work out:

$15,000	sale price of improved property
−6,000	payoff on existing mortgage
−4,000	down payment
−1,000	improvement cost
−900	realtor's commission (6% of $15,000)
−100	closing costs
$3,000	gross profit
−1,000	taxes (33% tax bracket)
$2,000	net profit

A net profit of $2,000 is not a great deal of money, considering the time and effort involved in getting it. If you want to earn a living fixing up houses, you would have to find quite a few of them each year to fix up and sell. Aside from the fact that you would always be busy fixing up houses, it is very unlikely that you would ever become financially independent this way. Since you would end up spending all your time working and paying taxes, you might as well go out and get a regular job and work and pay taxes. At least then you wouldn't have to worry constantly about finding houses, fixing them up, and then trying to sell them.

Let's see what would happen if instead of selling the house, you decided to refinance it. Here's how refinancing that same $15,000 house would work out if you got a sixty percent mortgage:

> $9,000 new first mortgage (60% of $15,000)
> −6,000 payoff on existing mortgage
> $3,000 gross profit
> −0 taxes (no sale, therefore no tax)
> $3,000 net profit

Notice that the gross profit is the same as the gross profit realized from selling the house. The big advantage in refinancing is that the money you do pull out of your investment is all tax free. By the time you have paid tax on the gross profit from selling, you actually net less than you would by refinancing your house. Mind you, this is how you profit if all you got was a sixty percent mortgage. If you were to get a seventy or an eighty percent mortgage, you could end up with $4,500–$6,000.

Right now you are probably thinking, "Sure, all that money sounds great, but I'm going to end up with higher mortgage payments." If you sell the house, you won't have any mortgage payments to make, right? If you mortgage the house, you still won't have any mortgage payments to make. The tenant makes the mortgage payments. The rent you receive from renting out the house should always cover all the expenses associated with owning the house, including the mortgage payments. Where else can you borrow money and have someone else make the payments and pay off the loan for you? No place that I know of.

If all this isn't enough to convince you that refinancing is better than selling, consider the following facts. Your house should increase in value every year, thereby increasing your net worth and making you wealthier. The write offs you will have should shield part of your income and thus reduce the amount of income tax you pay; they can even reduce your tax to zero. Even after paying all the expenses associated with the house, you should have a portion of the rent money left over to deposit in good ol' Hip National Bank (your pocket). Finally, as the tenant makes the mortgage payments for you, your debt will decrease and your equity will increase. If all this sounds familiar, it should. I'm talking about our four friends, appreciation, beneficial tax treatment, cash flow, and debt retirement. These are the four tireless, ever-working, never-shirking workers who put twenty-four hour days, seven days a week, fifty-two weeks a year into your gold mines every year. They never ask for anything except for the chance to make you wealthy. Use them, and don't lose them by selling your gold mines to someone else.

I should mention that the only possible drawback to refinancing is that you may not recover your original investment (down payment and improvement costs) along with your profit. In the example above (if you get a sixty percent mortgage), you received the net profit ($3,000) but didn't get back your down payment ($4,000) or your improvement costs ($1,000). This doesn't present a problem unless you are counting on drawing out an amount at least equal to your original investment ($5,000) and using it to repeat the whole process to acquire another property. Note, however, that $6,000 equity ($15,000 appraisal minus $9,000 mortgage) is an asset you could use to buy more property, but it is not considered here because it is not in the form of cash.

When you sell, you usually recover the net profit and all the other money invested, that is, if you as the seller don't finance part of the sale. If you sold this house and did finance an amount greater than your net profit ($2,000), you would walk away with less than the $5,000 cash you started with. Note, however, that the amount of the financing you would be holding is an asset that you could use to buy more property, but again it is not considered here because it is not in the form of cash.

The key to always getting all your money out of a property when you refinance is never to spend more for the house and its improvements than the amount of the mortgage you expect to get when you are finished. Every dollar you can stay under this amount is a tax-free dollar you get to put into your pocket.

Buying houses and fixing them up for resale could be a good way to raise seed money to start out your investment program, but it isn't an investment program in itself. Nor does it take advantage of the long-term effects of inflation. If we were to assume for illustration purposes that inflation averages seven percent a year, anything that you buy today will double in value (or cost) about every ten years. If you owned that $10,000 house in worksheet #2, let's see what would happen over the next ten, twenty, and thirty years. (Mortgages computed at a 10% interest rate for a 25-year term.)

	Appraisal	New Mortgage (60% of value)	Old Mortgage (Balance)	Net Profit	Equity
Now	$ 15,000	$ 9,000	$ 6,000	$ 3,000	$ 6,000
In 10 years	$ 30,000	$18,000	$ 7,614	$10,386	$12,000
In 20 years	$ 60,000	$36,000	$15,228	$20,772	$24,000
In 30 years	$120,000	$72,000	$30,456	$41,544	$48,000

As you can see, the house will be worth $30,000 by the end of the tenth year. If you got only a sixty percent mortgage on the new appraised value, you could borrow $18,000. After paying off the balance of your old $9,000 mortgage (about $7,614), you would be left with about $10,386 to do whatever you pleased. Since you have not sold your house, only mortgaged it, all this money is yours tax free. You could use the money for a new car, a boat, a vacation, or even another house or two. Now look at the $12,000 in equity you would have ($30,000 appraised value minus $18,000 mortgage). Nice, isn't it?

Now take a look at what you will be able to walk away with in the twentieth and thirtieth years. Can you imagine why anybody in his right mind would ever sell a gold mine like that? I certainly can't, but people do it every day.

Can you imagine what you could borrow if you were to shop and to get a seventy or eighty percent mortgage? It's enough to make you want to try, isn't it? Or is the thought of the mortgage payments on these great big loans killing all your enthusiasm right now? Well, according to today's standards, they would indeed be exorbitant. But when you get those new mortgages, the rents will have increased along with the price of houses. Yes, the payments will be higher, but as always the rent will provide more than enough money to make the payments.

About the only thing that you can't count on is that inflation will average seven percent a year for the next ten, twenty, or thirty years. Naturally, as an investor I would like to see an inflation rate of seven percent or higher (investors love to borrow money and then pay it back with cheaper and cheaper dollars while at the same time watching their investments grow in value), but that is not too likely. If we see an inflation rate that averages only five percent a year, your houses will still double in value about every fifteen years. You may have to wait a little longer when there is a lower inflation rate, but for that kind of money, I can wait a while, can't you?

MINING YOUR GOLD

There's no trick to getting your money and your profit out of your investments. You don't have to be a magician, and you don't need a magic wand. All you need is a little forethought. If you are going to be refinancing a house shortly after buying it, the way you buy the house can be very important. For example, you wouldn't want to get a first mortgage to buy a house and then turn around a month or two later and apply for and get another new first mortgage on the refurbished house. If this is the way you plan on getting your profit out of a house, you had better be prepared to pay a second round of closing costs and therefore lose a lot of your profits.

When I started out and didn't know any better, that is exactly what I did. I would buy a house with a conventional mortgage and then proceed to fix it up. After I was finished (usually a month later), I would apply for a new mortgage. After I got my new mortgage, I would use the funds to pay off my old first mortgage (the new lender actually does this for you so that he can be assured of being the first lienholder of record; thus a new first mortgage is created) and to pay off a second round of closing costs. I took the money that was left over and looked for another house to buy, so I could repeat the process all over again.

If for some reason you ever want to do the same thing rather than make use of the thirty-eight buying strategies we discussed, I will give you one good piece of advice. Never go back to the lender who gave you the first mortgage. In fact, don't go to any lender who uses the same appraiser as the original lender. The reason is that the appraiser will look at the house again, look at his original appraisal again, and then turn in another appraisal similar to that first appraisal (in other words, low). It's not his fault that he has a good memory and a copy of the first appraisal in his files. Although he will probably give you some credit for the work that you have done, believe me, it won't be enough.

I have learned never to go back to the same lender or any lender who uses the same appraiser. I have also learned that on the whole bank appraisers are just like bankers—they are very conservative fellows. If they want to keep their jobs, they darn well have to be. For them, going out on a limb and turning in a high appraisal is out of the question. If a loan were to go bad and the lender found that the house would fetch nowhere near the appraised value, the appraiser would probably be the second person to lose his job.

If you are applying for a loan and there is a difference between the selling price and the appraised price, the lender will almost always make the loan on the smaller of the two amounts. Going back to worksheet #2 again, let's assume that the bank appraisal was the same as the buyer's appraisal ($11,000). Let's also assume that the bank was making sixty percent mortgages. Since the house was purchased for $10,000 instead of $11,000, it would qualify for only a $6,000 mortgage instead of a $6,600 mortgage (sixty percent of $11,000). In this case, the lender completely disregarded the $11,000 appraisal the appraiser turned in and, in effect, penalized the buyer for getting a bargain. Had the bank's appraiser turned in a $9,000 appraisal, the lender would reduce the mortgage to sixty percent of the $9,000 appraisal, or $5,400. This time the mortgage would be based on the appraisal because it would be lower than the selling price.

However, you can escape this situation when you are getting a loan on a house that you already own. Since you are neither buying nor selling the house, there can be no purchase price to get in the way. The only figure the lender will have to work from will be the appraisal. Even if you bought the house one day and went in to see the lender the next day, the only criterion he would have for granting you the loan would be the appraisal. Since you will always be buying a house for less than its appraised value, you don't want to give a lender the chance to base your loan on your purchase price. And since you will be improving your houses, you'll probably want to wait until the work is finished before you apply.

Let's say that you have a house which is ready to be refinanced. You have shopped around and found the best interest rate and terms. You have also found at what institutions the more generous appraisers are employed. You are now ready to apply for the loan. There is only one more thing you have to do—find out how much your house is worth.

When you are filling out the loan application, the loan officer will probably ask you how much you think your house is worth. Since there is no selling price, he is probably trying to arrive at a figure that he can put in the space where the selling price would normally go on his form. Remember, your loan will be based upon the lower of the two figures (the selling price or the appraisal). If you give too low a figure, you will only be hurting yourself.

How do you arrive at a possible selling price? You ask your realtor. You may not want to ask the same realtor who sold you the house, for the same reason that you wouldn't want the same appraiser to appraise it after you had fixed it up. Many realtors will give you a free market appraisal of your house. This appraisal is not a formal written appraisal but a verbal estimate of its present value. Once you have this appraisal, you will be able to figure how much money you can get from the lender. If you know from shopping around that your lender is making sixty percent loans and you know from the realtor's appraisal that your house is worth $15,000, you know that your loan will be approximately $9,000.

Sometimes, instead of asking you how much you think your house is worth, the lender will ask you how much you want to borrow. Knowing the information above, you will be able to say, $9,000. Whatever question the lender asks you, he will ask his appraiser only one, "Is the house worth $15,000?" If the appraiser thinks it is, he will usually appraise it at or around that amount. If you had given the lender a figure of $12,000 on that same house, he would have asked his appraiser, "Is the house worth $12,000?" The appraiser would most likely respond that it was by appraising it for $12,000. In this case you would end up getting only a $7,200 mortgage instead of the $9,000 you could have had.

I found all this out the hard way, too. It wasn't until years after I started that I found out I could have gotten a lot more money if I had known what my houses were worth before I applied for a loan. Until my rude awakening, I thought I was a darn good appraiser. Every time a lender asked me what I thought one of my houses was worth, I pulled a figure out of the sky. Every time the appraisal came back, it was usually right on or close to my estimated figure. It wasn't until I was having all my property appraised by a realtor that I discovered a house that I had recently refinanced was appraised for almost twice the appraisal I and the bank had put on it. From that point on, I have always asked a realtor to give me a verbal appraisal before going to see a lender.

IMMEDIATE REFINANCING

If you are planning to buy a house, fix it up, and then refinance it a month or two later, there are several different ways you can go about it. Most refinancing involves getting a new first mortgage on your house and then using the funds from that mortgage to pay off whatever existing financing you have on the house. If this is your plan, make certain that before you buy the house you have done everything possible to assure an easy and economical transition when you apply for that new first mortgage. If you are going to buy the house in the first place by assuming the seller's mortgage, talk to his lender before you assume it, to see if an early payoff would be a problem. You should also get his lender to agree to the assumption in writing and have the document approved by your attorney. If there is a prepayment penalty clause, you may get the lender to drop it, especially if you make arrangements to get your new first mortgage through his financial institution. You may even get the lender to commit himself to giving you a new mortgage at that time. If current interest rates are higher than the rate of the assumed mortgage, you may also want to see what kind of blended rate (wraparound mortgage) the lender is willing to make.

If you are going to be buying on land contract, make sure that you negotiate a prepayment penalty clause out of the contract if there is one in there. If there isn't one in the contract, don't even bring the matter up. You should also check whether anyone else has an interest in the property. If there are any other lienholders or lenders, make sure that all the parties involved will accept payment in full when you decide to pay off. This is important because there is always an outside chance that someone may not want to accept his payment in full. This could create some problems and hinder your chances of getting a new first mortgage.

If you cannot or do not want to assume the seller's mortgage or buy on land contract, you have another very good option. You can buy the house outright for cash. Don't write this option off just because you don't have the money. You don't have to have the money because you can borrow it all unsecured by using one or more short-term loans or notes (see the section on how to get $10,000 in ten minutes or less).

I have purchased a number of houses this way and find it to be one of my favorite techniques. I borrow the money I need on both ninety-day notes and short-term installment loans. I always borrow more money than I need in order to cover any unexpected expenses. The extra money can also be used to make some of the loan payments until I'm ready to pay them off. Since I usually have my house ready in a month, I have two months before my ninety-day notes are due in which to find a mortgage. There is no prepayment penalty on notes and most installment loans, so I am never penalized for paying them off early. In fact, early payoffs help strengthen my credit rating.

Another way you can refinance your money out of your house is not to touch the existing financing. You may not want to lose it because of its low interest rate and/or low monthly payments. Instead of getting a new first mortgage at a higher rate, you may want to consider getting a second mortgage. Even though the second mortgage may carry a considerably higher rate of interest than a new first mortgage, when blended with your existing mortgage, it may actually come out to less than the rate you would have to pay on a new first mortgage.

Second mortgages are usually for a shorter term than first mortgages. Because of the faster payoff, your payments will automatically be higher than they will be if spread over a longer time. The payments may make your total outlay greater than if you were to get a new first mortgage, but the payments won't go on for as long either. If your reason for getting your money out in the first place is to use it to buy more investments, the additional income generated by the new investments may more than offset the higher payments and actually end up increasing your cash flow.

In many cases, you might not want to use a new first mortgage or second mortgage at all. Your best alternative would be to create your own paper (see chapter eight) using your newly created equity in the property as collateral. This paper will be as good as money, won't cost you as much, and will allow you to get up to one hundred percent of your equity out to use. Very rarely will a lender allow you to get all of your equity out on a first or second mortgage, so creating your own paper is an excellent way to get it out. Besides that, you should end up paying far less interest and getting much better terms on your own paper than you could ever receive on any mortgage from any conventional lender.

If any of the mortgages you have won't allow you to pledge your equity as collateral for any other loans or mortgages, you may want to refinance enough of your properties to get the cash necessary to pay one of your properties off. You can then use that free and clear property to create all the paper you desire.

The final option open to you for immediately refinancing your money and your profit out of a house is to lease the house from the seller with an option to buy. After the house is in shape, go out and shop for a mortgage. Once you find a mortgage whose terms you like, contact the seller and tell him you are ready to close. This differs somewhat from the lease with option to buy discussed in chapter eight. In the former case you buy immediately after finishing your improvements instead of waiting until the rents have helped you recover your investment.

FUTURE REFINANCING

If you're in no big hurry to refinance, time can be on your side. Interest rates fluctuate greatly, and if you can wait until money is more abundant and interest rates are lower, the money you borrow will end up costing you less. Since the interest you are paying for your borrowed money is usually your biggest expense, a small reduction in this one area can noticeably increase your cash flow.

If you turn back to the worksheets, you will notice that the interest on the $6,000 mortgage alone is the highest single expense. Even the total operating expenses (taxes, insurance, maintenance, and repairs) add up to less than the $600 in interest that must be paid on this small mortgage (the expenses on worksheet #1 are $480, and on worksheet #2 they are $540). As you can see, a small reduction in the interest can easily be worth more than a large reduction in any one of the items included in the operating expenses. Any time you want to increase your cash flow, you should start by looking for ways to cut your expenses. Interest should be the first one you try to reduce.

In addition to waiting until the lending institution with the best rate and terms has the money to lend, you can time some of your other moves as well. If you are scheduling any major improvements or maintenance projects, you can have them completed shortly before the appraiser comes out. Even if you have to borrow money to move the work up on your schedule, do it. You can repay any money you borrow once you refinance. Since the house will look better because the work has been completed, it should be appraised for a higher amount. A higher appraisal means a bigger mortgage and more money in your pocket.

If possible, you may want to have the appraiser come at the time of the year the house looks best. If there are some beautiful flowering trees or shrubs, try to have him see them in bloom. If the grass is particularly green after the rainy season, get him there then. If the yard is quite spectacular when all the leaves turn color, he is bound to be impressed. He will also be favorably impressed if your tenants have attractive furnishings. Granted, he is there only to appraise your house, but these things certainly can't hurt.

Finally, once you are financially independent and not holding down a regular nine to five job, refinancing could be a problem. Unless you have a paycheck coming in every week, bankers tend to get a little nervous. When bankers get nervous, they don't lend out money. So if you want to keep your bankers working for you, get as much as possible of your refinancing done before you become financially independent and retire.

There's a good saying in the financial community: borrow a little money and you have a serious creditor on your hands; borrow a lot of money and you have a partner who is interested in your future. Go out and get partners, not creditors.

POINTS TO REMEMBER

1. If you are planning to refinance a house shortly after purchase, don't buy a house using a new first mortgage because you will have another whole set of closing costs when you refinance; never go back to the same lender or to one who uses the same appraiser; make sure that there are no problems or penalties associated with refinancing and paying off the old lenders; and always know the new appraised value of your house before applying for financing.
2. Get as much as possible of your refinancing done before you become financially independent and retire.
3. Refinancing an improved house that you purchased below value

should net you at least the same amount of profit as you would realize by selling the same house.

4. There is no limit to the number of times you can refinance or to the number of tax-free dollars you can extract from your homes over your lifetime by refinancing.

CHAPTER TWELVE
RENTING IT OUT

Lord deliver me from the man who never makes a mistake,
and also from the man who makes the same mistake twice.

WILLIAM J. MAYO

No matter how careful you are and no matter how hard you try, the time may come when you get a bad tenant. There isn't a business or investment that you can go into that can promise you will never make a mistake, lose any money, or have a bad account every now and then. Rentals aren't any different. If you haven't learned by now that there is no such thing as a sure thing, you are either very lucky or you have never had the chance to meet an insurance salesman. I've had bad tenants, and you are bound to have your share too. However, you can cut your chances of getting one.

Fortunately, there are a lot of things you can do to put the odds against getting a bad tenant in your favor. One of the first and most important things you can do is have a house that is clean and presentable. If it is nicely decorated and recently remodeled, so much the better. If it is located in a desirable neighborhood too, the chances are you have a winner. Good people want and demand good housing. Good housing attracts good people. It's as simple as that. If your house is desirable, you will attract good tenants. Good tenants appreciate what you are providing and will take care of your investment for you. Good tenants also pay the rent on time.

On the other hand if you rent out dumps, you are very likely to attract bad tenants. If you are lucky enough to attract a good tenant, he probably won't stay very long unless there is a severe housing shortage in your area. Even so, he is likely to move the first chance he gets. As sure as night follows day, landlords who have crummy houses

223

eventually end up getting crummy tenants. The kind of people that are prepared to live in bad surroundings usually figure that since you don't care about the place, they needn't either. This kind of attitude eventually leads to damage and further deterioration of your house. Furthermore, tenants who aren't worried about taking care of your house usually don't worry about paying the rent on time either. A decent house won't guarantee you good tenants, but a crummy house will surely increase your chances of getting bad ones.

The rest of this chapter will show you how to increase even more your chances of selecting good tenants, keeping them with you, and keeping them happy. You will also learn how to handle repair problems and how to handle problem tenants. In addition to that, you will learn how to increase your chances of coming out of an eviction without losing a lot of money or sustaining a lot of damage to your house.

BEFORE YOU RENT

SETTING THE RENTAL AMOUNT

Before you purchased your house, you should have had some idea of the rental amounts being paid in the immediate area. Now that your house is ready to rent out, double check these rents. The place to start is the newspaper in the "houses for rent" section. Is the rental amount that you plan on charging below or at the market price being asked for similar houses? If you want to attract and keep tenants, you had better not be above the median market price. When your rents are too high, you will find your tenants constantly moving out on you. They will be moving either to a cheaper place or to one that gives them more value for their money.

After looking in the paper, drive by some of the houses that are for rent. You may have to call, or answer some of the ads to get the addresses. Check to see how they compare to your house in terms of curb appeal. Most prospective tenants will drive past a house before attending the showing. If the house doesn't have curb appeal (in other words if it looks like a dump), they may not even bother to show up for the appointment. If your house doesn't compare well in this respect, you need to do something about it as soon as possible.

If the newspaper and a drive by don't tell you enough, you may want to play prospective tenant. In this game, you pretend you're interested in renting some of those other houses that are for rent. This will give you a chance to see inside those other houses and see how they compare with yours. It will also enable you to meet some other landlords and give you an idea of what they expect from their tenants and of how they transact their business.

Once you have checked the newspaper, checked for curb appeal, and checked out the insides of a few of your competitors' houses, you will have a pretty good idea of where your rents should stand. Since you were able to buy your house for less than it was worth and then fix it up to make it worth more, you will be able to do something very few landlords can do. You will be able to adjust your rents downward if need be. Many landlords may have payments and expenses that won't allow them to do that. They may even be forced to charge a higher rent than you will normally be able to offer. When you can match or beat the competition, you won't be spending all your free time trying to rent out your house over and over again. Your rents will make your tenants want to stay put. That will give you the time and peace of mind to do what you want to do.

ADVERTISING

The first place most people look for a place to rent is the newspaper. The classified ad section has an up-to-date listing of most of the houses available in your area. There isn't anywhere else that you can advertise and be so easily found by so many people who are looking for what you have. In fact, the newspaper is going to be about the only selling-tool you will be using. Knowing how to use it effectively will greatly increase your chances of attracting a good tenant. It will also help you make more effective use of your time.

When you make up your ad, you want to include certain information which will keep you from wasting your time answering a lot of useless phone calls from people who wouldn't be interested in renting the house anyway. One of the most important questions you should answer in your ad is where the house is located. Although you shouldn't give the house number, you may want to give the street. If you give the exact address your prospective renter will end up driving by your house before he calls you. He may also stop and bother your present tenant at all hours of the day and night. You don't want this to happen. The main objective of an ad is to get people to call. If they sound as if they might be a good prospect, you want the chance to meet them and take them through your house. By giving the exact address, you would be defeating your purpose.

If the street is fairly well known, naming it in the ad should be sufficient. If the street runs on both sides of town, you should indicate its location by the section of town, for example, East 7th Street rather than West 7th Street or North Monroe Street rather than South Monroe Street. If the street is not well known, or if it is hard to find or just too long to give any indication of your house's approximate location, you should use a familiar landmark instead, for example, near the high school, close to the shopping center, on the river, or by the state park. If your house is in a particular area, you could give its location in that way, for example, east side location, west end of town, Cranbrook Estates, Woodland Beach, Riverside Manor Subdivision. Because people may want to be in a certain school district, be close to work or live in a certain area, location is very important. You want the people who call to be interested in living where your house is located. Give them an idea of the general area, but not your exact address.

Another question you should answer is how much is it going to cost? Always state the rental amount and note whether you require a security deposit. Since your rents will always be at market or below, you have nothing to be ashamed or afraid of. Landlords who leave the rental amount out of their ad usually do so because it is too high. They hope that by having the prospective tenant call to find out what it is, they will be able to sell him on the idea of paying their price. If you have to sell a tenant on paying the price, he will either end up moving or have trouble paying the rent. Since you don't want either problem, you should always put the rental amount in your ad.

Once your ad has answered these two questions, you can use the rest of your space to sell the good points of your house. Put in some of those amenities that make your house special and appealing. You definitely should include the number of bedrooms and bathrooms (if more than one); you should also include any extras your house has, like a family room, a fireplace, a garage, or a fenced-in yard. You could even list such things as carpeting, built-in appliances, type of heating, or the availability of city utilities.

If you are going to be renting to families with children, always list this winning extra—"children welcome." Some landlords will not rent to families with children because they think kids cause too much wear and tear on a house. About the only wear and tear I have ever noticed with my houses occurred in the yard where the children played. Grass seed is cheap. Whenever I have had any real damage done to any of my houses, it wasn't caused by the kids; it was caused by the adults. I have also found that when families with children find a landlord with a nice house they can rent, they know they have got something. And boy, do they take good care of it!

The last thing that you should mention in your ad is the time you want your prospective tenants to call. If you don't specify any times in the ad, you will find yourself either babysitting the telephone or worrying about the calls you are missing when you can't be by the phone. The hours you do choose will depend upon your schedule if you are going to be answering the phone yourself. If someone else is available, you can be more flexible.

Personally, I prefer to take calls between 4:00 and 7:00 p.m. and show the house between 8:00 and 9:00 p.m. that same day. This schedule works very well for me. I find that I don't spend my whole day answering the phone and running out to show the house. One word of caution: your showings should be scheduled during the daylight hours, otherwise your house may be difficult, if not impossible, to find.

Before you call your ad in to the newspaper, you should check out the ads that are already there. See if yours is as appealing as the best of them. If it isn't, do whatever is necessary to polish it. Notice what catches your eye and your imagination in the other ads. Copy their style, layout, terminology, or anything else that you like. Besides that, try to keep your ad short and sweet. It will keep the cost down and give you an extra point or two to mention when the prospect calls.

Finally, check to see if your newspaper arranges the ads in any particular order. If you are fortunate enough to have a paper that does arrange its ads, make use of the order, and try to get your ad at or close to the top of the list. For example, if the ads are arranged in alphabetical order, you could make the first word in your ad start with an "A"—*affordable, appealing,* and *attractive* are good words to use in a case like this. If your newspaper doesn't use any special order, make your first word a vivid or descriptive one. Here are just a few to consider: *colonial, Cape Cod, early American, quaint, cozy, charming,* or *distinctive.*

SHOWING THE HOUSE

I don't make appointments to show my houses. I show them for only one hour every day while the ad is running. I spent an awful lot of time early in my career running out to show a house any time a caller wanted to see it. This made life unbearable not only for me but also for the tenant who was still living in the house. To make matters worse, most of the time the caller didn't even keep the appointment. After spending my first few years running back and forth and waiting for callers who never showed, I decided that there had to be a better way. I believe that I have found it.

Now I use the "group showing" method. When prospective tenants call (between the hours stated in the paper), I tell them that I will be at the house later and give a time and that if they would like to go through it, they may do so then. The psychological benefits of a group showing cannot be overstated. When the prospective tenant arrives and finds that he is not the only fish in the sea, he is not likely to act as though he is God's gift to landlords and is doing you a favor by considering your house. Remember, you are not renting out an apartment or some crummy house; you are renting out a most desirable commodity, and if he has looked around at all, he darn well knows it. Let the prospective tenant sell *you* on why *he* should have the house.

When your prospective tenants show up, try to meet them at the door and welcome them. Tell them that you are glad they could make it and invite them to go ahead and look around on their own. Also mention that if they have any questions, all they have to do is ask and you will try to answer them. Quite often the questions you get have to do with the utility costs, so it is a good idea to have an idea of what they run. Even if you have just one prospect show up, don't follow him through the house. This tends to make people nervous. It also gives them the idea that you are afraid that they might get away. If he gets that idea, a prospective tenant might think he is the only fish in the sea.

After your prospective tenants have toured your house, ask them again if they have any questions. Next mention to them that if they are interested in the house, you have a rental agreement that they might want to look over. If they say that they are not interested, thank them for their time and say goodbye. If they are interested, give them a copy of your rental agreement to read. Tell them that if they have any questions about the agreement or any of its terms, they should just ask you. After they have read your rental agreement, ask them if they are still interested. If they are, give them an application to fill out.

After they have completed the application, go back over it with them. You need not go over it item by item. All you want to do is see that it is completed. If there are any blanks or incomplete answers or if any other information you will need is missing, now is the time to get it. Going over the application with them also gives you a chance to associate each applicant's name with his face. Later, when you get back home, you won't have any trouble trying to remember who went with what application. After this is done, thank them again and tell them you will contact them to let them know if they got the house or not.

If the prospective tenants ask you how long it will be before you decide on a new tenant, tell them you hope to know within two weeks. Tell them that you may know before that but that it will depend on how long it takes to check out all the people who have applied. You could also say that you always run your ad for at least nine days before you even start to check out all the applicants. Whatever you say, make sure it gives you enough time to wait until you have at least one good, qualified prospect who is interested in renting your house. You don't want to be forced into renting your house out to an unqualified party. It would be better to wait and have your house vacant than to end up with a bad tenant.

Don't be upset if not everyone who goes through your house falls in love with it. It may not be what some people are looking for. Maybe they came to see it on the outside chance that it could be what they want. Maybe your ad was so effective that they just couldn't stay away, or maybe they are just professional house lookers. These are people who entertain themselves by spending their free time going through other people's houses. No matter what the reason, don't take any personal offense.

SCREENING THE PROSPECTS

You actually start to screen your prospects the minute they call on the phone. That is why you want them to answer your ad before they get a chance to drive past your house. When a prospect calls, you should have a notebook by the phone, so that you can get his name and phone number. A notebook is not as easy to lose as a piece of paper, and it also provides you with a record of who called at what time and about what houses. It's a good idea to keep a special notebook for this purpose and to keep all the names and numbers for future reference. If any of the callers turns out to be an exceptionally good prospect but you don't end up renting to them this time, you can indicate this by his name. This way you can contact him next time you have an opening in any of your other houses. You can also indicate which callers you would definitely want to stay away from if they ever call again.

When you are talking to the callers on the phone, you may want to note if they are married, how many children they have, if they are on any government assistance program, unemployed or laid off, and how many people will be occupying the house with them. Most callers volunteer this information because they want to know if you will accept them under these conditions. If you will not, it is best to say that you would prefer to rent to someone who is not in those circum-stances, but add that they are still welcome to come and look at the house. Without having to come right out and tell him no, you have let these people know that their chances of getting your house are not too high. Not wanting to waste their time, they seldom come to view the house.

During this telephone conversation, you should not attempt to have the caller answer all the questions on the rental application form. Don't waste his time and yours; there will be plenty of time to get all the answers you need after he looks at your house. If you appear too nosey over the phone, you could lose a good prospect because some people tend to get a little upset when you ask too many personal questions too soon. Remember that the main purpose of the tele-phone conversation is to get the caller to come and view the house. If you can weed out a few of the undesirables at this point, fine. Just make sure you don't pull out any of the flowers along with the weeds.

When the prospects show up to go through your house, you have a good opportunity to tell what kind of people they are. Notice each prospect's car. Is it taken care of, or is it a wreck? Would you want it parked in front of your house? Notice the way the people are dressed. Is their clothing clean? Did they attempt to dress up, or did they wear their grubbies? Notice how they enter your house. Did they wipe their feet before entering, or did they track in dirt all over your carpeting? Notice their children. Are they neat and clean? Are they well behaved? Notice their smoking habits. If they are smoking, are they using an ashtray, or are they flicking their ashes on your brand new floor? If these observations don't tell you something about how they are going to care for your house, nothing will.

If a prospective tenant has passed the telephone test and the personal interview at the house, the rental application is his third hurdle. What you want to look at now is the applicant's rental record, his work record, and his financial record.

Rental record. How long has he been at his present address? If it has been less than two years, what was his address before that? Does he have a history of not staying in one place for a long time? If he does, this could indicate possible problems. Whatever the reason, try to find it out.

Work record. How long has he held his present job? If it has been less than two years, where did he work before that? Is he moving up each time he changes jobs? Is he changing jobs out of boredom? Does he have a problem holding a job? People who can't hold a job have a hard time paying their bills. Do you want to take a chance with your rent moneys?

Financial record. Does he have any open charge accounts around town? More importantly, does he have a savings and a checking account? People without these two accounts usually have money problems. If he has a checking account, is his next check number over 200? If it is, it shows that he has had it for some time, and his checks are likely to be good. Beware of checks with low numbers. Beware of people who try to give you one.

By the time you have gotten to this point with your prospective tenants, you should have a pretty good idea of what kind of tenants they will make. As soon as you have an applicant that looks promising, you should check him out the very next day at the latest. The method of checking him out I'm about to give you is one that I developed years ago and have used ever since. I have found it to be an almost foolproof method for screening tenants. In fact, the only times I have ended up with a bad tenant are the times I have not used this screening method.

Don't waste your time screening every application that you get, but only the promising ones. The screening process is very simple and doesn't take very long. The only thing it involves is stopping by the place where the applicant is presently living. Don't go directly to the applicant's residence. Stop by and see a neighbor first. Open the conversation by asking directions. Explain that the address you have is unclear. You can then ask the neighbor if he knows whether the applicant is home or not. If not, ask when would be a good time to catch him home. Explain that the applicant applied to rent a house from you and that you wanted a chance to visit with him. Once you have gotten this far, you can easily ask the neighbor how well he knows the applicant. This is a good time to verify some of the information on the rental application form, if the neighbor knows your applicant. Neighbors are a wonderful source of information, not only when you are buying, but also when you are renting your property. Always talk to at least one neighbor who knows your prospective tenant, and don't forget to thank him for his help and his time.

Your next step is to go and talk to the applicant himself. When he answers the door, reintroduce yourself and ask him if he has a moment or two to spare. Tell him that you were very impressed with him and that you have just a few more questions you would like to ask. At this point you will probably be invited inside. If you are not, ask if you should stop back at a more convenient time. If he tries to put you off, there is probably a very good reason. Most times when this happens, it is because his family is not made up of the world's best housekeepers. If this isn't the reason, it is probably because he misrepresented some of the facts he put on your rental application form. Either way, his refusal to let you in is a very strong indication that he may not be the great find you thought he was.

Assuming that you have been invited inside, the first thing that you should do is look for something to compliment your prospective tentant on, for example, his kids, his furnishings, his wife's decorating, anything at all, as long as you truly do admire it. Once the ice is broken, proceed to verify some of the information that you have on his application: his social security number, his full legal name and age, his place of employment, and his previous address if he has lived at his present address less than two years (get this information for both the husband and the wife). After you have gone this far, ask him if he minds your getting a credit report on him. If he says no, thank him. If he says yes, ask him why. Then tell him that you will be back in touch with him in a few days, and politely excuse yourself. This whole interview should take no more than ten minutes. If it does, you are doing something wrong.

The real reason for this visit is not to see if the applicant minds if you get a credit report done on him. Of course, if he does mind, you will be glad that you found out. The real reason is to see how the applicant is living. If his residence is clean and neat, he will probably keep your place clean and neat. And since people who take care of their places also tend to take care of their bills, there is a really good chance that your applicant will pay his rent. That a renter takes care of your house and pays the rent on time should always be your first concerns. This simple and easy screening process should assure you of both.

If you want to have a credit report on any of the applicants you are seriously considering, it is usually quite easy and inexpensive to get one. Go to your local credit-rating bureau and ask for a report. You will have to fill out an application stating your reason for wanting it and then pay a small fee to see the report. If you want a copy of the report, it will cost you an additional fee. It is really not necessary to get a copy. All you want to know is if your applicant is a good risk or not. The people at the bureau will be glad to explain how to read and interpret the information on the report if you are unfamiliar with its format.

RENTAL RED FLAGS

Besides all the screening techniques discussed so far, here are a few points to keep in mind before you make your final decision on any applicant:

1. **Beware of applicants who are not married.** I don't make moral judgments, but I do make business judgments. I have found that it is bad business to rent to unmarried couples. If they split up, you may find yourself in the middle of a great big argument, especially if one moves out and the other one decides to stay. The one moving out may claim the security deposit is his and want it back. The one staying behind may claim that he is not bound by your lease or rental agreement.

2. **Beware of applicants who want rent concessions.** Never make any concessions, no matter what kind, no matter how small. Once you concede on one point, your new tenant will push for other concessions. Once he knows that he can beat you, he won't give up. He will do it again and again and again.

3. **Beware of applicants who know it all.** These are the people who let

you know in no uncertain terms what you can and cannot do. Nothing is sacred or safe from these self-proclaimed experts. They know everything from law and business to home repairs and decorating. To them you are nothing but a bumbling idiot who had better take their advice, or else. These people may start out as a pain in the neck, but in no time at all you will change your mind and end up holding a much lower opinion of them. If you want to stay away from problems, stay away from them. Fortunately, this is not that hard to do. Most of these people would never consent to sign your rental agreement, and that's good. You wouldn't want them to.

4. **Beware of applicants with "crummy landlord" stories.** When an applicant starts telling you about all the crummy landlords he has had, you had better pay close attention. The next one could be you. These people probably have trouble getting along with everybody, and they always put the blame on the other guy. Don't try to be a knight in shining armor. As soon as you fall off your horse, you will be the next one they end up throwing dirt over.

5. **Be cautious about applicants with good references.** No applicant in his right mind is going to give you a reference who is going to bad-mouth him. If the reference is a friend or relative, it is doubtful that he will be completely honest. Even a former landlord can be evasive for fear of legal action if he is too honest about any problems he may have had with your applicants. His present landlord may even lie and tell you how great a tenant he is, just to get him off his back and onto yours (I once had a landlord do this to me).

All of these facts are darn good reasons for not relying on references to screen your applicants. Although you never tell your applicant that you are not going to use his references as references, you always want to get references from him for two very good reasons. One, you want to know if he knows at least a few people who will vouch for him. And two, you want to know at least a few people you can contact if ever you have to hunt down an applicant who skips out owing you money.

6. **Be ready for applicants who change their minds.** Every once in a while you get a new tenant all signed up, and at the last minute he decides not to move in. Whatever his reason, be thankful that he told you before he moved in and not after. Although there is no way you can ever really prevent a tenant from changing his mind, there is something you can do to prevent this from costing you any extra time and money. All you have to do is make sure you have at least two good prospects in mind before you make up your mind. If your first choice falls through, you can immediately turn to your second

choice without having to run a new ad, screen a whole new group of applicants, and try to explain to those repeat applicants that you didn't choose the first time through why you didn't call them.

7. **Beware of applicants with money in their hand.** Every once in a while you will have a prospective tenant go through your house and then tell you he is very, very interested. He may tell you how beautiful your house is and how much his wife and kids love it. He may tell you how much he wants or needs it. He may tell you anything, but he always ends up by pulling a wad of money out of his pocket and offering to take the house right on the spot. If you accept his offer, it may well be the last money you will ever get from him.

RENTAL APPLICATION FORMS

The application form on page 236 is one I use and find very satisfactory. It provides you with all the information you normally need to know in order to make a good decision. It also gives you all the information you need to know if you decide to get a credit report on any of your applicants. You can use this form if you like, or use those available at most stationery stores. Regardless of the kind of form you use, make sure that you do use one, and then file it with the signed lease or rental agreement that you have with your new tenant. A time may come when you need this information (when you are trying to find a skip, starting an eviction, or getting a garnishment issued, for example). Having all this information handy will sure make your job a lot easier.

COMING TO TERMS

LEASES

Leases are rental agreements that run for a specified time. One-year leases are the standard, but a lease can run whatever length of time the parties involved agree upon. Leases generally offer more protection to the tenant than they do to the landlord. This may sound contradictory to everything you thought about a lease, but if you examine the facts, I think you will agree.

The only protection that a lease offers the landlord is the knowledge that he can expect to have his place rented out for the term of the lease. Although he can expect this, he is not absolutely guaranteed that it will

RENTAL APPLICATION

Name _____ Date of birth _____

Present address _____ How long _____

Children (names, ages) _____ Phone _____

Your social security no. _____ Driver's license no. _____

   Present employer _____ How long _____

   Position _____ Phone _____

   Supervisor _____ Your salary _____ Other income _____

Spouse's social security no. _____ Driver's license no. _____

   Present employer _____ How long _____

Position _____ Phone _____

   Supervisor _____ Salary _____ Other income _____

Where do you bank? _____ Loans _____

Savings _____ Checking _____ Next check no. _____

List two local credit references

   1. _____ Purchased _____

   2. _____ Purchased _____

List two personal references

   1. _____ Phone _____

   2. _____ Phone _____

Present landlord _____ Phone _____

Auto make ____ Year ____

   License no. _____ Any Pets _____

Have you ever been arrested for anything other than traffic violations?

_____

If yes, explain _____

PLEASE READ CAREFULLY BEFORE SIGNING: THE UNDERSIGNED WARRANTS AND REPRESENTS, THAT ALL STATEMENTS HEREIN ARE TRUE AND AUTHORIZES VERIFICATION THEREOF.

Signed _____ Date _____

be rented. If a lessee decides to break the lease, the lessor can take him to court to force compliance, but if the lessee does not "stay and pay," the cost of enforcing the lease may be more than the amount that can be collected. In that case the lessor, if he has any common sense at all, will make an economical decision and decide not to prosecute.

On the other hand, the tenant renting under a lease has a lot of protection. He is guaranteed that the rent will not change for the duration of the lease. He is also guaranteed that the terms of the lease will not change, either. He may even be guaranteed the right to renew the lease automatically for another term.

The disadvantages of having a lease all seem to fall on the landlord. If the landlord decides to sell his place, the lease remains in effect and will be binding on the new owner. If a prospective buyer doesn't like the rental rate or the fact that he can't gain possession until the lease expires, he may decide not to buy. As you can see, a landlord in this position is unlikely to get the best price possible for his property and may not even be able to sell it at all.

Finally, if a lease expires and the tenant continues to make payments, it could be construed that the expired lease was renewed at the same rate and terms for another identical period. If you are going to use a lease and you want to avoid this happening, have your attorney put in an option to renew clause that will protect your interest.

MONTHLY RENTAL AGREEMENTS

Monthly rental agreements have none of the disadvantages of leases. If you want to sell your house, you can give your tenants a thirty-day notice to move. If you don't serve notice, the new owner is usually required by law to give them at least thirty days after the closing to vacate the house. Since neither you nor the buyer is bound as you would be by a lease, you will find it much easier to sell. You will also be more likely to sell for a better price.

Any of the terms and conditions of a monthly rental agreement can be changed with a thirty-day notice. If you want to raise the rent, you can do so. If you want to change any of the conditions of the agreement, you can do that, too. In order to change anything or even to terminate the agreement, all you need is to serve a thirty-day notice. This kind of flexibility makes the monthly rental agreement one of the best things you can have going for you.

The only advantage of a lease over a monthly rental agreement is the length of the contract. Although a lessee may sign a one-year lease (or longer) and stay the full term, he may be reluctant to renew his lease for a similar term. At this point you can either allow him to stay on a month-to-month basis or have him move. If he stays, you have no more guarantee that he will continue to stay than you have with a tenant on a monthly rental agreement. If he decides to move, he will probably do so before he normally would have, simply because his lease has expired or is about to expire. As for forcing him to stay until his lease does expire, forget it. When a person decides to move, he usually moves. A lease may keep him there longer than he wants only if you can convince him that you have the upper hand. I'm not much of a gambler, and I don't like to play showdown.

If you are really concerned about keeping a good tenant as long as you can, you shouldn't rely on either a lease or a monthly rental agreement. The only thing that will keep a tenant is having one of the nicest houses that tenant can possibly find for the rent he is paying. Besides that, make sure the rent is at or below the going market rate. And if you go about doing your business in this way, you will never have to worry about losing a good tenant to some other landlord. He will realize what he has, and he will never want to move.

The following monthly agreement is one that I use. I have found it to my advantage to make up my own monthly rental agreement rather than to use the standard forms available in most office supply stores. In this way, I can include certain protective clauses and conditions in my agreement that are not in the standard forms. You can use my agreement or make your own to fit your particular needs. Laws and regulations vary from state to state, so you should check with your attorney before you decide on any agreement.

The first five lines of the agreement are self-explanatory. That's where you put the date, your name, the tenant's legal name, and the address of the house you are renting out. The next line, rental starting date and terms, needs some explanation. Usually you will have your rent due on the first of the month. Once in a while you may have a tenant who would like a different rental due date because of his pay schedule. If that is the case, you want to use a due date that makes it easy for him to get his rent paid on time. Make a note of the date on the agreement. Next, you note the monthly rental rate. Even if you have to prorate the first month's rent because the tenant will not have been there a full month, put in the full rental amount.

MONTHLY RENTAL AGREEMENT

This agreement is entered into this _____ day of _____ ,
19 _____ , by and between _____ ,
hereinafter called Owner, and _____ ,
hereinafter called Occupant.

     Occupant hereby rents from Owner _____ ,
     in the city of _____ , State of _____ .

RENTAL STARTING DATE AND TERMS

The term of this rental agreement shall commence at 12:01 A.M. on the
_____ day of _____ , 19 _____ , and shall continue
from month to month at a rental rate of _____
dollars ($ _____) per month, payable in advance on or
before the _____ day of each month.

1. Rents paid and credited to the Owner's account by 3:00 P.M. of
the due date will be discounted by the amount of twenty-five dollars
($25).

2. If rents are unable to be paid in full within four days of the due
date then it is agreed that the tenancy will become a weekly tenancy
and rents will be paid every week at a rate of $_____ per
week.

3. To pay a security and damage deposit of $ _____ ,
said deposit to be refunded upon vacating if there is no damage
beyond ordinary wear and depreciation, and all rents and other
charges are paid in full.

4. To use said premises as living quarters for the residences of said
Occupants, being _____ adults and _____ children, and for
no other purpose whatsoever, and to pay to the Owner the sum of
$50.00 for each other person who shall occupy said premises with
Occupant.

5. Not to sublet said premises or any part thereof, not to keep any
dog, cat, or other animal or pet without the Owner's written
permission.

6. Occupant agrees not to violate any State law, statutes, or city
ordinances, not to commit, suffer or permit any waste or nuisance
in, on, or about the premises.

7. Owner may enter said premises at any and all reasonable times by himself or with others to inspect, repair, and maintain same, or to show the property to any prospective buyer or loan or insurance agent, and in the case either party has given notice of termination of this tenancy, to show premises to any prospective tenant.

8. Occupant agrees to maintain and keep, at his sole expense, the premises and furnishings and equipment, and to pay Owner on demand for all loss, breakage and damage occurring during Occupant's residence.

9. Occupant cannot make any alterations to the premises or do any decorating or painting without the Owner's written approval.

10. Occupant is responsible for all outside yard work and snow removal.

11. Owner shall not be responsible for loss, injury, or damage to the personal property or person of Occupant or his guest or visitors, caused directly or indirectly by acts of God, fire, theft, burglary, malicious acts, riots, civil commotion, the elements, defects in the building, furnishings, equipment, walks or landscaping, or by the neglect of other residents or owners of contiguous property.

12. This agreement is automatically renewed from month-to-month upon payment and receipt of rent, but may be terminated at any time by either party giving to the other in writing thirty days (30) prior notice of intention to terminate.

13. Utilities and services to be the responsibility of and paid for by Occupant include _____ , _____ ,
_____ , _____ .

SERVICES

BANK _____   FURNACE REPAIRS
    Contact _____   Contact _____
    Phone _____   Phone _____

EMERGENCY REPAIRS   SEWER CLEANING
    Contact _____   Contact _____
    Phone _____   Phone _____

SUMMARY OF CHARGES

$_____ Cleaning per Room (washing wall, floors, ceiling)

$_____ Painting per Room

$_____ Carpet Cleaning per room

$_____ Paint, permanent spot, or hole in wall, wallpaper, or carpet

$_____ Cigarette Burns (cost per burn)

$_____ Yard Clean-up

$_____ Sewer Cleaning (if obstruction is caused by Occupant)

$_____ Monthly increase in rent for each pet

$_____ Increase in Security Deposit for each pet

ADDITIONAL TERMS OR CONDITIONS

_____

_____

_____

Executed and entered into this _____ day of _____ , 19_____ .

David J. Grzesiek (Owner)
1715 S. Long Lake Road
Traverse City, Michigan 49684
(616) 941-8858

_____
Owner or Agent

_____
Occupant

_____
Driver's License Number

_____
Occupant

_____
Driver's License Number

Now, let's examine the terms point by point:

1. In order to encourage the tenant to pay his rent on time, you want to have either a late charge (e.g., a dollar a day for each day the rent is due and unpaid) or a discount (e.g., twenty-five dollars if the rent is paid on or before the due date). I prefer the latter because people react better to sugar than to vinegar. There is also some question in many states about the legality of penalties. You can work the discount in two different ways. If, for example, the rent you want is $100 a month, you can use $125 in your advertising and in your agreement. Think how excited your prospective tenants will be when they find that by paying on time, they reduce their rent to $100. The other approach is to use $100 in your advertising and $125 on your rental agreement. If a prospective tenant says he thought the rent was $100, tell him he is right. Tell him the rent is $100 if it is paid on time. Then ask if you were wrong in assuming he was going to pay his rent on time.

2. If the tenant is unable to pay the month's rent in advance when it is due, he should at least be able to pay a week's rent. If he can't do this, he is probably in deep financial trouble, and this will be your first clue. Set the weekly amount at at least one-fourth of the stated rental amount. In the example above you would take at least one-fourth of $125 and not of $100. In this case $35 would be a good weekly amount.

3. This item is pretty self-explanatory. You should check, though, to see if your state has any laws covering the handling of security deposits.

4. This is what I call my mother-in-law clause. I explain to my tenants that this is to discourage their mothers-in-law or anyone else from moving in with them. I tell them that if they were to have any more children, this provision will not affect their rent. Whatever amount you set as an extra charge, make sure it is enough to discourage them from having others move in with them.

5. This prevents a tenant from subleasing or assigning his rights to anyone else. Without this provision, you could find yourself unable to control who moves into your house. This clause also covers pets. Certain pets can do more damage to your house and yard than you would ever think possible. You want to be able to control what kind of and how many pets a tenant has. If you do allow a pet, always reserve the right to rescind your permission if a pet does any damage.

6. This states that a tenant will not permit or take part in any illegal activities or actions that will affect you or your property.

7. Without this provision a tenant could keep you from stepping onto your own property. If your tenant questions you about this provision,

explain to him that you will not be making unannounced visits or using this provision to invade his privacy. You just want to protect your right to maintain your property and show it to the individuals mentioned.

8. Again, this provision is self-explanatory. All it does is put the tenant on notice of his responsibility to maintain the property.

9. This provision is very easy to understand. It is also very important. If you don't want your tenants slopping paint all over and destroying the character of your house, you'd better explain and enforce this provision. If the tenant wants to paint, let him pick out the color, but make sure he understands that you must approve it before he buys it. (You should pay for it if painting is needed.) Only allow him to do one room at a time, and check each room after he is done, to make sure the job was done right. If you don't do this, you could find that you have to repaint the whole house to cover up his mistakes. If the tenant wants to do any remodeling, handle his request in the same way, and make sure he knows how to do what he proposes before he starts.

10. Again this provision is self-explanatory. You want the tenant to understand that the house he is renting carries the same responsibilities as his own house would. If he wants yard maintenance service, let him arrange and pay for it himself.

11. Although this provision will not release you from your liability, it does put the tenant on notice that you do not intend to cover his losses. If your negligence, either wilful or not, causes any loss, injury, or damage, you can be held liable. This is why you need to carry a good liability policy (see the section on insurance in chapter seven).

12. This is the provision that allows you to change or terminate this agreement at any time as long as you give a thirty-day written notice. It is also the provision that states the tenant must provide you with a written notice when he intends to move. As a good business practice, when a tenant gives you his notice, accept it and let him know how much you enjoyed having him. Don't get mad or upset.

13. This is the place to list all the services and utilities that are to be the responsibility of the tenant and paid for by him. If any of these items are billed to you because you are the landowner (city services are about the only ones that may be), let the tenant know that you will forward these bills to him for payment. If a tenant balks at this arrangement, tell him that if you have to pay these bills, you will have to increase the rent more than enough to cover the services. Explain to him that because he can control his consumption, by paying the bills himself he will be able to control his total cost.

Services. If you want to make your investments as trouble free as possible, you can find other people to assume some or all of the management responsibilities. If you delegate the tasks of rent collecting, emergency repairs, furnace repairs, and sewer cleaning, you will be able to use your time much more profitably and enjoyably. Having these services performed by licensed people also lowers the risk of your being liable in case of a lawsuit.

Bank. When you are ready to have a bank collect your rents for you, shop around and find the bank that offers the most services and the lowest rate. It is convenient for the tenant if a bank collects your rents, because he can pay by mail or in person at any of the bank's offices. It is convenient for you because you won't be spending a day or two (or more) each month running around trying to collect your rent. In addition, since tenants are naturally more concerned with paying a bank on time than with paying you on time, this arrangement is definitely a plus for you.

Emergency Repairs. When you dread hearing the telephone ring because you think it is one of your tenants with a problem, it's time to find yourself a handyman. If you don't know one, ask around. There are a lot of people out there who would be more than happy to earn a few extra dollars every now and then. Once you find a good handyman, treat him right. He'll take care of your properties, so that your properties can take care of you. If you are not using licensed people (who have workman's comp coverage), make sure you talk to your insurance agent about your liability.

Furnace Repairs. Your handyman will probably be able to work on your furnaces if he has to, but you will be further ahead if you find a licensed man to do most of your furnace repair work. If you have a number of houses, he may even give you a break on the cost. Even though he may seem expensive, his training and equipment will enable him to get the job done faster and better than an unqualified man. Changing filters and minor maintenance can still be done by your handyman or your tenant in order to keep cost down.

Sewer Cleaning. There are a number of small, independent sewer cleaners in every community. They usually work at it on the side, so their cost is at least half what the full-timers charge. In fact, some of them can do the job for less than you can do it yourself and give you a three-month guarantee to boot. Of course, if you have a pair of boots and enjoy wading around in sewage, you might want to rent a power snake. It's not my idea of enjoyment, but if that turns you on, go ahead and do it.

Summary of Charges. These charges are used to encourage your tenant to take better care of your house while he is living there and to leave it in good shape when he moves out. Spelling out all these costs beforehand also helps to eliminate misunderstandings when a tenant moves out. Set most of the charges at what your estimated cost will be. The tenant is charged for cleaning the sewer only if he causes the obstruction (for example, with toys, rags, or sanitary napkins). Your sewer cleaner will be able to tell you the cause. If the cause is roots or a broken line, you should pay the cost. Cigarette burns, paint spots, and holes should be assessed at a high enough price to discourage them altogether. The costs for damage by pets should be high enough to make the tenant think twice about getting a pet, but not so high that you may lose a good tenant over them.

Additional terms and conditions. Here you want to list any other provisions that you might think necessary. For example, you might add a stipulation that the security deposit will only be refunded after a minimum paid rental of six months. You might add a provision that allows you to use part of the garage for storage. You might add a clause that forbids the tenant to install any antenna on the roof. You can add just about anything to make the agreement fit each house you own. Just make sure that it is not illegal.

The signatures. Before your new tenant signs the rental agreement, make sure that you have gone over every item with him. Make sure that he completely understands which responsibilities are his and which are yours. Most disagreements occur because of lack of communication, and this rental agreement attempts to create understanding between you and your tenant. Remember, the best way to stay out of court is never to have legal trouble in the first place. A rental agreement that spells everything out will go a long way toward keeping you out of trouble.

When your new tenant signs the agreement, make sure he uses his full legal name. If he is married, have his wife sign also, using her full legal name (Helen W. Brown not Mrs. John Q. Brown). It's also a good idea to have all the adults who will be occupying the house sign the rental agreement.

COPING WITH BAD TENANTS

EVICTION

If you do a thorough job of screening your applicants, you may never have to worry about eviction. To say that you will never have to evict a tenant, though, is unrealistic. Therefore, it is necessary that you have at least a basic idea of what not to do in an eviction. Although many conditions can prompt an eviction, it is usually started because of nonpayment of rent. Damages and failure to comply with the provisions of the rental agreement are also grounds for eviction.

When you have a tenant you want to evict, never take matters into your own hands. A tenant could sue you for physical and mental damages, and you could end up losing a whale of a lot of money. Here is a list of rules that you must obey; otherwise, you will be acting unlawfully:

1. Never use force or threat of force.
2. Never remove, retain, or destroy any of the tenant's personal property.
3. Never change or add to the locks or other security devices.
4. Never board up the premises.
5. Never remove any of the doors, windows, or locks.
6. Never terminate or interrupt any of the services or utilities.
7. Never introduce any noise, odor, or other nuisances.

As you can see, any truly satisfying recourse is illegal. It is probably just as well, because any of these actions would invite retaliation from the tenant. Any retaliation would probably escalate until either someone was hurt or your house was destroyed. As undesirable as taking legal action might be to you, at times it may be your only viable alternative. Laws and procedures vary from state to state, so you should check with your attorney. He will best be able to guide you on which course of action to take in an eviction. Different circumstances will dictate different actions and remedies; have him inform you of your options.

Whatever the reason for evicting a tenant, it is best not to wait around hoping that the problem will somehow go away. If you don't act right away, the tenant may get the idea that you don't care. Once he gets that idea, he will think that he can push you around whenever he feels like it. If this happens, you have a real problem on your hands.

Always remember, the best way to solve a problem is to catch it right before it becomes a problem. Let the tenant know that you run a tight ship and expect adherence to the rules.

Sometimes a speedy and forceful response on your part will whip your tenant back into line. If a tenant's rent is unpaid by the third day after the due date, you should contact him immediately. If he can't pay the rent, remind him that he can go to a weekly rental (as stated in the rental agreement). Tell him that if either payment is not received right away, you will be forced to start taking legal action immediately. Be firm, be businesslike, and don't accept any feeble excuses or hard luck stories. If the money is not paid, start the eviction. Never back down; the tenant will take it as a sign of weakness. The only time you may want to bend and work with the tenant is when he has been with you for a while. If he is sincere and his problems surmountable, by all means be human.

The first step in an eviction is the serving of a notice to quit. The notice to quit is really a notice to pay. It gives the tenant the choice of paying up or moving out. These notices are usually for three, seven, or thirty days. Depending on the type of notice you send, the tenant has that many days to respond. If the tenant does nothing, your next step is to initiate summary proceedings and get a court date. The tenant is then served with a complaint and summons to appear in court. Unless the tenant thinks he has a chance to fight you, he usually doesn't show up at court. At this point the judge will rule in your favor, and usually give the tenant an additional ten days to move out. If at the end of that time the tenant still refuses to move, you can petition the court for a writ of restitution. A writ of restitution entitles the sheriff (not you) physically to remove the tenant and his possessions from your house. Once you receive the writ of restitution, it can be another ten days before the sheriff acts on it. This may not seem like a long drawn out process, but it can easily run three months or more if you have a belligerent tenant on your hands.

You can handle much of this legal work yourself, but it's best to have your attorney do it for you. As you can see, an eviction can be a long process. The lost rents, the court cost, the legal fees, and the possible damage the tenant can do to your house during this process can make an eviction very expensive. Many times a tenant will straighten up when he receives a notice to quit. If you don't dilly-dally around and get it out when you said you would, he will know you mean business. In a case like this, you won't have a great deal of expense. The longer you wait, the more expensive it is likely to be. Don't wait.

Once you start an eviction, you should be committed to carrying it to its conclusion. If there is any doubt in your mind about going all the way, don't even start. False or hollow threats can easily be spotted and will end up doing you more harm than good.

JUDGMENTS

A judgment is a ruling handed down by the court stating the tenant does indeed owe you a certain amount of money. Before you went to court, both you and the tenant knew that he owed you the specified amount. The judgment just makes it more official, but it's still up to you to collect the money; the court will not do it for you. Of course, having a judgment allows you to petition the court to attach some of the tenant's possessions or wages (garnishment). If the tenant is a real deadbeat, he probably won't have anything for you to attach or any wages for you to garnishee.

If your tenant has a good, steady job and he is not going to be running off somewhere you can't find him, you may want to get a judgment. You can usually file to get a judgment at the same time you file for an eviction. Doing so will be more expensive than just filing for eviction, but if there is a good chance of collecting, you may want to do it. Your attorney can best advise you about the cost and your chances.

If you decide to push just for an eviction, you can always go for a judgment after you have the tenant out of your house. You can go to a small claims court yourself (you do not need an attorney), and if the amount you are after is under the court's limit (usually $500–$1,000), you can sue. In many states you can wait up to six years and still be able to file suit. Once you receive a judgment, it is usually good for ten years. If your old tenant stays around long enough, there is a pretty good chance you will eventually get your money. The only question is, will it be worth all the time and effort?

If the amount that you are going after is over the limit set by the small claims court in your state, you will have to file suit in a regular district court. In this case, you will need an attorney. You must consider court cost, legal fees, and a possible judgment against you before going this route. Again, get your attorney's advice on what action to take, or whether to take any action at all.

THE EVICTION ALTERNATIVE

Yes, there is a better way than evicting a tenant to solve problems. Choosing to go the legal route, especially if you have to carry an eviction all the way out to the bitter end, usually ends up costing you. You are going to be out time, legal fees, court cost, and rents. To make matters even worse, the tenant is going to be mad at you for evicting him (even if you have a darn good reason) and he is very likely to take his anger out on your house. That means damages and damages mean more money, sometimes a lot of money. The only winners in a situation like this are the tenants and the attorneys.

The alternative that I am about to give you may go against every fiber in your body. You may think it is just a way of throwing good money after bad. No matter what you feel and no matter what you think, when it comes down to basic economics, it is good sense and good business. When you are faced with a problem tenant, don't get angry or hostile with him. It won't do much good, and you may find yourself facing a lawsuit because of your actions. The best approach is to sympathize with his plight and then tell him that you are having problems too. You might even ask him what he would do in your situation and how he would cover the payments and expenses that you can't ignore. You could go on to explain that all he faces is eviction, but you could lose your house if you don't make your payments. Explain to him how important it is that you find someone right away who can pay the rent.

Now he probably won't give a darn about you and your problems, but that's okay because you don't expect him to. The reason you give him your sob story is to get him into a position to buy your offer. What you are going to offer is this:

Dear Tenant,
    If you are out by _____ , I will return your deposit in full, so you can use it to find another place. If you clean the house before you go, I will also give you $100 that I usually pay someone else for the service.

The date you give for him to be out should never be over one week from the time you talk to him. If you haven't already started the eviction process (notice to quit), make sure that you tell him you are starting it immediately. This will help him realize that you mean business and give him one more reason to accept your offer.

The $100 (or whatever amount you set) you give him for cleaning the house really isn't for that purpose. The main reason for giving him that money is to discourage him from damaging your property (a disgruntled tenant could do thousands of dollars worth of damage). It also discourages him from leaving a truckload of garbage in the house when he moves out. Even if the house isn't that clean when he does vacate, give him his money and kiss him goodbye.

In case he says he can't find a place to move or he can't be completely out by the time the week is up, you want to include an additional provision in your offer. You will deduct twenty-five dollars (or any amount you think will light a fire under him) from his deposit for each day he is there after the week is up. You also want him to understand that he will lose his entire deposit if you end up having to evict him, and that he will also have a judgment made against him for all money you are due. For your own protection, do not give him any money until he is completely out and he has returned his keys to you.

As I said before, you may not like this alternative. Way down deep inside, I don't either, but it sure beats the time and cost involved in getting an eviction. Not every deadbeat tenant will go for this offer. Some will figure that they will be money ahead by staying until the day before the sheriff shows up to move them out on the street. Others, though, will look forward to the prospect of getting all that money in their hot little hand. When it does work, you will be glad you used this alternative.

KEEPING GOOD TENANTS—REPAIRS, IMPROVEMENTS, AND RENT INCREASES

REPAIRS

You want your tenants to call you (or your handyman) whenever something is in need of repair. You want them to know that you appreciate knowing as soon as anything starts to go wrong. The sooner you can catch a repair or a problem, the more likely you are to be able to stop it before it causes a lot of damage and becomes a big problem.

Little things left unattended can develop into big problems, and big problems mean big money out of your pocket. If not fixed promptly, a small leak in an upstairs bathroom can cause the floor to rot and the ceiling in the room below to fall. A job that could have been taken care of with only a couple of dollars could end up costing a couple of hundred or a couple of thousand dollars.

When a tenant calls, show your appreciation and then prove your gratitude by getting over there and getting the problem fixed as soon as possible. If the repair is due to normal wear and tear, you do not want to charge the tenant. In fact, you never want to charge the tenant for any repairs unless he is responsible for the damage himself. If a tenant gets the idea that you are going to charge him every time something goes wrong, he may never call. Not getting any calls may be great until the day you realize that you have some pretty big problems on your hands. You may even want to make it a point to contact all your tenants at least every six months and ask if they have any repairs that need attention. Sooner or later, they will get the idea that you care. And that's not a bad idea for them to have.

IMPROVEMENTS

Any time you improve your houses you increase their value and, therefore, increase their potential income. Many of the improvements you put into your houses you, and you alone, decide on. Every once in a while, though, a tenant will ask for some improvements. He could ask for new carpet, new fixtures, new cupboards, new counter tops, new anything. He could ask for something small or for something large like a complete remodeling job. No matter what he asks for, you should be glad to grant his every wish. Now you are probably saying, "Are you crazy? I can't afford that." Well, you're right. Maybe you can't afford it, but maybe your tenant can.

Take the cost of whatever it is he wants, and figure out how much you would have to raise his rent to pay for it in two years or less. Once you have the figure, tell him you will be glad to grant his wish if you could raise his rent by so much a month. If he doesn't like the idea, he will stop complaining and everyone will be happy. If he agrees, go ahead and give him what he wants, and everyone will be happy too. It's really not going to cost you anything, and it will end up increasing the value of your house. Besides that, you will get the additional benefit of being able to write off the improvement against your income at tax time.

If your tenant volunteers to buy all or part of the materials, so much the better. To reimburse him, you could lower his rent or promise not to raise it for a certain period. If your tenant does pay for any of the materials, make sure he signs a paper stating that whatever he purchased stays with the house after he leaves. You may also want to check to see if all the materials have been paid for, so that you don't end up with a mechanic's lien against your house.

If your tenant volunteers to do any or all of the labor, make sure he knows what he is doing before you accept his offer. If he does a bad job, you may have to go in and do it all over. It could end up taking more time to redo the job than you would have spent doing it right in the first place. You may also have to spend more money replacing materials he destroyed. Before you have a tenant do any work for you, always check with your insurance agent to see if you should get workman's comp coverage. If your tenant were to get injured while working on your house and you didn't have this coverage, you could find yourself looking right up the barrel of a big lawsuit.

WHEN TO RAISE RENTS

The best time to raise your rents is right after you have improved or upgraded your house. When the tenant asks for the improvements, it's always much easier. When you are making improvements the tenant didn't ask for, you may find some resistance. Some tenants would rather have things stay the way they are and not have to pay any more rent. Sometimes these tenants may even get upset and move.

If you have good tenants and want to keep them, the timing of your rent increase can be important. Certain times of the year are better than others. Most tenants are not fond of moving once their kids are settled in school. They are even less fond of moving in the winter months, especially around the holidays. Knowing this, you should time most of your increases to go into effect the first of the year. If you notify your tenants around Thanksgiving, your thirty-day notice will be easier for them to swallow. The weather and the holidays will take their minds off of looking for another place. By the time Christmas and January 1 roll around, they will have accepted the fact.

Most tenants expect rent raises to occur at the onset of a new year. Raises at any other time of the year don't make as much sense to them. What does make sense is that when spring is in the air, tenants get the itch to look around. The kids will soon be out of school, and the weather is just fine for moving. If you don't want to help push them out of the door, don't raise your rents then. Of course, if you do want them to move, this is the perfect time to give 'em a good one.

THINGS YOU DON'T WANT TO DO

1. Don't rent out a crummy house. Crummy houses attract crummy tenants.
2. Don't set your rents too high. High rents encourage tenants to look around.
3. Don't run yourself ragged showing your house. If a prospective tenant needs a place badly enough, he will make it to your showing. If he can't make it personally, he can have someone go in his place.
4. Don't ever let a tenant think he is doing you a favor by renting your house. It won't be long before he is telling you "Jump!" and you will be asking, "How high?"
5. Don't ever discriminate. You can pick the best tenant for your house without ever stepping close to a discrimination suit.
6. Don't use a lease. Use a month-to-month rental agreement.
7. Don't ever do anything unlawful when trying to evict a tenant. Make sure you know the seven things not to do, and don't do them.
8. Don't ever bad-mouth a tenant. If you are ever contacted for a reference and you can't say anything good about a tenant, simply say he didn't live up to the terms of your rental agreement. Don't say any more than that, or you might be sued.
9. Don't let repairs get out of hand. A small leak can end up costing a fortune. Get to them right away and show your appreciation to the tenant for notifying you promptly about a problem.
10. Don't supply appliances or pay utilities. Most tenants moving into a house have their own appliances (stoves, refrigerator, dishwasher, washer, dryer), and if they don't they can get used ones. The repair and maintenance on appliances can be high, and moving and storing them when a tenant doesn't want them can be a real hassle. If you pay utilities, you may find yourself stuck with supplying them to a tenant you are trying to evict. Remember, in many states you can't turn off the utilities when you're evicting a tenant. It's bad enough that he is into you for the rent; don't give him a chance to stick you for the utilities too.
11. Don't rent to friends or relatives. Believe me, it doesn't work out. You will both end up regretting the arrangement. You will also regret the day you became close personal friends with your tenants. Keep your distance, and keep the relationship business-like.

12. Don't say no when a tenant asks you, "Would you please raise my rent?" In effect, every time a tenant asks for certain improvements, that is exactly what he is saying. You should be more than happy he brought the subject up and more than happy to comply.

CHAPTER THIRTEEN

TAXES

Tax loopholes are available to the poor as well as the rich,
it's just that the poor choose not to make use of them.

ART BUCHWALD

Did you ever stop to think what you could do if you could keep all the money you pay in income tax? If you had only the tax you paid last year, you could probably do an awful lot. Income tax takes a good part of the average man's income. One of the best ways to escape from high taxes is to get your income from sources other than earned income. Income from real estate investments is one of those sources. Investing in single family homes can not only get you to the promised land of zero income tax, but it will also protect a good part of your income from tax while you are making the journey.

Would you believe that it is possible to borrow money interest free and in many cases not even have to pay back the loan? Sounds too good to be true? Well, it isn't. Uncle Sam has set up certain provisions in the tax laws that allow you to keep (borrow back from him) the money you otherwise would have to pay him in taxes. All you have to do is choose to take advantage of the benefits provided you by making use of depreciation, capital gains, and tax-free exchanges.

DEPRECIATION

One of the biggest single benefits of investing in real estate and in single family homes is depreciation. Depreciation is the decline in value of a tangible asset because of age and normal wear and tear. Tangible assets are such things as buildings, cars, tools, or just about anything else that can be weighed, measured, counted, or appraised.

255

Houses are tangible assets. And when you buy a single family home with the purpose of renting it out, you are allowed to depreciate it. For tax purposes you will want to attribute as little value as possible to the land, which you can't write off, and as much as possible to the structure, which you can write off. In most cases, the value of the lot a home sits on is worth between ten and twenty percent of the purchase price. Since you will want to write off as much as possible, attribute only ten percent of the value to the land every time you can. (It's not a bad idea to have a written appraisal stating the value of the land to be a figure equal to ten percent of the purchase price. This will come in handy if you are ever audited and have to substantiate your figures. You can usually get this appraisal at no cost from either your realtor or the seller's before the closing.)

Using the $10,000 house found on worksheet #1, let's see how depreciation works, using the simplest of all methods, the straight line method. According to this method, you divide the depreciable amount by the number of years over which it can be depreciated. If $1,000 or ten percent of the purchase price is attributed to the land, $9,000 is attributed to the structure. It's the structure that's depreciated, and it can be depreciated (written off) in as little as fifteen years. That means that $600 can be written off every year for the next fifteen years, until the full amount has been deducted.

"But wait just a darn minute," you say, "I thought houses increase in value each year, not decrease." You're right. That's why the depreciation write-off that Uncle Sam allows you to take is so darn nice. While a house is sitting there appreciating (creating wealth) tax free, you are allowed to depreciate it and write it off as a tax loss.

THE NEW ACRS

The Economic Recovery Tax Act of 1981 (ERTA) has radically revised the depreciation rules, thereby creating more opportunity than ever before for you to make money and keep your new-found wealth. The new ACRS (Accelerated Cost Recovery System) generally gives you much faster writeoffs, and it removes many areas of dispute that were in the earlier law.

Whereas the previous law stipulated that the cost of an asset be spread over its useful life, ACRS does not. ACRS stipulates that, except for allowable elections, assets must be written off over one of four recovery periods. Under ACRS you no longer have to decide the useful life of an asset or the method of depreciation you are going to use. You don't even have to decide whether there is any salvage value and, if there is, how much it will be. Financially and functionally ACRS is a superior system and a boon to the real estate investor.

The four recovery periods of some of the assets that you can write off under ACRS as a real estate investor are these:

1. **Three year property.** Tangible personal property with a present A.D.R. (Asset Depreciation Range) mid-point life of four years or less (autos, light trucks);
2. **Five-year property.** All tangible personal property except that specifically included in the three-year or ten-year class (heavy-duty trucks, furniture, fixtures, appliances, tools, equipment, office furniture and equipment);
3. **Ten-year property.** Tangible personal property with a present A.D.R. class life of more than eighteen but not more than twenty-five years (mobile homes, manufactured residential homes within the meaning of Section 603(6) of the Housing and Community Development Act of 1974); and
4. **Fifteen-year property.** Most real property (single family homes, apartment complexes, office buildings, improvements).

(Personal property is generally any property which is movable or which is not land or inseparably connected with the land; real property generally means land and anything permanently or inseparably attached to it, such as structures and improvements.)

First year recovery rate using ACRS. If you are a calendar-year taxpayer and you purchase a house and place it in service (rent it out or offer to rent it out) in January, you can take the full deduction of twelve percent (the first year's allowance shown in table 1). If you place it in service in February, you are allowed only eleven percent. Thereafter, the deduction drops one percent each month. A house placed in service in December would only give you one percent of its depreciable amount as a deduction.

THE STRAIGHT LINE METHOD

While ACRS is mandatory in most respects, you are allowed to elect the straight line method for the given recovery periods or to elect even longer recovery periods. The following table indicates the optional periods you may elect to use when using the straight line method.

CLASS	PERIOD
3-year property	3, 5, or 12 years
5-year property	5, 12, or 25 years
10-year property	10, 25, or 35 years
15-year property	15, 35, or 45 years

It should be noted that you can make these elections in the fifteen-year real property class on a property by property basis. In other words, you can elect to write off each property you acquire using the method and period you desire.

First year depreciation deduction using the straight line method. If you elect to use one of the straight line recovery percentages (15 years at 6.66%, 35 years at 2.86%, 45 years at 2.27%), the amount of your first annual deduction also depends on the number of months the property has been in service. If you are a calendar-year taxpayer and you place a house in service in January, you can deduct the full percentage. If you place it in service in February, you are allowed only eleven-twelfths of the applicable percentage. Thereafter, it drops one-twelfth each month.

COMPARISON OF ACRS AND THE STRAIGHT LINE METHOD

The following table gives a comparison of the ACRS rate and the straight line (S.L.) rate. I have used the house (structure) found on worksheet #1 to illustrate the dollar amounts. The value placed on the structure was $9,000.

YEAR	ACRS Rate	ACRS Amount	S.L. Rate	S.L. Amount
1	12%	$1,080	6⅔%	$600
2	10%	$ 900	6⅔%	$600
3	9%	$ 810	6⅔%	$600
4	8%	$ 720	6⅔%	$600
5	7%	$ 630	6⅔%	$600
6	6%	$ 540	6⅔%	$600
7	6%	$ 540	6⅔%	$600
8	6%	$ 540	6⅔%	$600
9	6%	$ 540	6⅔%	$600
10	5%	$ 450	6⅔%	$600
11	5%	$ 450	6⅔%	$600
12	5%	$ 450	6⅔%	$600
13	5%	$ 450	6⅔%	$600
14	5%	$ 450	6⅔%	$600
15	5%	$ 450	6⅔%	$600
		$9,000		$9,000

The ACRS, as illustrated above, allows a greater write-off in the beginning than the straight line method. These accelerated write-offs soon taper off and after the fifth year are less than the amount that would have been available if the straight line method had been used. The depreciation schedule you choose depends on your overall tax planning. You should always seek professional help about these matters, and you should direct any particular questions or special problems to a qualified C.P.A. or tax attorney. May I add that having a basic understanding of our tax system will help you make better use of their services.

In fact, there are several advantages to using the straight line method. The first and most obvious is that after the fifth year the writeoff ($600) is larger than the writeoff using the ACRS ($540, then down to $450). If you don't need large deductions in the beginning to offset other income, the straight line method may be to your advantage. The second advantage is that the straight line method will provide for a full capital gain return if you sell the property. If you use the ACRS rates in the table, any gain that occurs upon the sale may be wholly or partly taxable at ordinary income rates under the recapture rules. These rules will be discussed in a few minutes. The third advantage is that you can use different periods if you desire a longer writeoff. Most of the time it is to your advantage to use the shortest writeoff possible. Your accountant or CPA can best direct you in this matter once he knows your long-range goals.

RECAPTURE RULES

The gain (gains made on the sale or disposition of property) on any residential buildings will be taxed as ordinary income to the extent that the ACRS depreciation claimed exceeds the amount that would have been allowed under the straight line method. In other words, any depreciation that has been taken beyond what would have been taken using a fifteen-year straight line method is taxed as ordinary income.

The gain on any non-residential buildings will be taxed as ordinary income up to the amount of any ARCS depreciation claimed. This means that on non-residential property, recapture is not limited just to the excess claimed using ACRS over the straight line method. This can make using the ACRS on non-residential buildings very disadvantageous. Those of you considering investing in non-residential property, may therefore want to consider using the straight line method to depreciate your property. If you elect to use this method, there is no recapture, and all of your gains will qualify for capital gains status.

CHURNING

Before leaving the subject of depreciation, we must cover one more topic. Because members of Congress were fearful that many taxpayers and investors might try to take advantage of the higher recovery aspects of ACRS, they incorporated some elaborate anti-churning rules into the new tax laws. In essence, churning is the acquisition of property from a related party or user, with the intent of switching from an older, less beneficial depreciation schedule to a newer, more liberal one. Just about any property that was owned or used at any time in 1980 by the taxpayer or a related party comes under these rules. It should also be noted that the definition of a related party and user is very broad and encompassing.

Any property that you have owned since before 1981 cannot be depreciated under the Accelerated Cost Recovery System. It must continue to be written off on the same schedule you have been using. If you have any elaborate schemes for disposing of any of your older properties and then reacquiring them to take advantage of the new depreciation schedules, you should probably forget them.

CAPITAL GAINS

Your houses could appreciate hundreds or thousands or hundreds of thousands of dollars each year. All that appreciation would be yours to keep tax free, as long as you never sell the houses. You could even refinance them over and over again and never be liable for any tax on the monies you receive by doing so. The only time you will ever be liable for any tax is the day you eventually sell and realize a gain. Then and only then will you have to pay any tax, and even then the tax can be legally avoided or postponed in many cases.

The gain you should always be on the lookout for is referred to as a capital gain. The nicest thing about a capital gain is that it receives some very special tax treatment, especially if you held each house you sold for at least one year. A gain received in this way is referred to as a long term capital gain. For tax purposes, a long term capital gain is treated quite differently from a short term capital gain (a gain realized on the sale of a house you held for under one year).

Long term capital gains are subject to considerably less tax than short term capital gains. As of 1981, you have to claim and pay taxes on only forty percent of any long term capital gains. That's right, only forty percent. The remaining sixty percent is yours to keep, completely tax free. Short term capital gains, however, are usually treated as ordinary earned income when it comes time to pay your taxes. That being the case, you could end up paying dearly for any short term capital gains. That is why you should always attempt to take all your gains as long term capital gains.

Let's take a quick look at how a long term capital gain might be computed and how much tax might be due on that gain. Suppose you bought a house like the one appearing on worksheet #2, and sold it ten years later for $32,000. The first thing you have to figure out is your net sales price. This is done by taking the sale price ($32,000) and deducting all your expenses. Normally these expenses would include such items as your realtor's commission and your closing costs. If these expenses added up to $2,600, your net sales price would be $29,400.

Now you have to figure out the book value of the house. This is done by taking the price you paid for the house and all the improvements and deducting all the depreciation you have ever taken against these two items. Since you paid $10,000 for the house and $1,000 for the improvements, you have a total cost of $11,000. (Repairs are an expense and not a capital expenditure like improvements, so any money spent on them does not affect your book value.)

From this figure you subtract all the depreciation you have ever written off on the house and the improvements. With a value of $9,000 on the structure ($10,000 purchase price less $1,000 for the lot) plus the $1,000 in improvements, you have a total depreciable amount of $10,000. Of this amount, you would have written off $6,600 in the last ten years ($10,000 divided by a fifteen-year useful life comes out at $660 a year; $660 a year deducted for ten years comes out at $6,600). You can now calculate the book value by taking your total cost ($11,000) and subtracting your total depreciation taken to date ($6,600). The book value is thus $4,400.

Now you are ready to calculate your long term capital gain:

$29,400 net sales price
−4,400 book value
$25,000 long term capital gain

Notice that it doesn't matter that your house was worth $15,000 after all the improvements were in, nor that it more than doubled in value during those ten years. Even the amount of a mortgage (if in fact there is a mortgage or any other type of financing) isn't part of the calculations. None of these factors matters when it comes to figuring your capital gains. All that matters is the cost of the structure, the cost of all improvements, the amount you wrote off, and the amount you sold it for.

Now for something else that matters—the taxes you might end up paying on this $25,000 gain. Remember, this gain is a long term capital gain, so you have to pay taxes on only forty percent of the entire gain, or $10,000. If you are in the thirty percent tax bracket that means your tax is only $3,000 ($10,000 × 30%). Without the special treatment for long term capital gains, your tax could have been at least $7,500 ($25,000 × 30%). By choosing to get your income as a long term capital gain rather than as earned income, you end up saving $4,500 in taxes. In effect, you are legally choosing to pay less tax.

One of the nicest things about this tax break is that there are no strings attached. In fact, the higher your tax bracket, the bigger and better this break becomes. As fantastic as all this may sound, there are two ways to make it even better. The first is to have so many writeoffs that even when the taxable part of the gain is added to your income, your adjusted gross income is at or below the income level at which taxes are due. The second is to borrow the tax that is due on the taxable portion of that gain ($3,000 in the example above). This loan is interest free, and it has no monthly or annual payments that must be made. In fact, it may never have to be paid back at all during your lifetime. How do you apply for this loan? You apply for it by applying the concept in the next section.

TAX-FREE EXCHANGES

Section 1031 of the Internal Revenue Code allows you to exchange your houses for other property and not incur any immediate tax liability on any gain you may have made on the property you disposed of. Just as depreciation shelters some of the taxes that may be due on your income, tax-free exchanges shelter the taxes that may be due on your capital gains. Both of these shelters make it possible to borrow back from Uncle Sam the money you might otherwise have paid in taxes. Both of these loans are interest free and may never have to be paid back. Both of these loans allow you to preserve your investment capital, and that should be the number one objective of any investor.

If you don't want to dip into your capital as you are amassing your fortune, you will want to use the tax-free exchange provision every time you want to sell one of your houses. In order to qualify for a tax-free exchange, make sure that the house or houses you are going to get in exchange are of equal value to or greater value than the house you are exchanging. If you receive any "boot" such as cash or other property, all or part of the gain may be taxable. You should always check with your accountant whenever you get involved in a tax-free exchange, to avoid having some "boot" boot your tax savings out the window. ("Boot" is defined as any cash or additional property received in addition to the property exchanged.)

One of the biggest misconceptions about tax-free exchanges is the idea that you can sell your house and then have up to twenty-four months to reinvest your money. This may be true on the sale of your personal residence, but it is certainly not the case when you are selling a house that you are using as an investment. By correctly using the tax-free exchange rules, you can bypass the tax anyway, so this one disadvantage your investment houses have compared to your personal residence is minor. If you stop to consider that you can't depreciate your personal residence and that you can't write off any of its expenses directly against your income, your investment houses really provide you shelter—for tax purposes, that is.

Rather than get into all the intricacies of exchanging and how to do it, it would be far better if I just told you to talk to your realtor and your accountant if you ever decide to exchange any of your property. Knowing that you can do it and that it will keep you from losing your capital through unnecessary taxes should be all you need for now.

There is a Society of Exchange Counselors (P.O. Box 41964, Sacramento, CA 95841) which specializes in setting up exchanges anywhere in the country. These specialists will locate the people and the properties necessary to close any kind of deal you want. If you ever decide to exchange any of your houses, contact your local board of realtors for the names of the people specializing in exchanging in your area. If there is no one in your area, ask for the name and telephone number of the president of your state exchange group.

KEEPING YOUR INVESTMENT VEHICLE ON THE TAX-FREE HIGHWAY

As you are traveling up the road that leads to wealth and financial independence, it will pay you to keep your investment vehicle in good working condition. A tune-up that consists of filling out a financial statement (net worth statement) every six months and analyzing each of your properties (using the worksheet) every year will show you how to get the best performance out of your vehicle.

Your investment vehicle, like most vehicles, has four wheels. Each wheel has a name and these names are appreciation, beneficial tax treatment, cash flow, and debt retirement. Don't be too anxious to run out and sell a perfectly good vehicle just because someone says one of its tires is flat or going soft. Some short-sighted people can't see the whole vehicle, but only one wheel. When it happens to be the beneficial tax treatment wheel, such people may present a rather good but incomplete case for selling.

When your car gets a flat tire, you change the tire; you don't change or sell your car. The same holds true with your investment vehicle. If the tax benefits you once had are running out or running down, you can fix or replace them and still keep the whole vehicle intact. Here are a few of the things you can do to get your worn-out, overworked, or used-up tax wheel rolling again.

Fix the flat. You can fix your flat by fixing up the house in question. Either put in a lot of repairs (expenses that can be written off in one year), or put in some major or minor improvements (capital expenditures that must be written off over a number of years using the ACRS or straight line method).

Replace the tire. Instead of selling or disposing of a house, buy another house that will not only shield itself but the other house as well. The new tax law with its shorter recovery times makes this easier to do than it has been in the past. You could even buy more than one house.

You can also use this strategy to upgrade your portfolio of property. Instead of continuing to buy the same type of property, you could move up the ladder a step or two. Because of your situation and your experience, you could go on to bigger and better things, if you had a mind to. Although your profits may not be as high, you could also buy property that has already been improved or is not in need of any improvements.

Use road service. There are a lot of services out there that you could be making use of. Using these services will not only increase your expenses and provide you with more writeoffs, but they will also increase your free time. Such services include rental management, rental collection, and rental maintenance and repairs.

Use a jack. The greatest thing next to the leverage financing can produce is the leverage refinancing can produce. Refinancing will not only raise your expenses (you will pay more interest), but it will also raise all kinds of tax-free money for you to use for whatever you choose. Refinancing is a winner. You get higher writeoffs, you get lots of tax-free money, and you get someone else (your tenants) to pay back the loan for you.

Don't sell your investment vehicle just because one of the tires is flat. Find a way to take care of it and get it back on the road. You will never get really wealthy by buying one house and selling it to get another once most of its tax benefits are gone. You will end your investment career just where you started, with one house.

The same tax system that forces you to pay taxes can allow you to become wealthy if you let it. The choice is yours. If you want to pay no taxes legally, the system offers you not one but three alternatives: you can invest in real estate, you can improve the real estate you already own, or you can finance the wealth you created out of your real estate. Once you understand the system and put it to work for you and not against you, you will find that you love it. In fact, you will wonder why everyone doesn't feel the same way.

TAX TIPS TO REMEMBER

1. The money you receive by working for a living is taxed at some of the highest rates. The money you receive by having your money work for you (long term capital gains) is taxed at some of the lowest rates.
2. The money you receive by virtue of owning an appreciating asset such as a house is tax free until you sell it or until you die (even then there are options that make it possible to postpone or avoid the tax). The money you receive by refinancing any of your assets is all tax free, no matter how much you get or how many times you get it.

3. The capital gains exclusion (sixty percent of any long term capital gain is tax free) is an outright gift to you from Uncle Sam of any taxes that would have been due on that portion of the gain.
4. Tax-free exchanges allow you to borrow from Uncle Sam the taxes that normally would have been due on the remaining forty percent of a capital gain. This loan carries no interest charge and has no payments. It is usually due upon your death or upon your final disposition of the exchanged house, houses, or property.
5. Depreciation allows you to shield your income from taxes by creating a tax loss. The tax dollars you are able to keep because of this represent another loan with the same terms and conditions as the loan mentioned above (no interest, no payments).
6. All your expenses on your rental houses can be written off. Unlike expenses on your personal residence, every penny you spend on your rentals can be deducted from your income, and it can be done using before-tax dollars. The only thing that cannot be deducted is the cost of your own labor (except in some cases when you are incorporated).
7. In the past, putting your investment properties into a corporation generally lost you more benefits than you could hope to gain. Recently this all changed, and incorporation may be desirable especially if you could make use of a special type of corporation called a Subchapter S corporation.
8. Don't become a dealer. If you start buying and selling too many houses in too short a time, you will lose a lot of the tax advantages that you have as an investor.
9. No matter what your age, income, or tax filing status, you are exempt from paying any self-employment taxes (social security taxes) on any rental income, dividends and interest, and capital gains you may receive. If you are presently drawing social security and receive money (any amount) from any of these sources, your benefits will not be lowered or eliminated. On the other hand, earned income can be subject to self-employment taxes, and it can cause your social security benefits to be altered.
10. Buy a copy of J.K. Lasser's *Your Income Tax.* This is probably the best all-around tax guide you can find.

Note: The 1984 Tax Reform Act has changed the long term capital gain holding period from one year to six months for assets acquired after June 22, 1984. This change will remain in effect through 1987 only; after 1987 the holding period reverts back to one year. Also note that the ACRS recovery period has been changed from 15 to 18 years and straight line depreciation from 15, 35, or 45 years to 18, 35, or 45 years.

CHAPTER FOURTEEN
RULES FOR SUCCESS

The greatest thing in the world is not so much where
we stand, but in what direction we are moving.

OLIVER WENDELL HOLMES

In the beginning of this book I said that it was very difficult ever to earn enough money to become financially independent. I told you that the best way to get what you want out of life is to create or acquire enough wealth. Once this wealth is in place, it can grow virtually unaffected by taxes and be used to produce a tax-free income. I told you about the benefits of money earning money (capital gains) and the reduced income tax it pays. And I told you about people earning money (earned income) and the heavy penalties they pay through income taxes, self-employment taxes, and reduced social security benefits.

The knowledge and ideas you have picked up by reading this book will enable you to start and run your own investment program. Once your program is under way, it will grow as fast and as big as you let it. Your first house will help buy the second, the first and second will help buy the third, and so on. All the time this progression is making you wealthier, you will be able to do something else. You will be able to start shielding more and more of your income from taxes. As this happens, you will find that you have even more money to put into your investments or to enjoy. If you continue to nurture and care for your investment program, the day will soon come when you are both financially independent and exempt from paying any income taxes. At that point you can either continue with your investment program and become even richer or go out and live the kind of life you have always dreamed of living.

From worksheet #2 you saw that it was possible to achieve a one hundred percent or better return on your money. As unrealistic and unbelievable as this may sound (especially if you are used to your money earning five percent interest in the bank), it is nonetheless possible. Many of the houses that I have purchased have given me returns well over one hundred percent. Many have done even better. After buying, fixing up, and refinancing, I not only recovered every dollar (down payment and improvement funds), but I walked away with money in my pocket. Now it's impossible to figure a return on an investment that keeps making you money when you don't have any in it, but nonetheless it sure is nice. You can earn the same kind of returns. You can even have them be completely tax free. You can, in fact, double your money every year and end up wealthy in a relatively short time. Take a look at the chart below and see what happens when you just take $100 and invest it in something that doubles in value every year. Notice that you never have to add any more money, just keep reinvesting that original $100 along with its earnings.

YEAR	TAX FREE	TAXED at 30%	TAXED at 50%
1	$ 200	$ 170	$ 150
2	$ 400	$ 289	$ 225
3	$ 800	$ 491	$ 338
4	$ 1,600	$ 835	$ 507
5	$ 3,200	$ 1,420	$ 761
10	$102,400	$20,164	$5,783

As you can see, it can be very impressive to double your money, but only when you are able to do so tax free. Any taxes leveled against your earnings can make a drastic difference in what you actually keep and, therefore, what you have to reinvest. Investing in single family homes will not only allow you to earn fantastic returns, but it will also allow you to keep all or most of those returns tax free. If being a millionaire is your goal, you could reach it in just a little over thirteen years by keeping your investments in the first column in the chart above. If they stray over into the second and third columns, it is doubtful that you will ever live long enough to see the one million mark.

Before leaving the chart above, look back at it one more time. Stop to think what would happen if you started a program using $1,000 or $10,000. Suppose you merely started a new program with a new $100 every year. It's not hard to imagine, is it? It's not hard to double your money either, especially when you are starting out. Once you amass a great deal of money or wealth, it will become harder to find enough investments to continue at such a pace. Of course, by the time that you have that problem, you should be financially independent and not that concerned with increasing your wealth, but with preserving it and enjoying it.

Figures don't lie. Sometimes they may be hard to believe, but they never, never lie. The figures above and the figures that appeared on the worksheets probably seem as unbelievable and unrealistic to you as they seemed to me at one time. In the beginning of this book, I told you that when I figured out my original plan, it looked so simple and so unbelievable that I knew there had to be a catch. Just like my father's plan, it looked too good to be true. After I achieved my goal, I discovered I had a great faith in numbers that I just didn't have before. Of course, my faith is based on the fact that in order for the numbers to work, you have to work to make them work.

Ten rules of thumb. As you start your journey, there are ten rules of thumb you can use to bring you success. These rules are easy to use and easy to remember. They are all based on the number ten and have appeared throughout this book. I am consolidating and reviewing them here so that you can find them easily and look them over every now and then to refresh your memory.

1. Look at no fewer than ten similar houses before you purchase your first house. This exercise is vitally important. It will help you to remain unemotional and to be a better judge of value. It will also help save you from making a fatal mistake.

2. Make at least ten ridiculous offers each week. This exercise will get you out looking. Making this many offers will allow you to choose those you want to act on and turn down those you don't like. In addition, the sellers you are dealing with will be more willing to bargain because they'll know theirs isn't the only house you are considering.

   If you don't want to make ten ridiculous offers a week, at least make sure you have ten offers out at all times. This way the law of averages will be working for you. At the very least, one of those offers will come through and make you a lot of money. As a rule, make sure you use an escape clause in all your offers.

3. Act within ten seconds when a good deal comes along. He who hesitates is lost, and so is the deal. You aren't the only person who

will be able to recognize a bargain. When one comes along, take a deep breath and jump in with both feet. Remember, even if it is the buy of a lifetime, use an escape clause. Always tie up the deal without tying up yourself.

4. Always try to buy the house with ten percent or less of your own money down. By doing so, you will force yourself to negotiate and find better deals. You will also be able to make your money go farther and buy more.

5. Remember, ten percent of all sellers are "don't wanters." These motivated sellers will accept at least twenty percent less than their asking price. Many of these sellers will also carry the financing or accept just about anything as a down payment (cars, boats, motorcycles, use of your vacation home, your services, paper, or just about anything else you have to offer).

6. Borrow at least ten percent more than you need when obtaining home improvement funds. When you are getting a short-term loan, always borrow more than you need. The money helps to give you a feeling of security. It can also be used to cover the unexpected and to help make the payments on some of your loans until you refinance your profits out.

7. Most banks will lend you ten percent of your net worth, unsecured. Once you have established a line of credit at a bank, you may even be able to borrow more than that.

8. Always try to limit your improvement cost to ten percent or less of the purchase price of the house. Only in rare cases will you schedule more than this amount for improvements. Remember too that no matter what amount you schedule, always stay within the budget and attempt to get as much eye appeal as possible out of the money you spend. For example, you would be better off spending your improvement money on carpeting and paint than on a new roof. After the house has been reappraised and refinanced, you can put on the new roof. Patch it to hold until then.

9. Only about ten percent of all buyers shop for financing. Make sure that you are one of them. Interest rates, terms, and closing costs at various lending institutions can vary, and the availability of funds can vary. Learn to be a very smart shopper. And remember, when it comes to money, the quality is always the same; only the cost varies.

10. Only about ten percent of all the prospective renters who call will be good tenants. For every ten prospects who call, only about three will make it to a showing. Of those three, only about one will be top-notch material. You could get a couple of good ones right off the bat, or you could end up waiting a couple of days before a good

one shows up. In either case, make sure you have at least two good prospects to choose from before you commit yourself.

One more rule of thumb. This last rule isn't based on ten, but on one hundred. This rule says that you can roughly estimate the value of a house by multiplying its current projected rent by one hundred. For example, if the monthly rental income a house can generate is $150, the house plus all its improvements shouldn't cost over $15,000. If you pay over this figure, you will probably end up with a negative cash flow. Paying considerably less than this figure is called buying it right.

CHAPTER FIFTEEN
REACHING YOUR GOALS

It is a very funny thing about life: if you refuse to accept anything but the best, you very often get it.

W. SOMERSET MAUGHAM

There are people who make things happen, people who watch things happen, and people who don't know that anything happened at all. If you want to be in that first group, you have to be a person who sets goals for himself and then sets out to attain them. If you were to ask the president of General Motors how he got to be president, I'm sure he wouldn't say, "Well, I just showed up for work one day, and I kept on coming in, and, well, one day they just up and made me president." All successful people set goals for themselves, and you should too.

FINANCIAL INDEPENDENCE

I didn't end up financially independent by accident. I didn't end up owning all the property I own because I just happened to be in the right place at the right time. I had to go out and look for it and then act when I found it. I decided what I wanted, and I made sure that I was in the right place at the right time. I didn't end up financially independent because I was lucky, either. Just about every place I bought brought its share of misfortune. But I was able to take that misfortune and use it to help myself grow. I made mistakes, but I didn't let those mistakes stop me. I kept track of them so that I wouldn't make the same mistakes twice.

I had my share of obstacles, but I didn't let them overcome me. I learned to go over, under, or around them. If that didn't work, I went through them. I had problems, but I didn't let them overpower me. I found that problems are nothing but opportunities in disguise. I found that by solving my problems, I was able to attain even greater success. At times I even went out of my way to find problems, so that I could reap their rewards.

It's all up to you. Nobody can do it for you. You have to decide what you want out of life, and then you have to go after it. Nobody else knows your capabilities and your desires better than you. Nobody else knows what will make you feel successful and complete better than you. Sure, it's a big decision. But when it comes right down to it, would you really want to let someone else make it for you?

Many people don't like to make decisions, so they just don't. What they don't realize is that by not making these decisions they are deciding to let other people and conditions control their lives. They become victims of circumstance. They become misdirected. They feel unhappy with themselves and their lives. They may even feel unwanted and unloved, but most of all they feel inferior. Eleanor Roosevelt once said, "Remember, nobody can make you feel inferior without your consent." Decide here and now not to be like most people. Let them put themselves into the bonds of inferiority, but don't you do it too.

I used to have a terrible inferiority complex. Although it is somewhat better now, I never sought any professional help. I was afraid that my utmost suspicions would be confirmed. I was afraid that I would be told that I didn't have an inferiority complex at all, but that I was, indeed, inferior. I probably got this idea from looking at all the people who could do things that I couldn't do. Sometimes I had to look pretty far, but I always managed to find something. I eventually felt that life had dealt me a losing hand and that I would just have to play with the crummy cards I had been given.

I started losing some of my sense of inferiority when I finally took a good look at the hand I had been dealt. It really wasn't such a bad hand. All I had to do was arrange what little I had been given in the most effective way. I knew that if I used what I had (my intangible wealth), I could get what I wanted (tangible wealth). I knew that if I didn't, I would end up getting nothing and getting nowhere. I knew that the only people who didn't make mistakes were dead people, and I certainly wasn't dead, nor did I want to be. I decided then and there to give my hand a try. I knew that if I were to lose, I would probably be no worse off than I already was, and I would still be in a position to try again. I knew that if I should win, I would never live to regret the day that I had tried.

So, what is the alternative to trying? Not trying. And is that so bad? Yes. I talked to a lot of older people before I stuck my head out (remember that I don't have a lot of guts, and that's why I chose to invest in single family homes in the first place). What I learned from these people, especially the unsuccessful, was that the saddest four words in the English language, *I wish I had,* preceded all their stories about all the things they had wanted to do. These were the four words they used to sum up their life's experiences. These were the four words that I grew to fear.

I came away from all this determined not to live my life in such a way that I, too, would end up uttering these four sad words. I knew that I had only one shot at life. I knew that there was no way I could come back and do it all over again. There was no chance that I could be reborn into the right family, live in the right neighborhood, attend the right schools, marry the right person, get the right job, and make all the right investments. I realized that the only right there was, was right now. I couldn't be content with living this life in mediocrity. There aren't any second chances. I had to do it this time through or not at all.

What about you? Are you going to try playing out the hand you were dealt? Are you going to try to capture whatever it is you want out of life? Are you going to live the life you have always dreamed about? It's up to you. It's your decision. You have to decide whether you are going to direct your own life or let yourself be directed by other people and by circumstances. Not making a decision is, in fact, making a decision for the latter. By not deciding, you may be choosing the kind of life you don't want to live. You may be choosing a life that will end with those four words, *I wish I had.*

You know what you want out of life. You know what kind of life you want to live. Decide to go after it. Sure, there are no guarantees, but your chances of succeeding are darn good if you try. What guarantees and what chances do you have if you don't try? Sure, it may not be easy, but no matter how hard it may be, it will never be as hard as living a life you are not happy with. The odds are in your favor. Your chances of getting what you want out of life are good. Just look around you at the successful people you know. What do they have that you don't have? What can they do that you can't do? Aren't you just as smart and as capable as they are?

I hope that by now you have already set a goal to be financially independent by investing in single family homes. Reaching that goal should be easy and exciting. When I first set that goal for myself, I knew of no one who had ever set a similar goal or attained it. To me, it was much like the goal of breaking the four-minute mile. Until Roger Bannister broke the record and ran the mile in less than four minutes, many people thought that it was impossible. Since that day in 1954, hundreds of people have equaled or bettered his time. They were able to do it because they knew it wasn't impossible anymore. You now know that financial independence is not impossible and that it can be achieved by investing in single family homes.

Yes, you can achieve financial independence. You can accomplish the same things I have accomplished. In fact, I wouldn't be surprised if you go out and do a better job of it than I did. With the information I have given you, you won't have to waste a lot of time and effort spinning your wheels and getting nowhere. You won't end up making as many wrong turns or getting into as many accidents either. You will have a clear road ahead, a road that has by now been well traveled by many before you.

I used to think that financial independence was a rarity, something that happened to only a few people. Once I achieved it, however, I began to notice all kinds of people are financially independent. Most of these people were much better travelers than I and achieved success in less time than it took me. Many of them also achieved much greater success. Now, all of this could have brought back those old feelings of inferiority, but it didn't. Actually, it all made me quite happy, and it should make you feel the same way too.

Yes, there is a better way to live, and you can have it. Don't come down with a case of "paralysis by analysis." Don't be afraid to act or get started until you know everything there is to know. You don't have to know everything in this or any other book before you start. All you have to know is that success can be achieved. If you happen to know more than I did when I started out (which you already do), you will just be able to attain your goal that much more easily and that much more quickly.

Finally, don't write off the attainment of anything you want out of life simply because it looks or sounds too difficult. Nothing is too difficult. Anything that you want can be yours if you set having it as your goal and then break the process of attaining it into smaller steps. Most of us have at least forty productive years in our lives. You will never convince me that anyone, given that amount of time, cannot have whatever it is he wants out of life.

SEED MONEY

For many people the outcome of most of their income is zero. It doesn't seem to matter how much or how little they make, they always manage to spend it all. Most of these people find themselves living from paycheck to paycheck. Sometimes they even find it impossible to do that. The idea of putting anything aside for themselves is totally out of the question. It is a sad comment on their lives, but they end each year no better off than they began it. These are the people who, unwittingly, choose a life of slavery, in which all they have to look forward to is a hand-to-mouth existence.

Why would anybody choose to live this way? Apparently they do so because they don't think too much of themselves. Rodney Dangerfield, the comedian, put it rather aptly when he said, "They got no respect." They believe that the butcher, the baker, and the candlestick-maker are more important fellows than they are themselves. They even go so far as to prove it to themselves by taking each paycheck and dividing it up among these fellows. If there is anything left over, which there usually isn't, they get to keep it for themselves. If these people truly respected themselves, they wouldn't do it that way. They would pay themselves first, and then they would divide up what was left among the butcher, the baker, and the candlestick-maker.

Many great fortunes were started with a small nest egg that someone who was tired of being a slave had managed to save. (There is an "l" of a difference between slaving and saving.) Most of these fortune builders did not have above-average incomes or a rich uncle Harry who died and left them a lot of money. All they had was a determination to set a portion of their income aside. They knew that no matter how little they paid themselves out of each dollar they earned, it would eventually add up to enough money to start them on their way. They had faith in their plans, confidence in themselves, and the good sense to pay themselves first. If it is true that history is a good teacher, then this is a lesson well worth learning.

You don't have to be a Rhodes Scholar to put yourself on the road to wealth. All you have to do is get into the habit of paying yourself first. This money will help you break whatever bonds of slavery are holding you down. It should be kept in a safe place (a bank, not a mattress) and it should be used only for your investments. It should never be used as "mad money." Squandering it in any way will do nothing but re-shackle you and keep you down that much longer. The more you pay yourself, the sooner the day will come when you are a free man.

Deciding how much to pay yourself is a decision only you can make. How much do you think you are worth? If it is more than the butcher, the baker, and the candlestick-maker think you can afford, cut down on their services and not your pay. As much as you presently believe that you can't live without all the services and products they are now supplying you with, you can. Look at all the other people who earn less than you do. They get by on less. You can do it too. In fact, if you were given the choice tomorrow of taking a cut in pay or losing your job, you would be forced to cut back. You wouldn't like it, but you could do it. Why not take a voluntary cut, and pay yourself the difference?

So, how much should you pay yourself? As I said, only you can decide, but why not start out at ten percent of your income. It's not going to be easy at first. In fact, it's probably going to be downright difficult. Once you are able to do it, you will probably be amazed that you actually succeeded. Later you will even be amazed at how easy it is to pay yourself that amount. You may even be tempted to give yourself a raise. If you are tempted, go ahead; you deserve it!

TIME MANAGEMENT

A penny saved may be a penny earned, but a moment wasted is never returned. We all are allocated the same amount of time each day. How we spend that time is pretty much up to us. If we spend eight hours every day sleeping and eight hours working, that means we have eight hours left to ourselves. Even after shaving, showering, and eating, we still have a lot of time left. How we spend that time can determine to a great extent how our lives will turn out.

A few years after I had been in this single family home business, I decided to find out how much my time was really worth. Since I knew what my net worth was and how much it increased every year, all I had to do was divide my annual increase by the hours I had put in. Much to my surprise I found that my time was worth over fifty dollars an hour, and that was after taxes. At a time when most part-time jobs were paying less than two dollars an hour, I considered my hourly rate quite satisfying. Now that I am using my time more effectively, I find that I am able to earn many times that amount from my investment. Because of this, I am able to earn my living working even fewer hours than before. That's time management.

Time management consists of getting the most out of the time you spend. If you look at time as a commodity just like money, you will find that you can learn to spend it just as wisely as you learn to spend your money. You should always be interested in getting the most for your money, and you should be equally interested in getting the most for your time. You have probably heard the expression, time is money. For all practical purposes it really is. If you can find a way to do a job in half the time it used to take you, you will be able to double your output, and thus double your income from that job.

The whole secret of time management is to spend your time on the most important items and not to waste it on the unimportant. Many people do not organize a list of things to do and then work from that list. Even many of the people who do work from a list start by doing the easiest, the shortest, or the most pleasant tasks. Working with or without a list can be a waste of time if the most important items are neglected.

Getting the best use out of your time is really quite simple. All it involves is making up a daily list to work from and then arranging the items on that list in order of importance. This list can be compiled either the night before or in the morning before you start. On this list you should put down everything you would like to accomplish that day. After your list is complete, go back over it and number the items on your list according to importance.

As chance would have it, the really important items on the list always seem to be the most unpleasant ones. The least important ones are usually the ones you would like to do first. As hard as it may be, do the important ones first. If you do, you will feel a lot better when they are out of the way, and you will be able to coast through the rest of the day. You will also end the day feeling as if you really accomplished something.

If you don't get time to get to the less important items, that's okay. No harm done. Put them on the next day's list. You will probably find that the least important items either eventually get done by themselves or just disappear.

If you have been anxious to start but didn't know where you were going to find the time, now you know. Watch a little less television. If you have been wondering how you will get everything done in the time that you have, now you know that too. Use a daily list of "things to do." Using your time wisely has its rewards. Just remember, don't kill time; it has no resurrection. Time you are able to save can be used for the more important things in life, like enjoying yourself.

PERSONAL MANAGEMENT

I enjoy working for myself. I'm an all-around good egg and one of the best bosses a fellow could ever want. I'm easy to get along with, and I always let myself have my own way. If I want to take a day off or take off early, I let myself. If I want to take a break or an extended lunch hour, I never complain. If I want to take a two-week or a two-month vacation, I always say yes. Even if I want to work really hard or put in some very long hours, I never object. Yes, I'm a good boss now, but I haven't always been.

It's hard being your own boss at first. When you don't have someone over you telling you when to show up and what to do, you can become very lazy. You might find yourself getting up later and later in the mornings and quitting earlier and earlier at night. This is fine if you have nothing to do, but it can make all kinds of problems when there is work to be done. The hardest battle you may ever fight is the battle you have to fight with yourself, especially if you are not self-disciplined. If you are already self-disciplined, being your own boss will be a joy and a blessing.

If you are going to fight this battle, or, in fact, any other battle in your life, always keep your eye on the reward. Keep looking at what you have to gain by winning. If that doesn't work, keep remembering what you will have to go back to by losing. If neither of these two things does the trick and pulls you through, there is one surefire thing left. Try to imagine someone you thoroughly dislike or despise succeeding and winning the reward out from under you. If that doesn't work, nothing will.

FROM THIS POINT ON

I hope I have given you the basic knowledge you need to go out and become financially independent by investing in single family homes. I have tried to impart to you everything I wished I could have known before I went into the game. Had I known what I have told you, I would have made fewer mistakes and made much more progress in a much shorter time.

The basic knowledge that I have given you is just that, basic. Although basic facts hardly ever change, times and conditions do. For this reason, I encourage you to keep current and to keep learning. Laws, tax laws, the financial market, and the housing market are constantly changing. Being on top of these changes will keep you and your investments growing. The best way to keep current and to keep learning is to read all you can on these and any other subjects that affect you. Attend seminars and classes. Associate with knowledgeable people. And last of all, ask for advice whenever you can from people qualified to give it.

Investing in single family homes is not a get-rich-quick scheme. It is a safe and secure process that can make you financially independent. Just as in the fable of the tortoise and the hare, you will be able to move steadily along, building a sound investment program step by step. You won't have to take any unnecessary chances or go for broke as the big shooters do. In fact, you will probably end up in a much more enviable position than the people you now hold in high esteem. As for the few years it may take you to reach your goal, you will find that they will pass by all too quickly and probably end up being the most enjoyable and memorable years of your life. Have a good trip!

INDEX